MW00774124

The Day
I Became
a Runner

Celebrating
30 Years of Publishing
in India

THE New India
FOUNDATION

The New India Foundation, based in Bengaluru, uniquely matches public-spirited philanthropy with ground-breaking and relevant scholarship. In the seven-and-a-half decades since Independence, there has been a large body of work produced by Indian historians and social scientists. Taken singly, many of these studies are very impressive; viewed cumulatively, they add up to much less than what one might expect. The chief reason for this is the determining influence on the scholarly practice of one single date: 15th August 1947.

Given India's size, its importance, and its interest, and given that this is our country, the lack of good research on its modern history is unfortunate. It is this lack that the New India Foundation seeks to address, by sponsoring high-quality original scholarship on different aspects of independent India. Its activities include the granting of NIF Fellowships for highly researched original work, Translation Fellowships for bringing historical Indian language works to English, the publication of books on the history and culture of independent India, organizing the Girish Karnad Memorial Lecture, and the Kamaladevi Chattopadhyay Book Prize.

Advance Praise for *The Day I Became a Runner*

'With curiosity, sensitivity and agility, Sohini Chattopadhyay creates a sisterhood of Indian runners. These women's triumphs are incredibly hard-won, in life as much as in sport. Though some of this sorority are well-to-do, the image this fine and moving book leaves us with is: a lone woman at dawn, running barefoot on an obscure beach or rough playing field, underfed and inexperienced, her prospects daunting and her determination heartbreaking.'

—**Anjum Hasan**

'A hobby runner herself, the author weaves together the lives of nine notable Indian women runners to "trace the arc of citizenship in the Indian republic". Each of them has left their imprint on not just our athletic but also our social history—one is now my colleague in Parliament. Their achievements could not have found a better chronicler and analyst. The book is delightfully written, and it has been an education to read it.'

—**Jairam Ramesh**

'*The Day I Became a Runner* isn't just the best book ever written about Indian women in competitive sport, but it is the best book about India that you're likely to read this year. This vivid, moving, deeply researched and beautifully written book is a revelation. It's also unputdownable.'

—**Mukul Kesavan**

'Sohini Chattopadhyay's *The Day I Became a Runner* is a beautiful tribute to Indian women in sport. She skilfully interweaves her own relationship with running with stories of Indian women athletes from the 1940s to the present, demonstrating how women have creatively used professional sports as a way of creating space for themselves in the Indian republic. Chattopadhyay neither romanticizes the experiences of women runners, nor does she paint a picture of crippling oppression. Rather, she is able to explore the complexities of how women use their bodies to occupy space within the national imaginary in a manner that is often limited and at times liberating. This important work provides insights into the challenges women face, not only in India but across the region in terms of accessing public spaces in the face of patriarchal discomfort with women's bodies. *The Day I Became a Runner* is a history of India told through the lives of these incredible, boundary-pushing women. It is also a touching personal story of a woman struggling to connect with her body despite the odds.'

—Nida Kirmani

'This is what the "Big India Book" used to be, only better and more fascinating. Through running, Chattopadhyay traces a map of the country's dreams, fault lines and struggles, of gender, sport and nationhood. A work of incredible research, engrossing and powerful.'

—Nilanjana Roy

'I have had the great pleasure of having read, in manuscript form, Sohini Chattopadhyay's wonderful book on women runners in India. The book starts on a striking premise—that, since running is a solitary activity conducted in the public sphere, women who take up this sport pose a more direct challenge to patriarchy than those who play other sports such as badminton, cricket and tennis. This thesis is elaborated through a series of compelling case studies spanning the entire history of independent India and involving women athletes from a wide range of social and geographical backgrounds.

'Sohini is both a superb reporter and a beautiful writer. While the motif of struggle and sacrifice runs through the book, each story is moving in its own distinctive way. This is one of the finest works of non-fiction I have read in years.'

—**Ramachandra Guha**

The Day I Became a Runner is a searing comment on the harsh realities that women athletes face as they try to make their way in the sporting world. But this beautifully written book is not only about sportswomen, it is about all of us who struggle against stereotypes and the world's expectations of how women should live.'

—**Shobhaa Dé**

'A beautifully written and thoroughly captivating ode to the power of dreams and the pursuit of excellence.'

—**Sonia Faleiro**

'This remarkable and highly readable book braids together the lives of Indian women runners and the history of sport in a deeply gendered society. In so doing, Sohini Chattopadhyay also offers us a subtle and moving account of the meanings of freedom in India since its Independence.'

—**Srinath Raghavan**

'It is possible that many of us—particularly a generation of women— have willed this book into existence. Sohini Chattopadhyay gives us a history of Indian women in a manner never attempted before, without ever letting go of an opportunity to share a joke.'

—**Sumana Roy**

The Day
I Became
a Runner

A Women's History of
India through the
Lens of Sport

Sohini
Chattopadhyay

THE New India
FOUNDATION

4th

An Imprint of HarperCollins Publishers

First published in India by Fourth Estate 2023
An Imprint of HarperCollins *Publishers*
4th Floor, Tower A, Building No. 10, DLF Cyber City,
DLF Phase II, Gurugram, Haryana – 122002
www.harpercollins.co.in

2 4 6 8 10 9 7 5 3 1

Copyright © Sohini Chattopadhyay 2023

P-ISBN: 978-93-5699-462-1
E-ISBN: 978-93-5699-469-0

The views and opinions expressed in this book are the author's own
and the facts are as reported by her, and the publishers are not in
any way liable for the same.

Sohini Chattopadhyay asserts the moral right
to be identified as the author of this work.

Supported by the New India Foundation

For sale in the Indian subcontinent only.

All rights reserved. No part of this publication may be reproduced,
stored in a retrieval system, or transmitted, in any form or by any
means, electronic, mechanical, photocopying, recording or otherwise,
without the prior permission of the publishers.

Typeset in 11.5/15.7 Adobe Garamond at
Manipal Technologies Limited, Manipal

Printed and bound at
Thomson Press (India) Ltd.

This book is produced from independently certified FSC® paper
to ensure responsible forest management.

*To Santhi Soundarajan, who never stopped thinking
of the track as her home.*

CONTENTS

1

THE BENGALI WOMAN'S RUNNING DIARY[1]

Photo © Sohini Chattopadhyay

I BEGAN RUNNING, in grief and confusion, in 2008. My grandmother passed away suddenly one morning, a couple of days after my cautious and measured father allowed himself to tell me without a sigh that she seemed much better. A little over a week before that, she had been sent home from the critical care unit, and I had interpreted that as an unambiguously positive message. I decided then with relief to delay my visit home to Kolkata, so it would coincide with the holiday of a close friend from overseas. I would also use the visit to spend time with my grandma—it was convenient. The only doubt came from my mother, who spelt it out to me that an expensive trip home would be money well spent, even if I had to come again later to meet my friend.

She was right, my mother. She had the prescience of the carer who has done time by the hospital bed—she knew how fragile it all was. But the end was a surprise to her too.

Hindu rituals dictate that the body be cremated within twenty-four hours of death. At the time, my folks thought it would be a waste of money for me to come to see the body. I was, again, shamelessly relieved. I didn't want to see her body. My father had told me she had shrunk to 34 kg in hospital. How light she felt, my father said, when he walked the few ritual feet carrying the body on his shoulders with three others.

Hindu rites also do not leave much scope for women to mourn ceremonially or even formally—their duties are limited to the cooking of the mourning diet and cleaning. But most of all, at a time of rationalized, scientific and essentially Westernized mourning, it is difficult to be able to follow traditional rituals. My maternal uncle did not shave his head when his parents passed away.

When the priest insisted he should, my uncle cautioned him that another priest could be hired for the ceremony. This is not a criticism—it is merely a description and perhaps a question. My uncle works at an international organization, where a tonsured head will attract attention. But if you are grieving, is it not easier if you are marked visibly?

My father followed some of the rituals when my grandma passed away. He shaved his mostly bald head and I believe refrained from eating meat, but it is unlikely that we ate the ritual food of Hindu mourning—food cooked without onion and garlic, ingredients believed to trigger aggression. I was living in another city for most of the twelve-day mourning period; I was told not to follow the rituals. Better to not follow them than make a mistake with the details, my mother said.

So I didn't.

But grief without ritual can be bewildering.

I hear friends and acquaintances—on Facebook and in person—asking for recommendations to experience the 'authentic' Istanbul or Barcelona or old Dilli. We want to drink coffee at secret cafés brimming with character, eat at the fabled restaurants unlisted on tourist guides, shop where the people of the city do. We seek the rituals of belonging—we want to be, even if it is in passing, residents of the city. And in performing those rituals, we seek passage to a certain status, a certain identity. 'Tourist' is an unfulfilling identity. The tourist doesn't belong. The tourist is an outsider.

I, too, was in search of the rituals that marked belonging and status. I wanted to be in mourning. The rituals remind you of your loss, the austere diet marks you out as a mourner. And there is comfort in that belonging. The requirements are incomprehensible: Why must I buy puffed rice and white flowers? But, they tell you, you are not the only one to have lost—you are in the community of the bereaved. Ritual helps you cope. The bother of abiding by it is also a form of suffering—it can ease the guilt.

Running became my mourning ritual.

✤

I remember grief being heavy: I was carrying a dull, dead weight. It was enervating. I ran to shake it off. I ran persistently, seriously, which is to say that I turned up at the ground every day. But I could barely run 700 or 800 metres at the time, and far less than 500 metres at one stretch. I was lucky to live in a south Delhi colony with a couple of parks and jogging tracks. The park I ran in was popular—it hosted a busy cricket coaching camp, several walkers and a couple of joggers. The cricketers took over the better, more levelled half of the ground; the walkers and gentle joggers use the running track around it.

I was a lump in those days—a squat, easily breathless lump. I ran in the lower, unlevelled half of the garden. I didn't deserve to run on the jogging track—I wanted to be unseen. Some of this was the grief. I didn't want to *be*.

I come from a home that believes slimness is an inborn condition, like eyesight or hearing. Or, indeed, intelligence, for the Bengali. Either you were born with it or you were unlucky. My father watches sports on television tirelessly. His most frequent compliment is, 'What a beautiful physique', while bouncing his belly on his thighs happily, without a trace of resentment.

Running was horridly painful: a deafening lack of breath within a handful of strides, the feeling that my chest would burst, my heart thundering in my ears, and, invariably, a running nose. I had no rhythm, no stamina. I went full pelt those initial days, no half measures. I stopped more than I ran, but I went again.

The pain was penance: I was paying off my guilt. The pain was also a marker of my bereavement—I was here because of my loss, I was charging madly about a small patch of dusty green because I had to remember and grieve. It was my dawn cold-water bath, it was my white-flower puja with incomprehensible mantras.

This is what kept me running—the sense that I was mourning, that I was accounting for my loss.

It had been after breakfast, when the household was settling down to chores, that she suffered a heart attack. I would tell myself to go a little longer when I thought my chest would burst, to stop a little bit later. I made counting pacts—I would run till ten, then twenty. When I struggled to draw breath, perhaps I would intuit what her last moments were like. Perhaps I could be by her deathbed after all. I could grasp what death feels like.

Was there this deafening, rushing sound in your head? Did it tear open your chest? Was it anything like this, Tabba?

I could grieve after all.

✤

'When you are broken, you run,' wrote Helen Macdonald in *H Is for Hawk*, her majestic memoir of grief and falconry.[2] She meant running figuratively; I embraced it literally. Running was the only way out of the claustrophobia of my grief. But might it also have been a subconscious desire to live?

In January 2015, the results of an ambitious twelve-year study by the University of Cambridge were made public: Inactivity is worse than obesity, doubly so, in fact.[3] The lack of physical exercise, the researchers estimated, caused twice as many deaths in Europe as obesity every year. From the wasteland of my grief, had I instinctively reached for life?

I didn't make eye contact with anybody. I kept my head down and ran. I remember well the dusty, lumpy, green ground. Sometimes children would scuttle across my running path, but I didn't look up to smile at them or their chaperones. I spoke to no one. I ran alone in a busy park.

The haze started to lift after three months. I was still in shock. I cried easily and several times a day. I remember the feeling, distinct to this day, that I would cry if you shook me.

But I also found myself thinking of other things. I got a haircut. I bought some clothes because the running had made the old ones loose. I bought a pair of running pants and a set of loose, cheap T-shirts. Those were not bought with any particular thought except that I wanted to be comfortable. I didn't know my sweating patterns then—that I perspire especially in the upper body, that a good run particularly wets my back and chest, and marks out my bra line. Thankfully, a loose T-shirt sticks to the body less, especially if you keep pulling it down. I was to realize this, and many other things about myself, over the next months. Running offers many rewards, but self-awareness is the surprise gift.

I soon realized I was the only woman who ran in that Delhi park. The other serious joggers were all men. Some women walked furiously, others chatted on the phone or caught up with neighbours. They all wore salwar-kurtas. I hadn't learnt how to run long-distance then, yet, apparently, even a few weeks of single-mindedly charging around the ground can condition the body. I could go a few laps without stopping—five rounds or so of a 440-yard track. It was only a mile (1.6 kilometres), but I felt accomplished already—I was the only one of my kind. And I felt impatient, because I went faster than the male joggers who ran with rhythm. (It took only a few days to realize they were real, practised runners; I was an upstart novice.)

I noticed that I never asked to excuse myself when I needed to overtake men on the track. Instead, I would stop running, sidle past, then run again. It disturbed my running rhythm, but I was afraid to ask them to make way. Didn't it make me conspicuous? Didn't it make me pushy, insisting on the right to my space and telling others to move aside? Yet, when I had to bypass women walkers walking on the track, I said 'excuse me'. Politely, I believe.

I realized this was my pattern even when I was out in the city. On the craggy, steep, poorly lit footpaths of south Delhi, I did not request men to allow me to pass, even if they were lounging around, slapping backs, drinking alcohol out of cola bottles and taking up the entire footpath. I would rather jump off the pavement into the path of impatient autorickshaws, get squeezed with bullied cyclists into the slushy drainage conduit, and climb up again a few steps later. On the slim streets of Kolkata, where the footpaths belong to roadside entrepreneurs and thoroughfares boast a rich diversity of traffic, from trams to hand-drawn freight carts to pedestrians, I mastered the sideways trot. Yet, with women, I asked to be excused and strode past. When a couple walked side by side, I addressed the woman.

What if I annoyed a man with my Oliver Twist-like asking for more place, and he grabbed me? Followed me and pushed me into a side street, pinned me to a wall? I remembered the reports of acid attacks in the past five years. You may have read them too. Did you hear of what happened to the Hindi-film actor Kangana Ranaut's sister? She was attacked with acid some years ago.[4]

It was disappointing to accept how timid I was. A man I was falling in love with shook his head in annoyance when I told him why I avoided evening dos. 'Acid attacks are horrible, but why should you think about them? You cannot allow yourself to be afraid. I once thought I was about to be mugged in Philadelphia, but I turned around and asked "What?" to the guy who was shadowing me. He walked away. That's my attitude,' he told me. I told him I wanted to be like him, but I was held back by the things I'd heard over several years. Warnings, advice, news reports, paying-guest-accommodation rules,[5] living-room conversations. These had now shaped my anxieties. What kind of girl drives home alone at 3 a.m., like Soumya Vishwanathan?[6] She was shot dead by a gang of thieves when she was driving home after a late shift at work at the television channel Headlines Today in 2008.

'What will you do when your daughter comes home, squashed between unknown men in an office cab late at night?' an invigilator had tittered to a parent at the exam centre where I was writing the entrance test for a journalism course. A student had forgotten to bring her admit card for the test and her mother had run home to get it. When she returned with the card, the candidate was permitted to sit for the exam about forty minutes after the test began. Her mother, meanwhile, was greeted with this comment. I've never forgotten how casually this vicious comment was thrown at her. What made the man at the exam centre think of sex when he saw a young woman appearing for a journalism test? Why does working late outside the home carry sexual connotations for a woman?

My man's counsel had been to shrug off all the derision, well-meaning warnings, news reports—the irrational sum of my anxieties as he saw it—and look my potential assaulter(s) in the eye. To me, it was absolutely rational. But what is the fear of being mugged for a man who has grown up in India, where men own the streets at all times of day and night? Can it compare with the manifesto of avoiding sexual assault that women grow up with?

What is this country he grew up in? I wish I lived there too.

One thing is for certain—there are women who are braver than me. Does that mean they are not struggling with the same anxieties? A colleague of mine who drove home after the late shift at a newspaper desk said she was chased by a group of boys in cars around India Gate in New Delhi after midnight. She was forced to stop the car, but she did not step out. She locked herself in and remained on the phone with her sister throughout. She continues to drive home late after work. I admire her hugely.

But I knew how it exhausted me, this constant battle. And so, some things I have decided to let go. It is not the poster girl's choice, but is it not a valid choice too?

I would not have run outdoors in the city if I didn't have the privilege of a jogging track within my colony. Sometimes I ran on the roads inside the colony but never outside. Male colleagues told me how they started their days obscenely early, running on the still-dark streets of the sleeping city. On several days, I scolded myself for lacking their resolve: If I finished running by 8 a.m., I would have been a lot more productive with my day. One phlegmy Delhi winter's morning, when I finally awoke at a suitably unearthly hour, I left my apartment only to realize that I did not have the courage to run in the desolate streets outside. So I ran at 'decent', 'modest' hours, when it was light and there were people on the ground.

⁜

Yet I am grateful that I was able to run at all. It has put me in touch with my body, made me far more aware of it. As a teenager, I was so embarrassed by my stout frame that I was a stranger to my body. I took quick offence at its swells and bulges; I rarely made eye contact in the mirror. I have written in the past about how I have come to appreciate my squat but not unbeautiful runner's frame.[7] In a sense, it was the hard labour of running that helped me know my body. If this is how I looked after running long and hard every day, I was happy with the result.

I can tell how I am by the way I run. Most days I go at a steady clip. Some days I plod. And on a few days I glide. Plodding means I am tired, haven't slept well or have put on weight.

I am also much more aware of aches and pains, and my breathing. When my nose runs more than I do, I know I am coming down with a cold. As a patient of sinusitis, I have a chronic running nose. Running, in fact, has helped cope with this better, because the fluid drains out during my run. It has also made me less fussy: I blow my nose into my hand and shake it dry because there is only so much tissue paper I can carry. Contemporary research suggests it is good for our systems to muck around a bit, have soiled fingernails, not shrink from bodily fluids—it helps to keep our immune system alert and lucid. It guards against nasty autoimmune diseases such as lupus and asthma.[8]

When I started running, I couldn't hear my body. I ignored the creaks and cramps. I saw Rafael Nadal's bandaged feet and longed for such glorious trophies of my running routine. One morning in Delhi, my left butt seared with a piercing, blinding pain. This is it, I had thought with delight, I am a 'real' runner, and triumphantly continued running. Like everyone who thinks buying track pants and putting one foot quickly after another makes them runners, I, too, had read Murakami's *What I Talk about When I Talk about Running*,[9] I adored the maxim, 'Pain is inevitable, suffering is optional.' *This* was my moment of claiming the maxim, I thought proudly.

Later that evening, my leg froze while crossing a road, and a kind stranger helped me hobble across to my office. I couldn't even walk to the toilet. The kindness of strangers extended, implausibly, to colleagues that day: Someone called me a cab. An X-ray proved that I had worn my hamstring thin, close to snapping it. Hamstring strains are brutishly painful and an injury can put an athlete out of action for three weeks or more. They can also render you immobile on account of the hamstring's central, strategic placement in a group of three muscles that run along the back of the thigh.

It was a valuable lesson: Listen carefully to what the body says.

But that is not to say stop whenever it complains. Ignore the aches and niggles for the most part—it's only the body grumbling. It's good to be aware of it, though—it speaks of unfitness and a shameful lack of stamina.

Until recently, I did not run during my period—mine is a very painful and exhausting one. The water in the body makes my feet ache when I walk, I feel tired all the time, and a sharp, cruel knot twists meanly in my stomach. But the breaks destroy running rhythm. After four days off, I have to start again slow and heavy. By the time I build up to gliding form, it is time for another period. How is it for other women runners?

In 2015, tennis player Heather Watson garnered attracted global attention for her first-round loss at the Australian Open when she blamed her loss on her 'girl things'.[10] Her period. It opened up a conversation on menstruation and women athletes that, going by the media attention that followed, was clearly waiting to happen. Mainstream media in the United Kingdom, Australia and the United States followed up Watson's charming press-conference answers with discussions. Several prominent athletes in India spoke up about their own period problems in response. Star Indian long-jumper Anju Bobby George said she had lost at least two medals in her career due to period cramps. 'I was in top form in every other way, but the period made me feel weaker and there was nothing I could do about it,' she said. 'After the events, many people criticized my performance, but this is not something I could ever tell them.'[11]

This conversation is a happy thing, of course, but the tone of it is also a little startling. Did women athletes really never bring up the period before this?

Once I began running with my period, I realized it was not so bad, really. It's not very different from running after too little sleep or with hard, non-training shoes, or with a few hundred grams of excess weight. In fact, a run snaps me awake from the bloated daze of my period.

More often than I'd like to admit, I run with great difficulty, and zero rhythm and scarce breath, and I think then of my telomeres.[12] They are the X-shaped tails of DNA molecules, I learnt from reading popular science articles. The longer the telomeres, the younger the body cells.

I think also of the difficult conversations awaiting me—those two-minute conversations with bosses to ask for a raise or for different projects other negotiations, which invariably tend to conclude abruptly. Where the consequences dawn on us after we step out of the room. Or the conversations where we want to gently tell a friend that something they did upset us. I am very bad at these—my eyes smart with tears easily. It is my default reaction to stress. Then the focus of the conversation shifts quickly to how I use tears as manipulation.

I think ahead to these conversations when I run. I cut deals with myself. If I have the heart to go one more round, if I can summon up the breath to go faster, if I have the fortitude to abide the stiffness in the leg a bit more, then I shall have the energy to fling a sharp word back when one comes my way. I shall have the heart to accept a failure, I shall have the gumption to bear the embarrassment of my tears. It is true that I have become more confrontational after I started running, less afraid of unpalatable remarks, less worried about not being liked. Is this how the endorphin high plays out?

Like most Bengalis, I used to be a practitioner of passive aggression. I believed the dignified silence would merit deeply satisfying apologies. I have since realized that this method works best for Satyajit Ray heroines, whose photogenic brooding is lit by luminous close-ups.

I worry also about immediate concerns. The shape of my sweating—does it frame my bra line too obviously? Do my breasts bounce offensively? Is my T-shirt riding too high above my butt? Is my presence provocative? In essence, I want to be innocuous. And yet, I want to be complimented for the lightness and beauty of my running. I suppose I want to be a heroine in a Sooraj Barjatya film—beautiful and inoffensive, a tiny colourful budgerigar that chirps softly.[13]

❖

This is the runner that Delhi had made of me. This is, also, what I made of Delhi as a runner.

In spite of my resident anxiety, my running in Delhi was free of molestation. (Something tells me it is prudent to add 'so far' to this statement.) That event occurred in Amman, my first overseas city and, in every way, my most foreign destination. They speak Arabic there, their speech almost entirely untouched by English. My uncle quashed my enthusiasm to explore the city by bus and local transport. 'They don't feel the anxiety to speak English that we Indians do.' And Arabic, he said with an air of mild triumph, is among the most complex languages in the world.

Nevertheless, one morning I set out with the thrill of having learnt two Arabic expressions (*shukraan* and *hamdurilah*, both popular in Bollywood). Seven in the morning is early in Amman. On the expat colony streets, there were only the newspaper-delivery vendors and the dogs too unsocial to be taken out later. I strode ahead of my parents and smiled at a man delivering newspapers from an American-style pick-up truck. He smiled and waved, and I thrummed in the pleasure of the smile reciprocated in a foreign land. He was a sweet-looking young man and gestured to me to come closer. I stopped at the window of his truck, and he cupped my right breast and squeezed it. I drew back in shock. He spoke with what looked like urgency to me. I couldn't understand what he said, but I searched his face for clues. There was no embarrassment there, not even the awkwardness of a misunderstanding. He opened the front door and gestured to me to get inside his truck, repeating the movement with exaggeration. I kept saying no, with the congenital politeness I maintain for strangers, especially strangers in foreign lands. He then slammed the door shut and screeched the truck away.

I turned around in shame to see if my folks had noticed, and waved to them. When they waved back cheerfully, I was reassured that they had missed the encounter, so I started jogging, anxious to avoid immediate contact with them.

If that man mistook me for anyone, it would be a prostitute. Who introduces himself to a girl by cupping her breast? I was mortified, because my parents were in the background. But the truth is, I was also a little afraid for myself.

I did not mention the incident to my family, because they would have likely stopped me from stepping out unsupervised. I was twenty-seven years old then. Yet, I behaved exactly as if they had censured me. I did not run in the early mornings, choosing to step out only around 9 a.m., when the local school and college classes started. I never went out alone after dark, even to the supermarket around the corner. I abandoned the idea of exploring the city by public transport. The cultural gap, highlighted by my morning misadventure, seemed too daunting. I had imagined, from the stories of a gentle Islamic society that insisted on no more than a stylish hijab, that Jordan would be full of chivalrous but shy men of quaint graces. I had been anticipating the pleasurable irony of comparing them with Delhi's cavemen. And so I had smiled happily at a stranger.

Amman is a beautiful mountainous city with roads that ascend and descend steeply without apology. After the dusty flat grounds of Delhi, it was exciting running terrain. Beautiful too—sheer drops and clean, winding roads. But an anxiety had lodged itself in me and I ran with my eyes studiously to the ground at a quiet pace. I avoided eye contact, and I had lost that appetite to stop and observe the lifeworld of the streets.

But running brings its own gifts. Where the roads were deserted, I ran uphill at full pelt to see where my breath would leave me. The mix of uphill and downhill stretches evened out my breath nicely. The exhilaration of the sharp downhill stretches was delicious. It made me smile in spite of my anxiety.

I was a graduate student in Edinburgh for a year, back at university after eight years in the chaos of real life. I knew I had to run every day. I needed structure. And most of all, I needed a sense of who I had grown up to be after my student years. Graduate school has this nasty way of picking away at your sense of self.

Edinburgh is a stunning, proud, medieval city with magnificent ascents and descents. I anticipated the joy of conquering them. I smiled at the thought of the beauteous thighs I would acquire, sprinting up and down. Besides, the views would be memorable.

But the city was too viciously cold for me to run outside. Almost always there was a spiteful wind. And often, it rained too. I realized, for the first time, that running is not the inexpensive sport I had thought it to be: I couldn't simply step out kitted out in a pair of trainers. A regular running suit, offering protection from the elements, costs upwards of £90. In Indian rupees, this was almost Rs 9,000. The most expensive garment I had purchased for my student life abroad was a dense, waterproof parka priced at Rs 4,000.

My only option was the university gym. What a remarkable space it was—a state-of-the-art gym with rows and rows of individual, customized machines, where scores of people exercised in intimate proximity with no eye contact. Everyone sealed in a private bubble with his/her customized music or TV programming and training equipment. The gym is the public bath of this i-generation.

Once, a girl next to me didn't know how to increase the speed on her machine—I told her what I knew, but she couldn't hear me over her headphones. I had to gesture wildly before she acknowledged me. It was the tiniest thing, but she was intensely embarrassed. When did we become this self-conscious, I thought? When did neighbours become such strangers?

But it was freeing too. This was the first place where I had been able to check out other runners, other exercisers, with impunity. I didn't feel any gaze on me. I ran better. After the initial wide-eyed excitement of checking out others, I thought almost exclusively about my studies—the essays and dissertations I carried in my head. I sharpened arguments, reorganized paragraphs, moved them up and down, as I changed functions on the treadmill.

Some months after I arrived in Edinburgh, I noticed that my left breast was unusually itchy. On examination, I saw that it had developed red patches. I wouldn't have cared but for the posters at the local National Health Service (NHS) clinic of a splotchy, unhappy breast, with a note on Paget's disease—a rare form of breast cancer. I set up an appointment at my NHS clinic. When the attending physician asked me about my symptoms, I mentioned the itchiness and redness of my breasts.

'Sudden weight loss?' he asked, looking me directly in the eye.

'Not really,' I said, feeling some of my confidence at this fact ebbing at his direct gaze.

I checked my weight every week at the gym, optimistic that the scale would stop at a lower figure. But it stayed obstinately stable—56 kg at the lowest and 58 at the highest, the standard 1–2-kg daily range of fluctuation of the human body.

'Lie down,' said the doctor, and pointed to the examination table behind the curtain.

A female nurse helped me unfasten my bra and covered me with a sheet. After about five minutes of physical examination in silence, the doctor grinned. 'Congratulations. You are exercising regularly. That is good.'

His diagnosis was Jogger's Nipple, a benign condition that sometimes afflicts regular runners, a by-product of sweat and the body brushing repeatedly against fabric.

'Congratulations,' he repeated, when I was dressed and had said goodbye. 'Keep up the discipline.'

I smiled back in relief, and a bit of pride. But it was not the runner's trophy I had imagined. I couldn't show it off like a stressed hamstring.

⁂

Hamburg is the first European city I lived in at length. It is a graceful old city of large handsome public parks. I ran early mornings in these, with timid rabbits and intrepid red squirrels. These are the creatures I made eye contact with, and occasionally with one of the gleaming German dogs out for a run. A couple of years later, when I read Frantz Fanon and Ralph Ellison for a course, I wondered if I, too, had been rendered invisible, and swelled with indignation. At other times, I wondered if I was not a good foot (and a half) too short for the statuesque Germans to make eye contact with.

I was working in a fine-dining restaurant in Hamburg called the Bullerei then.[14] It was a new and astonishingly difficult world for someone like me, who had always worked a white-collar job, unused to the hard physical labour of the kitchen. In the restaurant kitchen, they are artists of the hands, foremost, and also of the legs, standing long hours and running across a damp, slippery floor. They are, of course, artists of taste. They worked with their bodies. I had to reorient myself to be there. How skilled their hands were, how trained their legs. My feet swelled like luchis with the hours of standing, my hands were useless blocks of wood when it came to chopping and peeling.

Running was my way of reclaiming my body from the humiliations of the kitchen, of feeling less alienated by its betrayals. *If I can run this much, I'm not entirely useless, am I?* It was also my way of inhabiting my body more fully, of setting it challenges and learning that it will listen to some things, after all. It gave me a certain fortitude to endure the hard, male, professional kitchen.[15]

By far, my happiest running ground has been Calcutta (now Kolkata)—my hometown, my first love. Calcutta is not a runner's city. In central Calcutta, where I lived, the parks were locked up all day except early in the mornings and late in the afternoons—like pet dogs who are let out twice a day. The grass in these is overgrown and unkempt; they do have a narrow tiled path curving around them, but it is too slippery to run on in the morning dew. The roads are full of impatient, restless cars from early in the morning.

Running, I realized, is a spectator sport here. I had found myself a strip of road to run on relatively undisturbed—the barricaded road leading up to the British Deputy High Commission and the American Embassy. When I ran up and down that stretch of

150-odd metres, the platoon of security men along the road watched me, turning their gazes as I changed direction, an exaggerated slo-mo version of the tennis-viewing routine. Several of them followed my progress with interest. One of the heads of the teams deployed there (or so I imagine, as he spoke with such authority) told me I should swim. 'It is the best full-body exercise,' he said, marvellously unembarrassed by his glorious belly.

It gave me joy to run among such potbellies—it melted much of my inhibitions away. I still wore the loose, inoffensive clothes and kept pulling my T-shirt down, but mostly I was confident. I was also something of a star there—a performer. Once, I overheard a cop scolding a driver for honking at me. 'Can't you see she is running?' It's the sort of tone I imagine A.R. Rahman's mother took when her son was in the music room.[16] Or any Bengali mother when her son is doing math.

The Long-Running Bias

Kathrine Switzer, one of the first women to run a marathon (Boston, 1967), by Memories of Pandora licensed under CC BY-SA 2.0.
Photo © Openverse.org

Have you seen this photograph from 1967?[17]

Kathrine Switzer, a nineteen-year-old student, is being pushed off the course by Boston Marathon official Jock Semple because women were not allowed to participate in the Boston Marathon, or any marathon, at the time. The Boston guidelines, however, did not mention this, presuming, perhaps, that women would not dare to sign up for or, worse, be interested in the Boston Marathon. Switzer registered for the marathon as 'K.V. Switzer' and was issued running number 261. Everything went swimmingly until about mile four.

In her memoir *Marathon Woman*, she writes about the moment:

> A man with an overcoat and felt hat was then in the middle of the road, shaking his finger at me; he said something to me as I passed and reached out for my hand, catching my glove instead and pulling it off ...
>
> Moments later, I heard the scraping noise of leather shoes coming up fast behind me, an alien and alarming sound amid the muted thump thumping of rubber-soled running shoes ... Instinctively I jerked my head around quickly and looked square into the most vicious face I'd ever seen. A big man, a huge man, with bared teeth was set to pounce, and before I could react he grabbed my shoulder and flung me back, screaming, 'Get the hell out of my race and give me those numbers!' Then he swiped down my front, trying to rip off my bib number, just as I leapt backward from him. He missed the numbers, but I was so surprised and frightened that I slightly wet my pants and turned to run ...[18]

Switzer was so agitated (bless that sentiment) by the attack that she kept running, determined to complete. She finished in four hours and twenty minutes, the first registered female participant to run in and complete the Boston Marathon.

In fact, a woman named Roberta Gibb had completed the Boston Marathon before Switzer. Only the year before, in 1966. But Gibb 'hid behind a bush at the start of the Boston Marathon' and ran on the sly, so to speak. Her request to enter the race had been refused with a note saying that women were not 'physically capable of running a marathon'.[19]

Even before this, there is the story of Stamata Revithi from the first edition of the modern Olympics in 1896. A report by a member of the International Society of Olympic Historians named Athanasios Tarasouleas documents that Revithi was not permitted to participate in the official marathon event on 29 March 1896 as women were barred from competition in the 1896 Games.[20] Nevertheless, she set out from Marathon at 8 a.m. on 30 March and got her start time attested on a document by a schoolmaster of the town, a mayor and a magistrate. Revithi reached the finishing point near a hospital in Athens around 1.30 p.m. She had the presence of mind to also get her finish time attested on a document by officers in Athens. Greek newspapers *Estia* and *Akropolis* carried mentions of Revithi at the time. But her name does not exist on the official Olympic record.

In 1974, the first international marathon for women was organized in Waldniel, Germany. World Athletics, then known as the International Association of Athletics Federations (IAAF), decided in 1983 to include women's marathons at World Cup competitions. The 1984 Olympics in Los Angeles became the first edition of the prestigious quadrennial Games where women were allowed to compete in the marathon.[21]

Right from the start of organized competitive sport at the close of the nineteenth century, running has been accorded high prestige. The 100-metre and 200-metre sprints are the primary showcases of the Olympics. Running and track events as a whole have thrown up several of sport's most enduring legends—on a par with the icons of sports such as football, cricket, tennis, baseball and basketball, whose exploits are easier to love and remember because they are wrapped in the emotive narrative of us-versus-them contests that the games offer. For instance, footballer Diego Maradona's beloved 'hand of God' goal is a cultural touchstone, as is heavyweight boxer Mohammed Ali's two fights against Sonny Liston. This kind of emotive association is difficult in athletics, which is pure sport—individual-based performances in competition with others, rather than in contest with one other. They don't offer the affecting drama of seeing your team (or player, in case of singles tennis) pitted against another.

Consequently, athletes evoke awe and respect but rarely love, barring very devoted fans. We watch Usain Bolt to be dazzled, but rarely with the kind of emotional investment we have for a football or tennis star. Athletics is more beauty and spectacle—a music video rather than an unfolding drama. Unless there is the political context, as in the 1936 Berlin Olympics, known as the Nazi Olympics because of the belief that Adolf Hitler's government would not permit Jewish athletes to participate, and used the Games as a whole to showcase the superiority of Nazi beliefs and systems.[22] The Black American athlete Jesse Owens's four-gold-medal haul at that Games—some of them accomplished as Chancellor Hitler watched from the stands—is among the most emotive stories of sport.

Even without such operatic context, running has given us memorable heroes and stories—Roger Bannister and the legend of the four-minute mile; Eric Liddell, whose story was filmed in *Chariots of Fire*; Carl Lewis (versus eventual-bad-boy Ben Johnson);[23] and, of course, Usain Bolt. Each one of them is a general-knowledge icon, if not a pop-culture one.

How many iconic women runners come to mind as easily? If you said the late Florence Griffith Joyner (whose 100-metre and 200-metre world records set in 1988 stand to date), you are possibly a competitive track runner yourself or a quiz-club veteran. (Much more likely, you have a smartphone with a solid, high-speed internet connection.) If you said P.T. Usha, the athlete who missed a bronze at the 1984 Olympics in Los Angeles by a fraction of a second, you are Indian.

Women have been systematically excluded from competitive running for most of the history of organized sport. For decades, the longest race women could participate in was 200 metres. This continued until 1960, when the 800-metre race was opened to women at the Olympic Games in Rome (and where, incidentally, Milkha Singh finished fourth in the men's 400-metre final).

Today the majority of participants in running events in the US are women. A *Wall Street Journal* report notes, 'Fast, slender men led the first American running boom, in the 1970s and '80s. But women of all shapes and sizes are leading the second running boom.'[24]

The sporting experience is not just officially separate, it is thoroughly so. The running body and its adventures are very different for a woman than they are for a man, especially in a place like India, as our dismal record in sexual violence would suggest. There is little room, and barely concealed impatience, for women in our public spaces and our public life. A woman who walks alone late in the evening is a slut. (A streetwalker is, in any case, a synonym for a prostitute.) A woman who runs? What kind of creature is she?

You, Me, Everyone

As I ran with no great gift but my resolution in places of varied climate and temper, it had occurred to me that perhaps running is the sport most suited to our i-shaped age. Run as long or fast or light or steady or quick or early or late as you like. In cities of cool air, or prickly heat. Accompanied by music, or just by hard, hungry breaths.

The figures bear this out. Over the past decade or so, the number of marathons has swelled. In the US, there were 300 marathons in 2000, in 2011 the figure was 1,100. The number of marathon finishers has also improved impressively—from 353,000 in 2000 to 507,600 in 2016.[25] If this increase does not seem as vivid as the surge in the number of marathons, it is important to remember that this represents the number of those who officially finish the marathon and not the number of participants.

The half-marathon is even more popular. Nearly two million people ran a half-marathon in the US in 2013,[26] up from more than half a million in 2004. The year 2008 marked the English-language publication of Haruki Murakami's memoir *What I Talk about When I Talk about Running*, which has become something of a popular cultural phenomenon. The news site FiveThirtyEight noted in 2013 that running, jogging and triathlons were growing in popularity, based on a five-year perspective comparing data provided by the US Sports and Fitness Industry Association.[27] A 2013 Bloomberg report estimated the running industry to be worth double the football industry.[28] This makes running a serious contender for one of the biggest sports in the world, notwithstanding football's massive popularity across the world.

In 2013, the Boston Marathon, the oldest existing marathon, became a terrorist target, a tragic but nonetheless telling marker of how clearly running has come into the public eye. Here, a distinction must be made from the terrorist attacks on the 1972 Munich Olympics, which was a mission to target elite athletes. This was the kind of terrorist attack that targeted the powerful and the influential—such as the bombing of the US embassies in Dar es Salaam and Nairobi in 1998, or the assassination of Rajiv Gandhi in

1991, a different generation of terrorism. Now terrorist attacks are directed at regular people—the train bombings in Madrid,[29] London and Mumbai through the noughties,[30] and the five contiguous blasts in bus stations and public parks in New Delhi on 13 September 2008. That the Boston marathon was chosen as a site of attack in April 2013 shows how regular marathon participation has become. As commonplace as train travel.

Indians, too, are signing up to run. The country's earliest marathon was the Pune International Marathon, which began in 1986. It was, however, the Mumbai Marathon, which started in 2004, that was the first big hit in public running competitions. There were 134 registered running events in India listed for 2023 on the website www.indiarunning.com. These include a catalogue of options, such as the 5k and 10k races, half-marathons, full and even ultra marathons. Uttar Pradesh even has a run called the Pardada Pardadi (great-grandfather great-grandmother) Half Marathon. Indian women, too, are running, albeit in far fewer numbers than the men, going by observation. There are, nevertheless, nine races earmarked specifically for women.

In the book *Citizenship and Its Discontents*, political scientist Niraja Gopal Jayal has written that women's citizenship in India was premised on the existence of two separate spheres—the private sphere of the home (of duties) and the public sphere of rights. Congress leaders in the national movement, including women such as Sarojini Naidu, held the 'curiously' bifurcated notion of separate spheres for men and women. The private sphere was seen as the domain of responsibilities towards children and families—by implication that of women—and the public sphere as the domain of the exercise of rights—that of men. Extending the vote to women was premised on the understanding that they would bring the values of the private sphere—of care, responsibility and domesticity, mothering and supporting good citizens—to the public sphere '*without in any way threatening* men's exercise of their rights and civic duties' (emphasis mine).[31] In other words, women are expected to be supporting actors in the public sphere—quiet, unobtrusive, retiring. Given this conceptual history, the public gaze that questions the presence of women outside seems natural and logical.

Is there anything for which women are seen as having a legitimate reason to put themselves out there in the world? The answer I have come up with is sport. Sport enables citizens to perform their patriotism. The high nationalism of sport bestows a certain licence to women to put themselves out there in the world in a way that almost nothing does. In particular, I chose to look at running because it is a basic, full-body, minimal-equipment sport. It doesn't need a team—you can run on your own. It is also public in a way that swimming—also basic, full-body, minimal-equipment—is not. Swimming takes bodies out of view. Running puts them on view.

In this introductory chapter, I have tried to map my own adventures and journeys as a hobby runner. Now I want to set out on a pilgrimage of runners—a project of both whim and ambition. *The Day I Became a Runner* is a history of women athletes in India, specifically runners, from the 1940s to contemporary India. Sport is an important and substantive part of my project. But running is also a lens for me to examine what it is like to be a woman in India, to put oneself out there, brushing up against the world, so to speak. In that sense, the ambition is to map a larger history of women in post-independent India, of the anxieties, aspirations and negotiations of being a woman in India. Through this book, I want to trace the arc of citizenship of women in the Indian republic.

I've arranged this book by chronology. First is Mary D'Souza, who ran for India at the 1952 Olympics. Then, there is Kamaljit Sandhu, the first Indian woman to win a gold medal outside India at the 1970 Asian Games in Bangkok. Next is the storied Olympian P.T. Usha, who ran twenty-three years on the international circuit and acquired over a hundred medals.

In the second section of my book, I tell the stories of the three Indian athletes who have been challenged and humiliated for their 'defective sex'—Santhi Soundarajan (2006), Pinki Pramanik (2012) and Dutee Chand (2014). Their experience underlines the central anxiety of competitive female athletes today: Are they female enough to compete as women? Do they meet the precise requirements of anatomy, chromosomes and hormones? Arguably, no other domain in the contemporary world maintains and polices the distinction between the male and the female as competitive sport does. The notion of fair play has led to two separate categories in sport— male and female—for which the biological markers of sex are closely monitored in women alone. Male athletes are not tested. There is no anxiety that women will sneak into men's competitions because they are biologically less powerful and, hence, not as fast.

This segment also doubles up as a study on the media. Its ravenous focus on athletes who are 'not female enough' has brought the issue of biological sex to the fore. But has it led to a better understanding of the fact that sex is not two fixed identities, but rather a spectrum of biologically determined identities that fall between the XX and XY chromosomes? Somehow, the media coverage feels like flashing a powerful torchlight on a person's face in a dark room. It makes the person in the line of the bright light wither, but it doesn't illuminate the room.

In the final third of my book, there is Lalita Babar, the daughter of small, impoverished farmers, who made a name for herself running marathons before switching to the steeplechase in 2014. Two years later, she became the second Indian woman, after P.T. Usha, to make the finals of an Olympic track event in the 3,000-metre steeplechase. Babar embodies a time when running is no longer an elite track sport. The marathon economy has made it a hobby sport, open to anyone who is interested, and its aspirational value translates to extremely good funding and media coverage. Consequently, marathons have broadened the possibility of sport achievement for non-traditional athletes and hobby practitioners as well as elite athletes. Runners in their thirties, for instance, tend to do well in marathons, an age by which most track stars retire. This offers an avenue for track stars once they are past their prime. Equally, it offers possibilities to non-traditional athletes who may not make the cut for track events but make for good long-distance runners.

The Sunrise Project is the story of an initiative to train teenage long-distance runners for this new marathon economy. It is based out of a rural residential school in the Marathwada region, known for drought, agricultural distress and farmer suicides. My chapter on this project chronicles a rural community and how the economic prospects of running have reshaped the lives of boys and girls there.

Finally, there is the profile of Ila Mitra, who was said to have been chosen to represent British India at the 1940 Olympics, which was cancelled because of the outbreak of the Second World War. She would have been the first Indian-origin woman to have gone to the Olympics. The 'missed Olympian' went on to become one of the foremost leaders of the Tebhaga movement, an agrarian protest movement in Bengal that emerged as a result of the Bengal famine of 1943, and asked tillers to give landowners no more than one-third (*teen bhaag*) share of their harvest. In 1951, she became arguably the first woman in the subcontinent to articulate her experience of rape in public when she gave testimony in court about her custodial torture.

She returned to India from East Pakistan for treatment, and later became a Communist Party of India legislator in West Bengal, serving for fifteen years. She was left with a lifelong limp, but Mitra would say that she managed to recover from her custodial injuries because of her fitness and discipline as an athlete.

I end with Mitra because the 2020s feel a lot like the 1940s in India. The wreckage of Covid is reminiscent of the devastation of the 1940s in Bengal, wracked by the famine in 1943 and the Partition in 1947. Pierre de Coubertin, the founder of the modern Olympics, said, 'The important thing in life is not the triumph, but the fight; the essential thing is not to have won, but to have fought well.'[32] Mitra, the missed Olympian, embodied the spirit of sportsmanship and the twin ideal of nationalism that shaped the twentieth century, working for the dignity of the citizens of Bengal on both sides of the border throughout her life.

Alongside this chronology is a more personal thread of time-keeping—my grandmother's story, my mother's, then mine, three generations of women in the same family living through the India of the 1940s to the India of the present moment. A private history of the republic, more or less.

It was 2014 when I began writing this book, the idea birthed in the collective anger I witnessed in the aftermath of the gang rape and murder of a twenty-three-year-old paramedical student in Delhi at the close of 2012. Marches and rallies filled the streets of Lutyens' Delhi, the heart of political and media (optical) power in India. I felt a sense of clarity at that moment of collective anger. For several years, working as a journalist in Delhi and Kolkata, I, indeed many of my women contemporaries, were asked to think of better ideas when we pitched stories of sexual assault. 'People are tired of your tear-jerkers,' my editors would say. It was then that I realized how much rage their dismissiveness had built up inside me.

My own reaction to the protests and marches in the winter of 2012–13 was an overwhelmingly physical one. I wanted to put myself out there on the streets with them. I wanted to occupy space in the world. I wanted to put myself, my body on view. I wanted to tell the world, 'I exist—so get used to me.' So no one would need to ask, 'But what was she doing there?'

Even in that moment of intense public anger, I heard that inevitable question rearing its head. In conversations within the rallies, and without: But what was she doing there? Why was the twenty-three-year-old paramedical student not home by 8 p.m. on a Sunday evening?

I call it the inevitable question because whenever a woman reports an assault or such an incident comes to public light, this question is unfailingly asked of her. It tends to carry two sub-questions: What was she wearing? Where was she going? Abhijit Mukherjee, the son of then President of India Pranab Mukherjee and a Congress MP from Jangipur in West Bengal, achieved his biggest moment in the public eye with his staggering remark that 'dented and painted women' were part of these protests.[33] Mukherjee never unpacked the term 'dented and painted' in the furore that followed, but what he meant was obvious—sex workers.

His comment was widely derided, but that was primarily because it was so cheaply phrased, I think. That inevitable question still remained.

My answer to that question is sport, the one thing for which women are seen as having a good reason to go out into the world. Sport is a project of nationalism. It offers women a solid, respectable reason to put themselves and their bodies out there in the world: for national service. For elite sportswomen, it is national duty. For fitness and hobby sport enthusiasts, it is national improvement. For both, sport appears to bestow a higher degree of citizenship in the public sphere to women.

This book is an exploration of this idea. What does sport offer women in a viciously gendered society such as India? Does it make us more equal citizens? How equal?

Some years ago, I watched the film *The Day I Became a Woman*, a trilogy of stories about a girl on the cusp of adolescence, a young woman and an old woman. The second of the stories is about a group of women who have a secret. They like to cycle. Down a gloriously empty road, they cycle like a pack of kites, their chadors billowing like powerful wings. But in an unforgettable drone shot, we see that each of them, the dozens of women cycling, is wearing a different pair of sneakers, their colours grinning insouciantly beneath their all-black uniform. What an incandescent sight it was, what a blazing protest!

When that day comes here, as it shall, will it look like this?

2

MARY D'SOUZA: THE WOMAN WHO DANCED HER WAY TO HELSINKI

Mary D'Souza. Photo © Goenchimathi.wordpress.com/

IN THE EARLY evening of 15 June 1952, Mary D'Souza put on a freshly laundered dress, dabbed on some lipstick, pinned up her hair and walked down to the St. Andrew's High School hall with two of her sisters, feeling distinctly uncomfortable. She was so used to wearing shorts that the fresh air around her legs made her feel light-headed in the dress. Was it supposed to feel like this?? Or was she wearing the dress wrong? She had to do this gamely, she told herself. She straightened her back, relaxed her shoulders and drew her elder sister, Rose, and her other sister closer around her. When you have eleven siblings, details such as names slip away sometimes, but she was glad for their presence. It made the day feel like a ceremonial occasion, warranting the lipstick and the dress. Her friend, Vincy D'Mello, had gone all out to arrange this 'whist and social', an evening of card games and dancing, for her trip to the Helsinki Olympics, and she was moved.

Truly, she was. Otherwise, would she have worn lipstick?

A fortnight earlier, Mary had met Vincy at the Gymkhana Club in Bandra, the east-Indian-dominated suburb of Bombay, for their usual game of table tennis. She had told him about her trip to Helsinki due that summer. That she was being sent as part of the Indian contingent to the 1952 Olympic Games as a member of the track team. She was thrilled excited, but admitted that she was a little sad too. The Bombay State Amateur Athletic Association was paying for her travel as a participant and she would be accommodated in the Olympic Village, but she had no money to cover any expenses there. That was when D'Mello got the idea for the evening.

At first, D'Mello's friends thought it was a whim. There were barely a couple of weeks before Mary was scheduled to leave.

He could be so excitable, like a breathless child running from fancy to fancy. But he was also full of punch and energy, known for being able to get things done. Later, he would be elected to the municipality, precisely on this reputation.

D'Mello and his friends settled on the assembly hall of the handsome grey-stoned St. Andrew's High School. It was a Catholic school and the fathers were pleased to offer a discounted rate to help the Bandra Catholic girl travelling to Helsinki to represent India. They agreed to the 5.30 p.m. slot, well before cocktail hour and dinner. But neither would be served, they decided—folks in Bandra loved their drink and there was no telling how much would be enough.

No, they would just enjoy an evening of dancing and cards, and raise a toast to Mary. A game of whist always went down well in Bandra, and if it brought in some of the older folks, why not? On little stubs of thick blue paper, tickets were printed in a smart black font, priced at Rs 2 each. Whatever money they collected would be set aside for Mary's trip. Mary danced gamely with the several men who sought her out that evening. As the evening wound down, around 8.30 p.m., they gathered around and toasted her with orange and lemon squash. Was this really happening? This dance, so many people, the songs and the laughter?

The next week, D'Mello handed Mary the hundred-odd rupees they had collected. So much had happened in the past couple of months. First, there was the letter informing her that she was going to the Helsinki Olympics on the track team. Then came the announcement that each athlete would have to submit Rs 5,000 for costs (and that was that, she had thought—a nice buzz while it lasted). Finally there was the news that the Bombay State Amateur Athletic Association would, after all, bear the expenses of the athletes. But only now, holding the money D'Mello had given her, did it feel real.

Just short of twenty-one years, she really was on her way to the 1952 Summer Olympics at Helsinki.

I first came across a photo of Mary D'Souza when I was scrolling through blogs and obscure websites. She looked straight at the camera, her head slightly cocked to the side, wearing a pair of high-waisted pleated shorts with a short-sleeved shirt tucked in. She had a full mop of curly hair secured with a thin band, and held a hockey stick in her right hand. 'Mary D'Souza was part of the 1952 Helsinki Olympics—the first time India sent women athletes to the quadrennial games,' read one blog post.[1]

But the websites carried scant references, no photo credits and insufficient punctuation. There wasn't even a Wikipedia entry on Mary, the minimum recognition for anyone or anything of substance today. Then I found a Facebook page with black-and-white photos of Mary running, playing hockey, sometimes grinning in a team shot. Mary D'Souza is India's first double international, it said. She played in two hockey world cups for women, ran in the Olympics and collected three individual medals over the first and second Asian Games.

Then I got lucky. A fortunate rearrangement of words in my search entry threw up a 2013 story in the *DNA* newspaper: 'Hail Mary: Hockey Player Mary D'Souza Being Honoured with Dhyan Chand Award.'[2] Sixty-one years after she travelled to the Helsinki Olympics, Mary was honoured with the Indian government's award for lifetime achievement in sport, incidentally named after the only major coach she had worked with—international hockey legend

Major Dhyan Chand. At the age of eighty-two, it was the first award she received for her national duties on the track and the hockey field. That summer trip to Helsinki had become a moment acknowledged in the nation's history.

I found myself suddenly moved, unprepared for this turn. I had thought I knew the way this story went—an unusual life lived with heart and fortitude, left unremembered. Instead, on 31 August 2013, Mary travelled to Rashtrapati Bhavan in New Delhi, dressed in a red sari paired with the navy-blue India blazer inscribed with the national insignia, and collected her award from then President of India, Pranab Mukherjee. At eighty-one, she was the oldest awardee by far, four years older than the President himself, who had spent more than forty years in public life. Virat Kohli, one of India's biggest sports stars and one of the greatest batsmen in the world, was among those honoured with the Arjuna Award in the same ceremony. As is the norm with lifetime awards in India, the entire hall stood up to applaud Mary as she went on stage. Later, I would learn that the guests, senior Indian bureaucrats, ministers and their spouses, crowded around Mary after the ceremony, fawning over her, more than they did for Kohli (whose stardom was perhaps more intimidating).

It was a year after she had received this award that I first read about Mary. When I wrote to the Facebook page that carried the photographs, her daughter Marissa responded. Mary was alive, but she was in hospital then. She was having gall bladder surgery. She lived in Atlanta with her daughter's family. Just my luck, I thought, but she was eighty-two, after all. I crossed my fingers.

Mary made it. Ten months later, when I telephoned her for the first time, making an international call from India, I found myself crossing my fingers again. An air pocket swelled in my chest as I prepared mentally for my first conversation with her. In the intervening months, her story had taken root in my mind, and grown into a giant.

How many of us live to see mighty governments scramble to make amends for what they had forgotten? How many stories peel away some of the cynicism that has settled around us? Every journey needs a totem, and I found mine in Mary D'Souza—the first woman who represented India at the Olympics and at two hockey world cups in England and Australia.

'How did you come to hear of me?' Mary asked right after we exchanged greetings. She chuckled as I told her, apparently tickled that anyone would spend time searching for information about her. Then she said, 'Don't mind my asking, dear, but are you married?'

'No,' I said, puzzled. 'Not yet.'

'That's why you have so much time to chase me,' she said.

After this, it was impossible to be intimidated by her.

And the air pocket in my chest dissolved for good.

In the summer of 1952, when Mary got the selection letter for the Olympics, she was preparing to leave for a job in the hill station of Ooty in the state of Madras. A school there had offered her a salary of Rs 250 a month for the position of physical training instructor. She had quickly agreed—her job at St. Joseph's Convent in Bombay paid her Rs 100. She would also get a room to herself there. Mary had always had to share her room with a continent of siblings. It sounded irresistible.

The letter for Helsinki felt unreal, like a lottery ticket. Mary had begun sprinting only two years before this. In her first year of competition, she had won third place in the 200-metre event in Bombay and was selected to represent India at the inaugural Asian

Games in 1951. She had gone to New Delhi, travelling third-class on the train, and came back with a bronze for the 200-metre sprint. And now, there was a call for the Olympics.

When the notification asking for a submission of Rs 5,000 towards her cost of travel for the Helsinki Olympics arrived, it felt like life had come back to normal. 'There was no question,' she told me. 'I didn't have the money. Daddy had fed twelve of us and my mother on a single income. I had just begun to earn, one of my brothers had left for England—it was our time to contribute to the household. My parents, they never saw me run or play because Daddy was always out and Mummy was cooking. We ate our meals, paid our bills, and that was it—there were no savings.'

On the sports pages of *The Times of India*, a terrific scramble of preparations was being reported within various sports federations and the Indian Olympic Association (IOA) as India readied to send her second delegation to the summer Olympics as an independent nation.[3] It was the first time the country would send women to the Olympics, and perhaps *that* was seen as an invitation to a free-for-all. Over April and May 1952, a number of federations such as the wrestling federation, cycling association, rifle association and the boxing federation rowed within themselves and with the IOA over sending representatives of their sport to Helsinki. Some of these federations, such as the one for cyclists, decided to ask selected participants to pay Rs 4,000 each for their passage. In *The Times of India*, Leon, who went only by one name and wrote the no-holds-barred weekly column 'Bori Bunder Gossip', alleged that there was also a terrific scramble among sports officials to enjoy a free trip to Helsinki.[4]

'I remember going to school in the mornings, training and playing hockey in the afternoons. And preparing for Ooty—that was the main thing then! I had bought warm clothes, and I was learning to cook simple things, in case I needed to. I didn't bother about the Olympics because no one thought we were going.'

Even at twenty, she had a certain detachment, a distance she retained through her life. No ambition had that close a hold on her heart. She was practical. When you have ten other siblings, a father on the verge of retirement and no family savings, there is no time to brood. Mary was a stoic. In the impoverished, wretched sports establishment in India, perhaps this is the most important gift of all.

Then one day, a note arrived from the Bombay State Athletic Association, informing Mary that their Olympic uniforms had come, and that she was to go and collect hers. The set comprised a white shirt, a pair of divided shorts, a light-blue sleeveless Nehru jacket with the India crown on the breast pocket, and a white salwar-kurta for the opening ceremony. (The men wore white shirts, white trousers and light blue blazers at the ceremony.)

'I thought it was a consolation prize, because they couldn't send us to the Games,' Mary told me. 'Frankly, that made sense, because those days no one travelled abroad ... unless you got a job on a ship, like one of my brothers did. And why would we go to the Olympics? To come last?'

But along with her clothes was her ticket to Europe. The state association was paying for her travel to the Olympics. In fact, they would spend a couple of weeks in Copenhagen before the Olympics. The Indian contingent would first train there, then travel to Helsinki for the Olympics. This was, after all, the first time most of them had set foot in Europe. Only Lavy Pinto, the champion sprinter from Bombay, had been sent to London for training almost a month ahead of the Games by his employers, the Tatas.

Copenhagen would be the first time she would work with a coach in her athletics career. They spent time on her starting position (the crouch on the ground before the sprint) and on moving her legs in a cycling motion at full pelt. These were little things that made you look good, more professional. A fortnight was too little for anything meaningful, but it was a nice gesture from the government, she felt.

She met most of the sixty-four-member Indian contingent on the special chartered flight to Copenhagen. Aside from the men's hockey team, which had been flown to London for the 1948 Olympics, no one had flown on an airplane before. The general nervousness meant an excellent ice-breaking session, as boisterous or as quiet as you wanted to be—people were either too excited or too uneasy to judge. Of the sixty-four members, four were women. Besides herself, there were Nilima Ghose, her partner in athletics—a square-shouldered, quiet girl from Calcutta—and two swimmers, Arati Saha and Dolly Nazir.

The summer was beautiful that year, as hot as Bombay but with that glorious clear light of European summer. A couple of days before the Games, they reached the Olympic Village in the Käpylä district outside Helsinki and were thrilled with the arrangements—the neat, hygienic rooms, the tureens of inviting new foods, the many nations and peoples they met. She had expected to be overwhelmed, and she was. No one she knew had gone to the Olympics, and the newspapers did not write about food and living provisions, not unless there was a problem.

'I turned twenty-one on 18 July, but I don't know what I did for my birthday. It was thrilling to be outside India, so far from home. If I remember right, it was the day before the Games opened. We must have done a rehearsal of the march past. Balbir Singh, the hockey vice-captain, was our flagbearer. It was very stiff and formal; we marched in the India colours behind Balbir Singh holding the tricolour aloft.'

The next day, at the actual opening, a light rain fell. The heat was gone. A man walked in front of Balbir Singh with a placard that said 'INTIA'—it was not a typo, but how the Finns (and the Inuit) spelt India. Something clicked into place within her. Her excitement stilled. The foreign trip, the crisp delicious summer receded. Her back straightened, her shoulders squared. Everyone's did, she thought. Perhaps it was the ceremony of national representation that made them feel a certain purpose.

The Indian hockey team, then in the middle of its six-golds-on-the-trot spree, was expected to play for glory. For everyone else on the Indian contingent, their role was to save face—justify the passage from India to Helsinki, the trip's expenses plucked from the coffers of an impoverished nation.

She had no chance of winning. Or even qualifying. Mary knew this with the clarity of basic arithmetic—she had done 100 metres in 13 seconds in her national record-breaking effort that year. And Marjorie Nelson-Jackson of Australia, the principal contender for the 100-metre gold (and eventual winner), was doing 11.6 seconds.

A difference of 1.4 seconds in athletics is the distance between the First World and the Third World. Marjorie was years ahead of Mary in training, support and equipment. She had a personal coach and first-class training facilities. Mary had two years of self-coaching, and a pair of spikes.

On Monday, 21 July 1952, the heats for the 100-metre sprint for women were held. There were twelve rounds of heats—Mary's was the ninth. She carried her new starting blocks, said a prayer and hugged herself close. *Don't slip, don't fall ... God, let me not do anything idiotic.* Her breath felt trapped against the walls of her chest. Nothing else of the day remains with her—the sun, the people, whether she had lunch or not. It was as if the day had condensed to the inside of her chest—the loneliest day of her life. She came last in her heat, doing 13.1 seconds. It was a little worse than her best, but it wasn't the worst in the competition. Out of fifty-six contestants, five finished with worse time than her. One of these was her compatriot, seventeen-year-old Nilima Ghose, who clocked 13.8 seconds in the first heat.

The heats for the 200-metre were held on Friday, 25 July. Seven heats for thirty-eight participants. Mary's was the third, a tough round with Marjorie Jackson, the eventual winner of the 100-metre and 200-metre events that year. Mary came last in her heat again, with a time of 26.3 seconds. She was fifth from the bottom out of a pool of thirty-eight contenders.

The Indian Olympic contingent returned with one gold for the men's hockey team and one bronze for K.D. Jadhav for wrestling. Leon described India's show at Helsinki as 'comic-opera exploits' in his Bori Bunder Gossip column. 'Actual events served to demonstrate in as clear a manner as possible that our contingent should have comprised only a hockey side and Lavy Pinto; everything else was superfluous …'

Interestingly, Leon didn't count K.D. Jadhav, the policeman who won bronze for wrestling at Helsinki, as one of the worthy passengers to Helsinki. Jadhav was the first Indian to win an individual medal at the Olympics. Technically, the first Indian to have a medal listed against his name in the Olympics is Norman Pritchard, but Pritchard had British parents and was only Indian to the extent that he was born in Calcutta.

Mary nodded when I read Leon aloud to her. 'He's right, this Leon. We had no chance.' She was quiet for a bit, and then she spoke again. 'But this is what the Olympic spirit is about, no? To see what excellence is, to learn from seeing it. If it were about winning, there would be only three to four countries—America, Russia, Germany and Britain. What an Olympics that would be!' she said, laughing.

In truth, the Olympics is much more than a competition in sport—it is equally about competing political systems and performing nationalisms. The great Cold War rivalry of the US and the Soviet

Union was perhaps most evident in the Olympic results. In the 1952 Games, the Americans and the Soviets were first and second, with not much separating them. The Americans had seventy-six medals (with forty golds) in all, and the Soviets seventy-one (with twenty-two golds). For a new nation such as India, emerging from the Independence struggle, the Olympics was an arena to say: Here we are now, our own people with our own flag, staking our own place in the world.

It was also a message, Mary thought, to send women to the Olympics. It was the charismatic Prime Minister Jawaharlal Nehru's way of reaching out to Indian women—telling them they, too, were this country, that they, too, could go to the Olympics, or indeed, anywhere in the world, that they, too, held sovereign rights over their lives. Perhaps Mary had thought less about this than another woman might have. She was Catholic—she'd have worked some job anyway. They all did. Mary's neighbours, sisters—they were teachers, secretaries, saleswomen, typists; one of her sisters had even cracked the civil service exam. Only her mother didn't work outside the home. She was from the previous generation, which stayed home.

'You know what I was thinking before the Olympics? What would happen to my job in Ooty. I asked my neighbour, Yvonne D'Souza, if she would go in my place. She agreed, and I wrote the school a letter saying I was very sorry, but I was going to the summer Olympics. Could I join them two months later in August?'

The Helsinki trip shifted something in Mary, though. Flying home deep in the August rains of Bombay, she decided she wouldn't take the job in Ooty, after all. She was more than a PT teacher, she had realized. She would do whatever it took to be a full-time athlete. She would stay back in Bombay and give that life a shot.

🔱

Mary's sports career was unplanned, largely bereft of financial support, and for a long time, a source of annoyance to her family. The only thing you could say was that her family did not actually stop her from playing. Her father, Francis D'Souza, had moved from his ancestral village of Aldona in Goa to the sleepy Portuguese Catholic suburb of Bandra in Bombay after the birth of his sixth child. Goa was part of the Portuguese colonial empire in India, and Bandra remained with the Portuguese, even after Bombay was gifted to the British as part of an enormous dowry in the marriage of Catherine of Braganza, a princess whose looks alone were considered inadequate to net a good match, to Charles II of England.

Francis secured the job of a motorman in the Indian Railways in 1933. Mary, his seventh child, was born in Bombay in 1931. She was followed by four more children in the D'Souza family. Mary and her sisters went to a Catholic missionary school in the neighbourhood, St. Joseph's Convent. Girls were taught to be ladylike and proper— there was no question of showing their legs shamelessly and running around like boys. Yet, for their exploits in the sack race, spoon-and-potato race and three-legged race, Mary and her sister Rose, elder to her by four years, managed to gain the monikers of Junior Champ and Senior Champ.

One evening, a man named Emil D'Souza (no relation) showed up at their door. He had set up a women's hockey team in Bandra, called the Suburban Elles. Three of his sisters were on the team, and he was scouting for other girls from the neighbourhood. He had heard of the two racing champions of St. Joseph's Convent. Would they be interested? The sisters had never held a hockey stick in their lives, but were thrilled to be invited. Francis shrugged—he didn't think much of any project that *invited* his daughters. Still, he thought, it might ease the terrific racket at home in the evenings. Emil bought them hockey sticks, and taught them to play.

This was the beginning of Mary's sports career. Every day after tea, she would walk from their house at 20 Hill Road to a large municipal school ground that the boys in Bandra took over to play hockey. Mary would be the sole girl in sight. The neighbourhood noticed. She acquired the reputation of a tomboy, and Francis wasn't pleased about it. Mary was never home in the evenings, he fumed. 'If you have to get exercise, why can't you help your mother in the kitchen?' he told her. 'Grind the masalas, sweep the floor, mop the house.'

Later, when Mary made the headlines on the sports pages of Bombay's newspapers, she would see Francis cut out the stories to show his friends on the Bandra promenade, where he walked every evening. He had retired by then, and somewhat mellowed, but not enough to tell Mary himself what he thought of her achievement. They were not that kind of people. He died not long after his retirement, before he could watch Mary run or play hockey.

Like hockey, athletics just happened to her. One day her cousin, Maxi Vaz, showed up at her home and took her to the Brabourne stadium, where the Bombay State Athletics Meet of 1950 was being held. Maxi played hockey, and had been impressed with Mary's speed in the game. He'd told Mary that she should give running a try, but she hadn't realized he was serious. He put her name down for the 100- and 200-metre sprints. Mary had never seen a track competition, or even an oval track before this. When she saw a man putting three girls through stretches and exercises, she thought it was stupid. Let them tire themselves out, she thought, she'd beat them easily. They were Roshan Mistry, Bano Gazdar and Pat Mendonca, well-known athletes in the Bombay circuit, and they beat her in both the 100- and the 200-metre.

But Mary managed a fourth-place finish in one of the races. Mistry, Gazdar and Mendonca were so well known on the Bombay circuit that as the newcomer who came close to beating them,

Mary made an impression too. A couple of newspapers made mention of her the next morning.

Mary decided she wanted to beat those three. She had learnt that the Brabourne ground was open for training in the morning, and started going. Mistry, Mendonca and Gazdar would be there too, training with the man she had seen on the day of the competition. This was their coach, Jal Pardiwala. The girls never spoke to her, nor did Jal, and she didn't speak to them either. Yet, a training regimen began: Mary did whatever she saw them doing. She ran the number of rounds they did, and followed their stretching exercises. The results showed. Next year, in 1951, Mary finished second in the 200-metre sprint.

On the basis of this performance, she was selected for the inaugural Asian Games, and travelled on a third-class train ticket to New Delhi. She came third in the 200-metre sprint, and with her Bombay rivals Bano Gazdar, Roshan Mistry and Pat Mendonca, won silver in the 4x100-metre relay. This was what earned her the ticket to the Helsinki Olympics.

It is hard to understand how much of a thrill foreign travel was in the 1950s in India, when no one except the Prime Minister, some Cabinet ministers and a handful of elite business families travelled anywhere. The first Indian film to have a sequence shot abroad would come several years later, in 1964. *Sangam* was a big-budget Hindi film made by the Bombay film industry, the country's richest. Through those years, Mary travelled repeatedly across the world—to Finland, the UK and Australia.

Sport was a precarious, non-glamorous and often-heartbreaking career in the 1950s. (Seventy years later, it is still a damned brave choice in India, more so for women.) It would be three decades before the government started sports promotion schemes for women in the early 1980s. The only support for sportspersons at the time was the employment that Indian companies such as the Tatas and the Mahindras, and the Indian Railways offered. Sport in itself paid no money. When Mary travelled for a hockey match or a track competition, she would get a third-class train ticket in India; she would sleep on bedrolls in government schools and colleges. Essentially, you played for the honour of wearing the India colours.

Still, it was a remarkable life, rich with adventure and the glamour of travel. Very, *very* few women, in any case, played a sport in the country then. It meant performing in the public sphere, and most Indian families did not permit this. The ones that did were mainly Catholic and Parsee families. You see this in the sports pages of Indian newspapers of the 1950s—full of D'Souzas and Fernandeses and, to a lesser extent, Nazirs and Mistrys.[5] Very occasionally, there was a Nilima Ghose or an Arati Saha or an Ela Sen—girls from the very rare, likely very liberal, Calcutta families.

Not long after she declined the job at the boarding school, Mary got a call from the Tatas, the largest, most prestigious industrial conglomerate in India at the time. They offered her a job in the sales department of Lakmé, their cosmetics wing, to market lipsticks. Her office was in the handsome Taj Mahal Hotel, now imprinted in history as the site of the 26/11 terrorist attacks in Bombay. She signed in at 10 a.m., worked until lunchtime, changed into her training clothes and left for the Brabourne cricket ground.

Like many women athletes in an era when women's sport was seen as a forum for participation, D'Souza competed in more than one sport. She was an attacking centre-forward, an integral part of the first women's hockey teams in India. Three days a week she ran track and three days she played hockey. At 3 p.m., when her training slot started, the sun was at its highest, hottest and most injurious in Bombay. But it was this or nothing—the only time slot available for women was 3 p.m. to 5 p.m. In all likelihood, it was not even a slot, but a time of the afternoon when no one dared to brave the heat.

There were no women's bathrooms in the stadium either. After practice, Mary would wear her track pants over her shorts and take the train home in her sweaty clothes. Perhaps this was what she remembered the most about the Olympic Village at Helsinki—the abundance of showers and changing rooms, and the hot water that never ran out.

Still, these were the best years of her life. There were evenings when Mary would go out—she loved dancing and jazz at the Taj Mahal Hotel, though she had to leave just as the dance floor was filling up, because she needed her sleep. She couldn't drink too much. Running was the opposite of fun. It was enervating, solitary and exacting, eating up her energy, eating into her evenings. Its joys were too slender, its demands constant. It was only the thought of being the best at something—the fastest woman in India, perhaps Asia—that kept her at it. Standing on the tallest square of the podium.

From 1952 to 1956, Mary was the fastest woman in India, undefeated at the national games. She was also a well-known hockey player, known for her terrific speed and attacking game, and represented both Bombay and India at the sport for more than fifteen years. In 1953, she travelled to the UK by ship to play in the unofficial women's hockey world cup—the International Federation of Women's Hockey Association tournament—at Folkestone in Kent, England. In May 1956, she travelled to Australia for the second edition of the women's hockey world cup. And she was expecting to make a second trip to Australia that year. The 1956 Olympics were slated for Melbourne that November.

Soon after she returned home from the hockey tournament, the Bombay State Amateur Athletic Association sent Mary and a select team of Bombay athletes first to the former Czechoslovakia and then to London to train for the Olympics. The fastest Indian of the time, Lavy Pinto, was also going. Pinto had trained in England before the Helsinki Olympics too, and he had been the only Indian athlete to make it through two heats right up to the semi-final in Helsinki. There was another young woman in the London selection, who, too, was called Mary. Mary Leela Rao.

Mary D'Souza's own speed had improved by a full second since Helsinki—she was doing 12.1 seconds for 100 metres then. If the London training went well, perhaps she could shave off another tenth of a second. She had a chance, she thought—an outside one, mind you—of doing well in her heat and qualifying for the semi-final in the 100-metre.

It was autumn by the time the Bombay bunch reached London, and the grey cold had set in. Mornings were chilly and fretful, and the gloomy evenings slipped in by 3 p.m. But Mary was unaffected—she was at the peak of her running form then. There is joy in a fit body, a synergy so sublime that it feels like song. On 24 September 1956, a curious report appeared on the sports page of *The Times of India*. Four Bombay athletes, it said, were in danger of losing their Olympic berths if they did not report for a training camp in Patiala in the first week of October.[6] Over the past few days, the newspaper had carried a string of reports on the growing number of Olympic aspirants, the straitened finances of the Indian Olympic Association and the strict rationing of funds by the Indian government.

In London, a different story reached the athletes. Mary was told that women would not be sent on the Indian team to Melbourne as the government was short of money. She was taken aback—she had been informed of her provisional inclusion in the Olympic squad back in March. The news upset her, and she decided to stay back in England. Her Bombay teammates Alex Silveira (who once defeated India's legendary sprinter Milkha Singh at his pet event, the 400 metres[7]) and the other Mary, Mary Leela Rao, left for India.

Over October and November 1956, until days before the Olympics began, the reports about the severely restricted Olympic budget continued. Initially, seventy-nine sportspersons were expected to travel, but only fifty-nine made the actual journey. And one woman did travel to Melbourne, after all—Mary Leela Rao.

On 14 November, a short report appeared in *The Times of India*, describing Rao as one of the 'loveliest athletes in the village': 'This slender student has drawn admiring glances whether in the dining hall in her midnight blue sari and gold-studded sandals or on the track in her black track suit with the unusual appendage of earrings and bangles.'[8] On 25 November, the sports-page lead story was about Rao: She had pulled her thigh muscle and fallen flat on her face as she had started her 100-metre heat.[9]

Understandably, Rao failed to qualify.

'Can you believe that? She literally fell on her face,' Mary said, unusually forcefully. 'I now think: Why didn't I push for myself? Why didn't I ask some more questions? After all, Mary Rao went. I could have put my foot down and argued that I had better timing than her. I lost my mind, thinking it would be better to stay back in the UK. I missed my chance.' Clearly, it was a memory that still moved her, and she spoke with a vehemence that I didn't see in her either earlier or later.

Mary effectively gave up running after this. In 1957, she decided to get married. She'd known her husband for a year by then—he had nothing to do with sport, but he made her laugh. When she became pregnant soon after, she was relieved that she had a reason to ease out of running. In truth, something had shifted irreparably and she wasn't enjoying herself as much as she once did. It was only work now—the thrill and anticipation were gone. She would continue playing hockey until 1968, however, long after her daughter Marissa was born.

In Atlanta, where she has lived with Marissa for more than a decade, she spends many hours in solitude, completely on her own. Every day but Tuesday, Mary would go over to the local senior centre in Atlanta, play bridge and chat. In the afternoons, she would lunch alone. Marissa left her a cooked meal—she just needed to heat it. Then she would nap. Later, she would go for her walk and by the time she returned, the family would be back. She took long, rambling, luxuriously undisturbed walks, and found her thoughts going back to her playing days. For many years, she hadn't wanted to remember these days.

Tuesdays were the days we usually spoke. It would be late evening for me, and post-breakfast for Mary in Atlanta. She always appeared cheerful, energetic, slender, taut-skinned and in excellent health. She seemed content, and I complimented her for enjoying her eighties—an age that hollowed out three of my grandparents who made it to that age, not only physically, but also emotionally.

The Indian government award, my questions—these had brought old memories back, she told me. Perhaps she could have tried harder? Fought and pushed to go for her second Olympics in Melbourne? Had she let go too easily? Had she really made a kind of history? Why didn't anybody tell her then?

'I have been lucky, you know,' she told me one day. 'I came up fast. In my second year, I was winning medals at the Asian Games. People take years to come to the top. I did work, but perhaps it was easier in my time. Fewer women tried out sport. I see my grandson today, how much he trains. He measures his food, his carbs and proteins, he goes to sleep early—he's so disciplined. He's much better than I ever could be, but he will never make the Olympics team. It breaks my heart sometimes,' she said.

I felt a stab of envy amid my admiration for her. I was weathering a stubborn bout of anxiety and depression when I met her. Nothing exceptional, the squalls of any human life: My father was terminally ill, I was falling in love but afraid to say it out loud, a close friend had stopped speaking to me. Every life has these afflictions, yet I was often unable to sit still and face mine. Why couldn't I have some of Mary's cheer, I wondered? Why couldn't I break off some of that fortitude for myself?

※

In the summer of 1952, when Mary became one of the first women to represent India at the Olympics, my maternal grandmother, Dipti Banerjee (nee Mukerjee), became the first woman in her family to pass the intermediate examination, the equivalent of the Class XII university-qualifying degree. Though she was the fourth-born of her siblings, and the third of the sisters, she was the first to graduate with a Bachelor of Science degree in 1954.

Dipti enrolled for a chemistry honours degree in Bombay's Siddharth College, a new co-educational college set up by the great scholar, reformer and Constitution-maker Dr B.R. Ambedkar. It wasn't that the Banerjees were liberal enough to permit their daughter to choose a co-ed college for herself, or that Dipti insisted. Dipti's eldest brother, Pronab Deb, had enrolled for his bachelor's degree at Siddharth, having quit his apprenticeship in a huff. With their eldest son on hand, the Banerjees felt their daughter would be better monitored on the same premises than if she studied in a girls' college by herself. Later, Dipti's sister Tuhina, returned from a failed nuptial mission, and enrolled for a humanities degree at Siddharth as well.

With or without their brother, the sisters were fully committed to being good girls. They attended all their classes, carried tiffin from home, declined invitations to watch films and saved their pocket money so they could pitch in with the household finances. Every morning, Dipti took the train from Bombay Central to Churchgate to attend college. In the evening after classes, she went straight to the kitchen to help her mother.

It was like this that Dipti became the first woman in the Banerjee family to earn a university degree, along with a lifelong reputation for being clever. Dipti's first nephew was born the year she graduated, and her eldest sister suffered from devastating post-natal depression. Dipti, only eighteen then, gave herself wholly to the child's care. There was no question of getting a job—no women from good Hindu families worked in those days. The main thing was to get a husband. She was a slender girl with a swan-like neck, unusually tall for an Indian woman, at five feet five inches, dusky and very pretty. Her lips were full, her cheekbones high, her cheeks taut, her oval face had a poised beauty fit for a painting. And she was a graduate to boot.

What a catch she would be on the marriage market!

One evening, as Dipti was crossing the street, a motorbike skid and hit her. She was twenty-one then. When she fell, she hurt her head and the doctor advised her bed rest for a year in full darkness. So she lay almost a year in a solitary room, the curtains always drawn, eating meals brought to her on a tray. Perhaps the accident dented her chances of marriage. No offers came her way for the next three years. But there was another nephew in the apartment, brought to Bombay for the chance to study in an English-medium convent, who needed a mother's care. Besides, Mrs Banerjee was getting old, Dipti's father, Tom Banerjee, was retired and increasingly irritable, the household still large and its finances stretched. As soon as Dipti recovered, she went back to her household duties. She woke up before dawn with her mother to collect water before the municipality stopped supply, and slept after 11.30 p.m., after everyone had been fed and the dishes done.

Her daily chores included taking her nephew to school, and she often chatted with his teachers at the missionary school. Soon, one of them offered her a teaching job, and she was panic-stricken. She couldn't say no, but in class she found herself imagining the dust gathering on the shelves at home, the clothes piling up for washing. When a month had passed, she felt she had done enough to honour the priest's request and asked to be excused. That night she slept well for the first time in weeks.

In 1959, at the age of twenty-five, she was married to Brojoraj Mukerjee, my grandfather, older than her by eleven years and the star of his eight-sibling family in Calcutta. He had a taste for tailored suits and cocktails, a job in a British firm called Avery and membership of the Calcutta chapter of the Freemasons. She was a Bombay graduate, and carried the label of a cosmopolitan girl throughout her life, though she chose to devote herself to scrubbing and dusting the home, sewing, managing the kitchen and transferring leftover food from large utensils to smaller ones. She gained a reputation for being smart, managing to keep Brojoraj's impulsive spending in check. Through her life, across both her own and marital families, and a large network of family friends and neighbours, she was consulted for her quick wit in the present and wise view of the future. Property sale? Dipti. Court case? Dipti. Marriage? Dipti.

Soon after she arrived in Calcutta, she was offered a job to teach maths at a high school in north Calcutta, close to her large, shambling conjugal home. Her mother-in-law, a conservative, taciturn woman, was uncharacteristically in favour of the job, but Dipti declined. She preferred looking after the accounts of the household, she said, and taking care of her three youngest brothers-in-law, all teenagers then. Later, when her own children were older, her daughter's school asked her to teach physics and chemistry in Class XI and XII. She cut an unusual, impressive figure among the mothers, the rare woman with a degree in science and perfect fluency in English. But she refused.

When I heard these stories for the first time, I thought there was something she was holding back. Dipti and I have never been close, but I knew her as a woman of thoughtfulness and courage. There was pressure from home, I thought—she doesn't want to give my grandfather away.

But with every telling, as I pushed her for her reasons, I came away at first surprised, then disappointed. Her world was in the home, she told me. The thought of working outside filled her with anxiety and ate away at her sleep. What if she failed? Who would dust the sofa and match the cushions? Would her husband and children get their meals as hot as they liked them? Who would put away the leftovers in smaller utensils?

Four years before she passed away, I moved in with Dipti in her new convenient flat after I quit my job in Delhi and returned to Kolkata to get married, a commitment that was eventually called off. In our new live-in intimacy, I noticed things I hadn't before: She could not abide the thought of her help eating at the table with her, though she depended on them; she ignored her bank correspondence and tax filings because she hadn't been used to dealing with them; she avoided the camera, e-mail, the mobile phone—the simplest technology unsettled her. Most of all, she was terrified of the inevitable onset of age with its physical and mental frailties.

In a series of novellas written at the turn of the twentieth century—*Nashtoneer* (*The Broken Nest*), *Chokher Bali* (*Eyesore*) and *Ghare Baire* (*The Home and the World*)—Nobel Prize-winning author Rabindranath Tagore wrote about the evolving identity of women as education and modernity brought them to the threshold between the home and the world outside it. In writing about his heroines

Bimala, Binodini and Charulata, Tagore drew a vivid picture of the evolving position of women in Indian society with the advance of modernity. By the end of each of these novels, his heroines had taken their first tentative steps outside the home and into the world. But my grandmother Dipti never did, though she arguably received a far more Western education than they did.

I know this business of comparison is a bogus one. No life can really be measured against another, so what good does it do except point out facile differences? Yet, when I think of Mary, I can't help but think of Dipti. They grew up in the same city, within a distance of ten miles and a couple of years of each other. Perhaps they crossed each other's paths at Churchgate station, or even spoke in passing while waiting for or travelling on the local train. Yet, how distinct Mary's tryst with modernity was. How calmly she made her way into the world and her home in it. How bravely she recognized and accepted her limited prospects, embracing the adventures of third-class train travel and dancing her way to the Olympics. What a chance she got at history and what a terrific gutsy swoop she took at it.

3

KAMALJIT SANDHU:
THE WOMAN WHO TOOK GOLD
UNEXPECTEDLY

Kamaljit Sandhu. Photo © *Hindustan Times*,
issue dated 24 December 1970

THE MORNING OF 13 December 1970 in the capital of Thailand saw heavy rain, the majestic downpour of the tropics where the music of water returning to earth stuns you into a daze. By late afternoon, though the rain had stopped for hours and the running track had dried out, small puddles remained in places. This was the day Kamaljit Sandhu ran a full second slower than her best time, but still fast enough to win gold. But it wasn't just the water that slowed her down.

Since morning, she had experienced the familiar trance that came over her on competition days. The voices around her were muffled, the words garbled. The faces of people appeared as masks, one indistinguishable from the other. Only her breathing was audible to her—calm, rhythmic and amplified, as if there was a microphone attached to her lungs. The air around her seemed rarefied, sealing her inside a capsule of pure focus. Kamaljit felt pleased—she was in the groove.

Later in her career as a coach, she would learn that those were her hormones responding to the anxiety of the race, locking her mind in concentration. But at the time, she thought it was something spiritual, a cosmic design that propelled her performance. She had woken up that morning and immediately felt in the groove, as if someone had turned on a switch when she was sleeping and the universe had receded into a muffled hum around her.

It was day four at the 1970 Asian Games in Bangkok. India had sent a contingent of 150 persons to the Games. That was the number that marched in blue blazers, white trousers and blue turbans at the opening ceremony of the Asian Games on 9 December. Of the 150, only two were women—the second was Manjit Walia, who had won bronze at the 80-metre hurdles in the 1966 Asian Games.[1] Kamaljit had been picked for the 400-metre sprint.

'You know that the Olympic-medallist will participate, after all?' someone came up to her and said. Kamaljit looked in the direction of the voice and saw a vaguely familiar face. 'Oh,' she replied. The face said some more things in response. The sound reached Kamaljit, but the words themselves were garbled now. 'Oh,' she said again, and then her boarding-school politeness kicked in. 'Good luck,' she said, and returned to warming up.

The top contender in the 400-metre event was Chi Cheng, a Taiwanese athlete who had won bronze at the 1968 Mexico Olympics for the 80-metre hurdles. Over the past year, she had set a new world record in the 100-metre hurdles and equalled the world record for the 100-metre sprint at 11.6 seconds. In Bangkok, she had already won gold for the 100-metre sprint and was widely expected to sweep her other events. But she had run with her left leg strapped in bandages in the heats and was reported to have strained her leg even further.

Earlier that year, Kamaljit had represented India in Singapore and Malaysia in small events, and won. She thought she had a chance in Bangkok too. When the starting pistol went off, Kamaljit's eyes locked on the runner in lane 8 on her right. It was an old habit. The first time Kamaljit had run on an oval track was in high school at the convent in Hyderabad where she had studied for just a couple of months. Still, she had learnt a lesson here that she would remember all her life. She hadn't known then that the innermost lane meant running the least distance around the bend of the track, and the outermost lane meant running the widest arc of the curve. That is why the runner in outermost lane starts furthest up the tracks. Kamaljit, who had always raced in a straight line before this, panicked to see how far ahead the outer-lane runners were, and went flat out to catch up with them. By the time she had crossed the first bend, she had taken a big lead. Relieved, she paced herself to the finishing line, maintaining her first position.

That memory—of panic, then relief—stayed with her. It became her style. She would go flat out into the first bend, then take stock of her position and pace herself to the finish. The 400-metre race is not a pure sprint like the 100-metre. It has to be paced.

That afternoon in Bangkok, she had barely taken the lead when a figure from the left overtook her. Kamaljit was pushing to accelerate further when the figure on her left crumpled and fell, inducing a momentary sense of vertigo in Kamaljit. Startled, she slowed down, gathered her breath and ran until she breasted the tape at the finishing line.

The world switched back on. It was as if someone had unmuted the sound. Now Kamaljit could hear her voice being shouted from the stands, and turned to look. Some of her team members from the Indian contingent were waving. She looked for her coach, Ajmer Singh, but he was already at her elbow. She was first, he informed her—she had won gold, running with a time of 57.3 seconds, even though the woman who had won silver had also clocked 57.3 seconds.

When she looked at the silver medallist, she realized this was the face who had come to tell her about the Olympic-medal winner. Alvin Balass from Israel. 'Congratulations, Alvin!' she called out, feeling a sudden dip in her mood. She remembered that the woman who had fallen had overtaken her to lead the race. 'What happened to that girl?' she asked Singh. He pointed, and she saw Chi Cheng hobbling towards her, leaning on a man for support. 'Congratulations,' Chi called out to Kamaljit.

'It was your race, you know,' Kamaljit replied, taken aback.

'These things happen in sport,' Chi said. 'Whoever wins is the winner.'

Later that evening, there were telegrams from Prime Minister Indira Gandhi and President V.V. Giri. Kamaljit Sandhu had made history, the first Indian woman to win a solo gold for track and field at an international event. Many years later, she would remember Chi Cheng's words and take comfort from them when disappointment threatened to overwhelm her. The world is what it is. Whatever happens is meant to be. It is destiny.

In December 1970, the news in India was glum all around. The political uncertainty brewing in erstwhile East Pakistan would eventually lead to a war with India in 1971 and the birth of Bangladesh. In Bengal, supporters of militant Left ideology known as the Naxals had launched violent attacks on government functionaries and properties. The staff of the country's sole airline, Air India, were on strike, leading to crippling losses for the national carrier. Workers in jute mills were agitating for better pay and working conditions; cotton supply stocks in India were running so low that cotton mill owners were taking out advertisements in the newspapers to complain about their situation. The optimism of independence, of a new beginning, that was palpable through the 1950s had long worn away.

Perhaps, for this reason, Kamaljit would be a fixture in the newspapers for weeks and months after her success. The gold medal in Bangkok landed her on the front first page of *The Times of India*, Bombay, and *Hindustan Times*, Delhi. Two days after Kamaljit won, there was a picture of her reaching the finishing line. The day after that, there was one of her on the podium with her gold medal, alongside the silver and bronze winners. When the Indian contingent arrived in Delhi after the Asian Games, she was the only member of the team photographed at the airport—in a sari, with a bindi on her forehead, and her long, straight hair loose. She looked stunning, no less than a film star. Some months later, when the national honours were announced, Kamaljit made the list for a Padma Shri, among the youngest winners in the history of the Indian republic. In a special edition of *The Times of India* in 1972, marking twenty-five years of India's independence, Kamaljit Sandhu was the only woman on the sports page.

The only other Indian woman to appear on the news pages was Prime Minister Indira Gandhi, dominating headlines, being photographed at official functions and occasionally playing with her grandchildren. Her male colleagues were never photographed with their families.

The women you typically saw in Indian newspapers at the time were on advertisements for textiles, detergents and medicine. In detergent ads, women gave advice on how the product cared for their hands. In garment ads, they posed seductively next to suited men or wholesomely held the hands of dressed-up children. In pharmaceutical ads, they looked pleased with themselves for knowing how to take care of their loved ones.

Like Indira Gandhi, daughter of India's first and longest-serving Prime Minister Jawaharlal Nehru, Kamaljit, too, was a princess of sorts. In fact, there is no one quite like her in the history of Indian athletics. Women's athletics in India is largely the story of women from impoverished backgrounds who benefited from the jobs that the Indian state and some large private companies handed out as encouragement to sportspersons. Kamaljit had never thought she would work—she saw herself spending her life as someone's wife, like her college-degree-holding paternal aunts. In her circle, it was what the 'modern' families did—they educated their girls with university degrees and then got them married.

Kamaljit Sandhu, born in 1948, was the daughter of an affluent military officer, Mahinder Singh Kora, who had served in the Second World War for the British Indian Army, and his wife Rashpal Kaur Cheema, who was a housewife. Unlike her sisters-in-law,

Rashpal had only studied until Class VIII in school. Kamaljit was the second of four sisters; they had no brothers. To this day, most South Asian families have such a strong preference for sons that they do not stop trying until they beget at least one son. With ultrasound technology, this practice saw an update—female infants were aborted in the womb, which, in turn, alarmingly skewed India's sex ratio. The government then banned the use of ultrasonography for sex determination. What this means is that radiologists must withhold information about the sex of the foetus from the parents until it is too late (medically unsafe) to abort. In truth, there continues to be a roaring practice of sex-selective abortion, and India has one of the most worrying sex ratios in the world, along with China. The Koras, however, stopped trying after four daughters, and brought them up no differently than they would have their sons. All four sisters were sent to elite boarding schools. This was unusual, as money was more often only spent on the education of boys, and girls were rarely sent away from home to study.

Kamaljit grew up in a large house built by her grandfather in one of Chandigarh's most handsome localities, a part of which she inherited after her parents' death. Her grandfather, a veterinary doctor who worked with the British Indian Army, had also educated all his children, including his daughters, who went on to complete university degrees just like his sons. 'My grandfather was a "forward" man. That is why my father educated all four of us sisters and sent us to the best schools, *hai na* [isn't it]?' Kamaljit said.

Mahinder Singh Kora played centre-forward for the Khalsa College team in Amritsar, a team whose hockey rivalry with the Sikh Government College in Lahore was legendary in the 1930s and the 1940s. Kora captained the college team and was christened 'Mahinder Ghora [horse]'. Once the ball was with Mahinder Ghora, it was said that there was no stopping a goal—he ran like a horse, and no human could catch up with him. From 1928 to 1936, an Indian team made up of players from the subcontinent and those playing under the British Union Jack won three consecutive Olympic golds at hockey. Naturally, Kora thought he stood a good chance at making the Indian hockey team. The best route for this was joining the British Indian Army, where the training and diet were geared towards Olympic sport. Kora was selected as an officer.

But the Second World War broke out in 1939, and the 1940 London Olympics were called off. The 1944 Olympics, planned for Tokyo, were also cancelled as the war continued until 1945. Twelve years passed between the Olympics of 1936 and 1948, a substantial time in sport, and Kora's Olympic dream, too, passed. What remained was the love for sport. Whenever he was home, he would gather his girls and the neighbourhood children for no-fuss, no-equipment games—races, high jump, long jump, tenniquoits. The reigning champion of her father's track and field events was Kamaljit, and she never forgot the look in his eyes as he watched her, both proud and wistful, when she ran. Perhaps he saw himself in her, and the dream of a career in sport that had slipped past him.

The boarding schools he sent Kamaljit to, first in Hyderabad and then in Gwalior, were modelled on English-style public schools that encouraged sport. The first high school she went to was St. Anne's, a convent in Hyderabad. She could only stay there a couple of months because her grandfather died suddenly and she was summoned back to Chandigarh. In Class IX, her father admitted her to the residential Scindia Kanya Vidyalaya school in Gwalior, run by the royal family of the state. The city had the first college exclusively dedicated to sports education, the Lakshmibai National Institute of Physical Education, and Kora took her to meet the famed founder of the institute, Raja Karan Singh, who was heir to a small kingdom in Rajasthan. Kora took special permission from her school to allow her to go to the sports college for coaching in the evenings.

Kamaljit did a bit of everything—sprinting, jumps, basketball—and excelled at everything. In schools such as these, romanticized in the works of authors such as Enid Blyton and J.K. Rowling, and British classics such as *Tom Brown's School Days*, sport is the epicentre of life. Kamaljit loved sport, and the attention it drew to her. Everyone knew her, students in other schools too, because she was the sports champion. But beyond the framework of school, there was nothing—no government-organized sports competitions, certainly none for girls.

A series of fortunate incidents in college, however, put Kamaljit on the team for the 1970 Asian Games. The Government Women's College in Chandigarh, where she enrolled for a degree in fine arts, had a full-time physical education teacher on its staff, though there were no sports classes in the curriculum. Kamaljit signed up for everything the sports teacher asked her to—basketball, sprints, and a bunch of field and track events. She shone at everything. In 1969, her final year in college, the teacher put her name down for the 400-metre sprint at the national open athletics meet in Jalandhar. The college assigned a female chaperone to accompany her.

A curious thing happened here. It was the first time she was running in any serious competition—she had no spikes, no starting blocks, no idea even of how to run the 400 metres. She had never run more than 200 metres at college events. She took her usual start, eyes glued to the runner outermost on the oval, flying to take the lead. But 50-odd metres before the finish, she found herself on the ground, her legs slumped under her. In her mind, she was racing to the finish, yet she lay in a heap on the ground. The incongruity of it made her laugh out loud.

When a number of coaches came to look for her after the race, Kamaljit felt embarrassed. Had it looked that bad? Did they think she had fallen ill? Or was it the laughing that had appeared unhinged?

It turned out that the lead she had taken before she fell had been remarkable. Among the coaches present there was Raja Karan Singh, her old teacher at the Lakshmibai National Institute. He told her that he was pleasantly surprised to see that she was still active in sport. The raja had already trained a number of male athletes who represented India. One of them was Ajmer Singh, who had won two individual medals at the 1966 Asian Games—a gold for the 400 metres and a silver for the 200 metres.[2] He, too, lived in Chandigarh. He was aiming for another medal at the 1970 Asian Games. Would Kamaljit like to train with him, the raja asked her.

Every morning before classes, Kamaljit would go to the university ground in Chandigarh, where Ajmer himself trained. He wasn't a coach—he was an active athlete. Besides, he had no idea about how to train a woman. He told Kamaljit to follow what he did. And so she did: when he did endurance running, she followed; when he did strength-training, she followed; when he did sprints, she followed. There was no question of asking him for rest when she had her period—it was a topic rarely broached even among female friends. She realized, in fact, that her cramps and bloating were reduced after exercise, a lesson she carried throughout her life and later offered to her own trainees.

It was an unusual arrangement, one that is likely to scandalize South Asian parents even today. A young unmarried woman, training alone, unsupervised, with a man only slightly older than her. On 15 August 2014, Prime Minister Narendra Modi referred

to the unequal citizenship of men and women in perhaps his most
celebrated public address to the nation:

> I wish to ask every parent that when your daughters turn ten
> years, twelve years of age, you become so vigilant. 'Where are you
> going? When would you come back? Call us, inform immediately
> when you reach'. You ask your daughters hundreds of questions.
> But have any of you parents ever dared to ask your sons, 'Where
> are you going? Why are you going? Who are these friends of
> yours?'[3]

But Mahender Singh Kora was thrilled at the opportunity Kamaljit
received to train with Ajmer Singh. 'It was a privilege to be noticed
by a famous coach, trained by a national athlete such as Ajmer Singh,
who played for India and won medals. My father was very proud,'
Kamaljit said when I asked her how the arrangement went down
with her family. 'No one we knew had been selected like this, he told
me. My whole family was impressed, actually, probably because my
father was so impressed. It was destiny, hai na?'

Kamaljit came from the rare family in the subcontinent that
permitted their daughter to go where her destiny took her. From a
spectacular collapse on the tracks in her first serious competition to
the top of the podium in a foreign city. The front page of newspapers
in India. A place in history as the first Indian woman to win an
individual gold outside India.

And then her destiny, it seemed, left her there--on that podium
in Bangkok, a December's day in 1970 when it rained a lot and an
Olympic medallist slipped and fell, startling Kamaljit.

When I met Kamaljit Sandhu in 2019, it was nearly fifty years
since her moment of history in Bangkok at the Asian Games.

She lives most of the year in Canada now, and it took a year and a half for me to fix a meeting in Chandigarh, where she lives in her ancestral home for a few weeks of the year. Before we met, she asked that I send her a photograph of myself. It was an unusual request, one that I have never encountered with any of my interviewees, not in this book nor in my career as a journalist. In the images I have seen of her, Kamaljit Sandhu is astonishingly attractive. I remember standing up in the dusty National Library in Kolkata to peer closer at one of her photographs in the worn black-and-white newsprint. She seemed to light up the page, and I stood up to read that it was really her, an athlete, and not a film star of that time. So I sent her the best portrait I had of myself, shot by a professional photographer. When she typed back that I was young and pretty, I felt unexpectedly pleased, as if I had been approved by a very good-looking mother-in-law.

All the pictures of Kamaljit that hang in her handsome Chandigarh mansion are of her as a stunning young woman, the most recent one at least forty years old. There is no picture of her as an older woman. She has naturally put on some weight, lost that stunning sharpness that made me pause when I saw her pictures in the newspaper archives. Today, though you can tell she is the same person whose photograph you have seen, it is as if the focus of the camera has now blurred. There is also a palpable sense of disappointment that hangs about her.

Her life is too privileged to be considered tragic, and she has the self-awareness to know this. Kamaljit Sandhu is not Miss Havisham, broken and bitter, but Rip Van Winkle, baffled at how the years have just passed by. In some ways, Mary D'Souza was a disappointed woman too, although some recognition had come to her in her eighties, taking away some of the sense of loss. By voicing her disappointment, Mary seemed to have somewhat diminished that sense of waste. She gave it shape in words, and then put it away to one side.

But here the unsaid seemed to envelop me too, and I found myself slipping into a sort of gloom. I asked the questions I had come prepared with, and Kamaljit answered them—yet something was always left unsaid.

At the 1968 Olympics in Mexico, Colette Besson of France won gold in the 400-metre with a time of 52 seconds. Kamaljit Sandhu's best time in 1971 was 56.3 seconds, a continental difference of 4.3 seconds. Of the eight finalists at the Mexico Olympics, seven had been Americans and west Europeans, from what was called the First World, and one from the former Soviet Union (Russia). At the time, the Soviet Bloc was considered the 'Second World'. But for all practical purposes, Russia was a First World country in the 1960s. After all, in 1961, the Russians beat the Americans in sending the first man to space—cosmonaut Yuri Gagarin entered the record books twenty-one days before the American Alan Bartlett Shepard Jr (and the term 'cosmonaut' entered public discourse alongside the more popular American term 'astronaut').

After her Bangkok win, Kamaljit got an opportunity to travel to the First World to try and bridge the gap of 4.3 seconds. The Indian government sent her on an exchange programme to the country then known as West Germany, one of a group of Indian artists and sportspersons. It was her first time in the West, and Kamaljit was thrilled. Her family was impressed too. Who got the opportunity to travel abroad for weeks on end in those days? Who'd have thought she would be travelling the world on her own like this, on her own ticket, not one paid for by a husband or her father?

Even though there was a lot more sightseeing than sports activities on the itinerary, Kamaljit enjoyed herself. Some sights she was unprepared for, such as when she opened the dormitory door and found a young man and woman undressed, kissing each other. There were a couple of exhibition events, and Kamaljit performed well enough in these to catch the eye of a sports scout from the US. She received an invitation to train with an amateur athletics club in Los Angeles over a few months in 1972, all expenses paid. Those were charmed times, as if the world had arranged itself to pave the way for her. 'If I could touch 53 seconds, I thought there was a chance at the Olympics,' Kamaljit said. I asked if she meant a medal. 'No, no,' she said. 'I am a practical person. How could I think of a medal against the Europeans, Russians, Americans? I thought if I could make it to the finals—the first Indian woman in an Olympic final—that would be my history, my place in it.'

The LA Mercurettes was an elite track and field club in the US that exclusively trained women athletes. In the 1960s and the 1970s, thanks to the performance of its athletes, its name featured regularly in major US newspapers such as *The New York Times* and *Los Angeles Times*, and in the premier sports magazine of the world, *Sports Illustrated*. The first American woman who qualified for the 400-metre sprint final at the Olympics, Jarvis Scott, trained at the Mercurettes. What's more, Chi Cheng had trained at the Mercurettes for several years in the 1960s, which culminated in her Olympic bronze for the 80-metre hurdles.

More than anything else, this seemed like a sign. If not here, Kamaljit thought, then where?

When you leave the familiar for the foreign, the small pond for the ocean, you know there will be change. You prepare to be humbled, to learn that you are not as big a fish as you thought. And yet, when it happens, it takes you by surprise. It still hurts. America!

Just the thought of it had been metamorphosis. She would it give it her everything, she had thought. If they broke her, she would make herself unbreakable.

One evening in particular has stayed with Kamaljit. The training with the coaches took place in the evenings because most of the athletes there were American, who were in college and had classes during the day. Kamaljit was used to doing four or five repetitions of 400-metre sprints in an hour's training. The expectation here was twenty reps, with approximately a two-minute break after each sprint. After her eighth rep, Kamaljit swallowed her embarrassment and confessed she couldn't run any more. The coach told her to decide—do the reps or pack her bags for India.

She learnt to do the twenty reps. She shaved off 2 seconds to reach a timing of 54.3 seconds, even though she did it at an internal training session, unrecorded on the books. She had a lot of time to herself there, and she arrived at a difficult realization—that she was good, but she was not among the elite athletes of the world. She would never get an Olympic medal. Perhaps she would never reach the 53-second mark she had set for herself. She was twenty-four years old then—still young, really.

In India she had always been the biggest fish in her pond, and here she felt adrift, abandoned. A spare-time charity project for the Americans—no coach took charge of her training in the way they mentored their own athletes. They turned to her once their work with their main athletes was done, and she learnt what she could. She felt ashamed to ask for more than she was given. Was it possible that you could be living what you thought was your dream—training in First World facilities in the most powerful country in the world—and still feel it was all a mistake?

'The truth is, why would they promote an athlete from a Third World country? They had their own people, their protégés—

the coaches wanted them to do well. When I think back on my life, I realize I should have insisted on going there with my own coach. If there was no funding for that, I shouldn't have gone. That's when it makes sense—their facilities and your own coach. When you are young, you travel abroad as a tourist—you take a couple of flights, you see a boy and a girl kissing and you think you know what the world is about. But, really, you are just another young person who thinks too much of herself,' Kamaljit told me.

What shifted something in her irrevocably, however, was a letter that never came from India. Kamaljit was waiting to hear from the IOA about the Indian team selections for the Munich Olympics. The days lengthened, summer arrived, the Mercurettes who had been selected for the Olympics intensified their training and then left for Europe to train in similar conditions before travelling to Munich. Kamaljit swam in the mornings or ran long-distance for two hours. She trained in the evenings with any coach who had time to spare. She reminded herself that the Indian postal service was notoriously late sometimes, that perhaps there would be a long-distance call instead.

Back home in India, her family kept an eye on the newspapers. There were reports of the Indian teams selected for the Games. There was no mention in them of Kamaljit Sandhu. She was not among the best in the world, Kamaljit knew this much by then. But she was the best in India. She deserved to be on the Indian team to Munich. If they were indeed dropping her, would the Indian authorities not even inform her?

A dullness had come over her, and she could only think of putting an end to this chapter in her life one way or another—either she knew she was going for the Munich Olympics and left for the Games, or she left to return to India. It was only the long hours of intense activity that kept the loneliness from slipping into depression.

Back in India, her father took matters into his own hands. He approached the then president of the IOA, Raja Bhalindra Singh of Patiala, who asked Kamaljit to meet him in Munich. She bought a ticket to Munich with money that her father sent her, and met the former raja. It was brief and pleasant. The former king informed her that she would indeed represent India at the 400 metres, and that she was to join the Indian contingent and collect her India uniform.

Yet, it filled her with sadness to think that her father had to arrange this meeting using his connections, as if she had been permitted to represent India as a personal favour. In just a few months, it seemed, her destiny had changed. A few months ago it had felt like the world was hers, fitting itself around her needs, priming her for the Olympics with the opportunity to train in a reputed athletics club in the US. Now she couldn't even merit a response from the Indian sports establishment on her own. She joined the Indian camp, and marched with the Indian team on the opening day. It was a moment she had thought of often since she had stood on the podium in Bangkok. But when it came, she found no joy in it.

On 2 September 1972, a beautiful cool day in Munich, Kamaljit laced up and ran her 400-metre heat. She felt neither excitement nor fear, just a leaden weight in the chest that she should not shame herself. How lonely she must have felt in that moment, stepping out to represent India at the largest platform for sport and knowing that she was far from her best, the training of the previous months having been eroded by the uncertainty of recent days. Running in lane 7, Kamaljit finished with a time of 57.74 seconds, 0.4 seconds slower than her time in Bangkok in 1970, seventh place out of eight contenders. She felt relieved, the kind we feel when an exam is over, even though we know it went badly.

Three days later, on 5 September, Kamaljit stepped out for breakfast in the Olympic Village. But no one was eating or serving—

they were all staring in the same direction, at the building in front. At first she saw nothing. Then she noticed. There was a man in a ski mask and dark clothes on a balcony looking out of the building. There were slits for the eyes—nothing else of the face was visible. It was an eerie, cruel visage. She had no idea what the figure in the mask meant—terrorism was not a word that was in currency then. There were no movies about terrorists, or plane hijackings, or prime ministerial assassinations, or flights crashing into buildings at the time. Those were still many years away.

Minutes later (or was it seconds), another masked figure appeared outside another part of the building. The two masked figures convened for a quick talk before they disappeared from view. Sometime afterwards, she heard gunshots.

They were not the first shots of the day, she learnt. Gunfire had been heard intermittently from early that morning. The building in which the masked men had appeared was the Israeli team's quarters. Word was put out that no one was to go out. Kamaljit remained in the breakfast room the entire day until past 10 p.m., locked in with everyone else who had been in the room. But for several hours there was no clear statement on what was going on, only rumours of attacks and hostages. In the afternoon, finally, there was a statement: Eight Palestinian terrorists had attacked the Olympic Village, killed two Israeli athletes and taken another nine hostage. Sometime later, the television was switched on—the German police was attempting a rescue and the operation was broadcast live on TV—the first time a terrorist attack was broadcast live.

The next day, Kamaljit learnt that seventeen persons had been killed—all eleven Israeli athletes, five Palestinian terrorists and one German policeman. The Munich Olympic massacre, as it has come to be known, is the deadliest, most audacious terrorist attack on a prominent sports event to this day.

The next day, the Olympic flag flew at half-mast. The Games resumed, but people walked around in a daze. Everyone spoke to everyone, even people who had never smiled at mealtimes. What happened? Did you know them? Were you there? How could it happen? Do you think you might have been hit if you were there? It was just talk without answers, again and again, without direction.

To Kamaljit, it felt like the fog in her mind had spread over the entire village. It was a time in her life when little in her life made sense, and the Munich massacre echoed her sense of meaninglessness. If anything, it helped provide a cover for the strange feeling she had been carrying around in herself. In 1973, months after she returned from the Olympics, she retired from track athletics. She was twenty-five years old at the time.

❧

Kamaljit's time of 57.3 seconds for the 400 metres stood as the national record in India until 1979—almost a decade—even though Kamaljit herself had retired from competition in 1972. It confirmed what she had thought—the central aspiration of Indian sport in those years was participation, and this was especially true for women's sport. Kamaljit didn't want to participate, not any more. She had trained with the best, even if she realized she wasn't in their league. She had lost the taste for participation. The woman who broke Kamaljit's record in 1979 was her student, Rita Sen, whom she trained as a coach with the Netaji Subhas National Institute of Sport in Patiala, popularly known as the NIS, Patiala.

'There was nothing for me to do—there was no proper training, no regular competitions, nothing proper, you can say. Ajmer Singh was in Chandigarh, although he, too, had retired from athletics. I did go to him, though. But the thing is, it becomes difficult to learn from someone when you realize you know more than him. That thing was gone—the basic teacher–student relationship. I still respect him—to this day he remains the coach who got me my gold medal. But the athlete–coach relationship is a very special thing—I know this as a coach myself. A coach and an athlete spend much more time together than a teacher and a student. You have to *know* that your coach knows more than you. You have to believe it, otherwise you cannot accept this person as your coach. Perhaps it was my time in California that made these things become problems for me—there has to be a method, a system, a plan,' Kamaljit said, her hands drawing a series of steps in the air.

She had seen what it took to compete at the highest level—the facilities, the systems, the planning. In India, a series of lacklustre competitions took place annually, dictated by habit, not drawn to a plan. There was no objective, only whim—and the occasional alignment of talent and good luck, such as hers. Unlike Mary D'Souza and, indeed, most other athletes in India, she didn't need the government job. Or any job, indeed any of the meagre enticements that Indian sport offers its participants. So she stayed home and completed a master's degree in fine arts. Later, her family tasked her with helping her sister during a difficult period early in her marriage. Kamaljit agreed.

A couple of years into her retirement, Kamaljit received a call from the NIS in 1973. Some of the coaches there remembered her from the training camps before the Asian Games. The institute had started a year-long diploma course for sports coaching and they thought she would be a good fit. It was a gesture that took her by surprise, and pleasantly so. She hadn't had the easiest time at the institute. There were whispers about her when she had attended the national camps at the institute—that she was too privileged to have the winner's hunger. Too posh. Too proud. For a brief moment, it did cross her mind that this was their way of rubbing her nose in it, her brief career. But she completed the year-long course, one of the first batch of trained women coaches in India. Two years later, she was appointed as permanent faculty.

She was the first woman in her family to work at a job. Her father's sisters, all university graduates, tended to home and brought up their children after they married. Her mother's side of the family was less modern in this sense—the women still observed the purdah. Kamaljit found herself enjoying the job. She liked the majestic campus of NIS, which was part of the palace of the erstwhile Maharaja of Patiala. The campus had a new sports science department, where they had started the study of exercise and its relationship with the body. It was there that she met her husband, a sports scientist. Work was relaxed because there was no organized sports training for women, except the national camps before sporadic international events that Indian women were sent to. In these years, Indian women's sporting events were like the flower shows or cultural performances put on by the wives of bureaucrats—a signpost to the West that said Indian women were not just baby producers and domestic workers. They also grew flowers, danced and sang, and participated in sports.

And then, one afternoon in 1980, Kamaljit changed the history of women's sport in India simply by speaking. The Union minister who was assigned to look after the 1982 Asian Games, Vidya Charan Shukla, had called a meeting of coaches, bureaucrats and sports associations at NIS to discuss the forthcoming Asian Games. India had won the bid to host the 1982 Games in New Delhi. It was going to be a display of India's ability to pull off an international event, and in time it would be recognized as the most ambitious Asiad held until then. The Indian government didn't want to lose face with a pathetic display on home ground. In the 1980 Olympics in Moscow, India won a solitary medal—a gold in hockey, their eighth gold since India started playing in the Olympics in 1928. In fact, even the 1980 hockey gold felt like a somewhat lucky triumph—about sixty countries boycotted the Games that year to protest the Soviet Union's invasion of Afghanistan.

It was post-lunch when Kamaljit brought the meeting alive. Perhaps it was the slowness of an afternoon after a big meal or perhaps no one really had any idea to offer, but Kamaljit broke the silence: 'We should look at women,' she said. 'We could double our medals if the women do well.'

Shukla, who would head the Special Organising Committee of the '82 Asian Games, liked the idea. The 1982 Asian Games is reported to have cost Rs 700 crore, and was the first sports competition to be telecast live in India. India ranked fifth in the final medals tally, just one better than their sixth-place finish at the 1978 Games, but they doubled their medals tally from twenty-eight in the previous round to fifty-seven, as Kamaljit had suggested. The women won at least fourteen of these medals, with eight in athletics alone.[4] Among them was P.T. Usha, the sprint queen from Kerala, who won two silver medals in the 100- and 200-metre sprints. She also broke the 400-metre sprint record in India, that had recently been set by Kamaljit's student Rita Sen. M.D. Valsamma was the sole Indian woman to win an individual gold in track and field at the Games, at the 400-metre hurdles. She was from Kerala, like Usha. Two years later, Usha would become the first Indian woman to qualify for an Olympic final in this very event—the 400-metre hurdles. With this one bureaucratic move, calculated to boost national ego, women's sport in India took its first steps towards an organized, systematic movement. At the 1984 Olympics in Los Angeles, P.T. Usha became the first Indian woman to qualify for the finals of a track event. She finished fourth, missing the medal by a fraction of a second, and captured the imagination of the nation.

In the last week of March 2019, I went to Chandigarh to meet Kamaljit Sandhu. The north Indian weather was still cool then. In the evenings you had to turn off the fan, though the large landscaped areas of the city were beginning to take on the colours of summer. Chandigarh, designed by the well-known French urban planner Le Corbusier, is the first planned city of independent India. Wide roads meet in neat radials, traffic behaves, the footpaths are paved and substantial, and sometimes blend into patches of neatly trimmed grass. Slum-like settlements and accumulated garbage waiting to be collected—routine sights in Indian cities—are far less visible there. Large segments of the city are cordoned off as open grounds, as in European cities, grounds that are open for citizens to run, play, walk or simply sit in. At night, the grounds are lit up and filled with people who couldn't make time during the day. Even today, Chandigarh feels half a century ahead of the crumbling, collapsing mess that is the usual Indian city.

It is also a union territory, governed directly by the Union government with far more resources at its disposal than the straitened means of state governments in India's federal structure. These resources include a greater number of personnel for law and order and internal security. Political unrest—strikes, riots—that has visited so many towns and cities in the country has been noticeably less in evidence here.

In the 1960s, when Kamaljit was growing up in Chandigarh, I imagine it gave wing to her dreams. Vast, landscaped, beautiful, hopeful—the sort of city where it was plausible to think that you stood a chance in the world. This, too, was to Kamaljit's advantage, I thought, besides her natural athletic talent. That she lived in a place like Chandigarh. And she had a family that permitted her to go where her destiny called.

In 1970, when Kamaljit burst into national news, my mother Supriya was one month short of nine years old. Kamaljit Sandhu's gold-medal news did make it to the papers in Calcutta, but it did not register. The first half of the 1970s was a horrific time for Calcutta, which was the epicentre of a campaign by Leftist radicals to overthrow the government, provoking a stunningly bloodied reprisal from the state. The Leftists were known as Naxals, after Naxalbari, the tea-growing region in which the movement was launched. Calcutta newspapers then were full of accounts of murderous attacks by Naxals on professors, government officials and police officers—and of midnight arrests, rounds-ups and crackdowns on the Leftists.

There was also the imminent war with Pakistan, which brought waves of refugees into Calcutta and Bengal. It was a time of intense pressure—on the state, the resources of an already stretched society and, most of all, the minds of people.

'I remember those days as a time when Baba was home by 7 p.m.,' my mother told me. 'I would come home from school, take some rest in the afternoon and then sit down with my studies. Those were years of massive power cuts. I wanted to finish before the power went out. There was also anxiety if everyone was not home before dark. It was fun to gather around candlelight and battery-operated torches. Sometimes, in the dark, we would hear knocks on the doors of houses nearby, and our hearts would quicken. You heard stories of knocks on the door and men barging in with guns or daggers—sometimes it was Naxals on the run from the police, sometimes it was the police come to search a house for Naxals hiding inside. Sometimes Naxals would force people to allow them to hide. We residents were caught in the middle, harassed by both sides. If there was an unexpected knock on the door, I remember the dread I felt and the relief when the visitor was known. We never had a Naxal or a police visit, but the anxiety was huge. We slept by 10 p.m. Sometimes, we thought we heard gunshots in the distance.'

There is a sort of thrill when my mother recounts these stories. What she left unsaid was the constant monitoring, the curbs on movement, the watching-over that never stopped. She was never allowed to walk alone anywhere, even with her younger brother. Her father dropped her to school, a domestic worker fetched her home. For tuition, teachers came home. She was never sent to the shops to fetch things, unlike her younger brother. Never for a moment was she allowed to move around alone. There was no question of playing outside or chatting with the girls in the neighbourhood either. Girls in Calcutta stayed home to do their homework. When my mother was in high school, my grandmother Dipti was offered a job to teach maths and science in the same school, but she refused. She wanted to stay home.

It is in the teenage years that we begin to break away bit by bit, start to shape our own lives, especially those of us whose lives are tightly hemmed in. The violence of the 1970s in Calcutta provided a rationale to control the lives of young women even more. What is the effect of extreme violence on women in a society? In times of war, there are reports of rape, sexual assault and other forms of violent physical harm. But what happens to those who are locked in, policed, chaperoned and never allowed to step out alone for fear of violence? They do not face sexual assault, but what does this incarceration do to them? Calcutta was a pressure cooker, and of the things locked inside, the women were the ones pushed down deepest, squashed the most.

The claustrophobia of those years is captured nicely in the film *Ek Din Pratidin* (*One Day, Every Day*) by Mrinal Sen (1980). By this time the Naxalbari movement had been brutally crushed, a Leftist but less extremist party had come to power and taken some steps towards the dreams of the revolution. Yet much remained unresolved, much unspoken. The greatest sense of disillusion with the revolution was felt by women, who found themselves trapped under the crushing load of unpaid household labour and policed by savage expectations of patriarchy. 'Udayan wanted a revolution,' Jhumpa Lahiri wrote in her novel *The Lowland*, which is set during the Naxalbari years. 'But at home he wanted to be served.'

In *Ek Din Pratidin*, a young middle-class woman doesn't come home from office one night in Calcutta. The household runs on the earnings of this young woman, Chinu (Chinmayi). The tension that grips the neighbourhood that night is partly the anxiety of what might have befallen the family's main source of income, but for the most part it is that old patriarchal panic around the female body. Has she been raped? Has she eloped? Does she have a boyfriend she never told them about? What will people say?

Before they start to worry, the family is actually angry with Chinu: Why is she being so irresponsible? Chinu has an elder brother who does nothing, earns no money and routinely returns home around midnight. But his absence, his late nights and his general irresponsibility arouse no worry or censure. Her younger brother gets hurt playing cricket on the streets, but nobody scolds him for being out on the streets, playing as he likes. The difference in the family's, and society's, expectations between girls and boys, women and men, is sharp.

Male family members and some neighbours visit the police and the mortuary, and come back with no news. In the mortuary, they are pointed to an unidentified woman's corpse, but find it is not her. When morning breaks, Chinu returns, but no one asks her any questions. Her mother tells her, rather sharply, to come in and not make a fool of herself.

The film, in fact, does not offer any explanation for Chinu's delayed return. But it leaves a clear sense of the tightly leashed lives women live in Bengali society. The Bengali title of the film sums it up beautifully—One Day, Every Day. This is the story of the everyday lives of women there, who live with censure, questions and the ever-present fear of bodily harm. Interestingly, Chinu is a working woman. She has a life outside the kitchen, the home. At the turn of the twentieth century, Rabindranath Tagore wrote about how modernity had brought Indian women to the threshold between domesticity and the world outside—a subject he explored again and again in his writing. In *Ek Din Pratidin*, the woman has crossed this threshold; in fact, she is the primary breadwinner in the family. Yet, her life is claustrophobic—it has not expanded with freedom as much as it has filled with responsibility. Her family is happy to let her work because they live off her income, but they are uncomfortable, even unhappy, with the independence that entails.

A later film, Tapan Sinha's *Atanka* (*Terror*), released in 1986, is a political take on the tyranny of communism, but its most chilling comment is on women, how fragile their lives are in this society. A teacher witnesses a murder and reports it to the police. To threaten him, the murderers throw acid on his daughter's face. The sight of the young woman's disfigured face haunted me for a long time. Perhaps, it still haunts me, it's why I like to hurry home when I am outside. What if that acid fell on me—somebody taking revenge or sending a threat or marking turf on my face. The woman's body is the site of conflict.

My mother's life was shaped in these years, when the fear of bodily harm was ever-present. Dipti was also a believer in classical patriarchy. When Dipti's mother would serve Supriya half an egg and her grandson a full egg, Dipti never objected, although Supriya would ask her about the disparity. Much later, when Dipti was in her eighties, she told me that she believed that girls/women didn't go out like boys/men do, to play and to work, and hence need less nutrition. It was clear to Supriya, even if Dipti had not said so in words, that her son would be given the best possible education to ensure he could have the career he desired.

In response, Supriya excelled in class, yet Dipti patronizingly called her 'first girl'—an epithet that implied she was just good at exams, so she came first in class. She wasn't special. The one with the real intellect, Dipti said, was her son, who would eventually need a hefty capitation fee to study the subject of his choice in college. She praised her son as creative, and her daughter as studious. She thinks too highly of herself, Dipti's sisters would say about my mother, because she showed no interest in cooking or serving them tea. Dipti never objected to this kind of talk—she seemed to agree.

Supriya studied with something akin to frenzy, and got into Presidency College, the top college in the country at the time, to study economics. She aspired to be an IAS officer—a special cadre of elite government officers who are recruited through a tough entrance examination. The government gives these officers large houses to stay in, cars, security, staff to wait on them. Even today, when an IAS officer arrives, doors are held open, people carry bags and files for them, there is a flurry of activity to mark the moment. For a girl who grew up valued at half an egg in a city that savagely showed women their place, it is not hard to see why this would be the dream. Prestige, the feeling of being valued and the security to go outside without fear of harm.

But Presidency is a co-educational college. Dipti asked her to reconsider her decision, to go, instead, to a girls-only college. Supriya refused. Dipti set out to look for a suitable boy to arrange her marriage—the idea of an unmarried young woman in a place with young men of similar age made her anxious. One day, when a male classmate accompanied her home to borrow her notes, my grandfather asked him a series of questions. Did you not attend class? Is this book not available in the library? Where do you stay? Is there no local library there? Why can you not study in class?

The classmate made light of it. They laughed in college about strict fathers. But in truth, Supriya was stung by embarrassment. Dipti put out an advertisement in the newspaper seeking a groom, and when the first reasonable match appeared, Supriya agreed.

It was 1981 then, the year Kamaljit Sandhu's protégés first started making their mark on the track in India, beating her record, setting new records. And my mother, in her first year in college, became the youngest girl in her class to get married. To her it seemed that the most patriarchal institution in the world, marriage, was a better choice than staying in her stifling home.

4

P.T. USHA: THE WOMAN WHO CAME FOURTH

P.T. Usha. Photo © P.T. Usha's Instagram account

WHEN I WAS around four, I used to run with Pilavullakandi Thekkeparambil Usha, India's greatest woman sprinter, every weekend. I would wait for her after *Spiderman* on Saturdays and *He-Man* on Sundays, and when she would appear, glistening in the rain, deer bounding in the foreground, and holding up a flaming torch in her right hand, I would run circles around my living room, pacing my steps with the music. In my hand, I had a plastic mace, the closest thing I possessed to a flaming torch. It looked a bit like a torch too, the top red and rounded, and the handle white. I don't know if I loved running then, but Usha was the only woman I knew who ran, and when she appeared, deer leaping around her beautiful arching strides, it felt like a call.

In that 2.36-minute video made by the Indian public broadcaster Doordarshan to promote national unity, there are twenty men and three women. Each of the men—most of them cricketers but also a couple of footballers, and tennis and badminton champions—appear on camera for several seconds. Two women get less than a second each. Only Usha receives eight seconds of screen time and bounding deer as her co-stars.

The 1980s were a good time for Indian sport. In 1980, Prakash Padukone won the prestigious All England Open Badminton Championships, the first Indian to do so; and in 1981, he won gold at the World Cup in Kuala Lumpur. In 1983, the Indian cricket team won the World Cup unexpectedly in England, and a bunch of little-known names became household ones. And in 1984, P.T. Usha became the first Indian woman, and the fourth Indian ever, to qualify for an Olympic athletics final for an individual event. She missed the bronze in the 400-metre hurdles by one-hundredth of a second—

her timing was 55.42 and the bronze winner's 55.41. That year, her presence also galvanized the Indian women's 4x400-metre relay team to qualify for the Olympic final—the first and last time ever—and they eventually finished seventh.

In 1982, India had hosted the Asian Games, the country's first major international sports event. It had also hosted these Games in 1951, their first edition, but that was only four years after Independence, when the nation was impoverished and barely out of its momentous freedom struggle. The 1982 Games is known as the first televised sports event in India. It was the first time the country broadcast in colour, and 50,000 colour-TV sets were permitted to be imported into the country. The number of TV sets was reported to have gone up to 100,000 within a year, such was the interest in the Games and the thrill of watching the action in colour.

Sport on TV was transformational, for it was being *watched* by Indian people now, not just followed on the radio and the newspapers. The 1982 Asiad was the first time women were *seen* competing in sports by a large number of Indians. In the early hours of 9 August 1984, when Usha ran in the Los Angeles Olympic stadium, thousands of Indians tuned in to watch her on their own television sets or a neighbour's. Arguably, no Indian woman had been watched by so many Indians, or had such a large audience in general, in a setting as grand as the Olympics, as Usha did that afternoon in Los Angeles.

What does the act of seeing do to us? From India's dismal sporting returns in the next twenty years, it would seem nothing. There was only P.T. Usha whom one could talk about. But from the decade of the 2000s onwards, something has shifted visibly. In 2000, Karnam Malleswari won a bronze in weightlifting at Sydney and became the first Indian woman to win an Olympic medal. In 2002, the women's hockey team won gold at the Commonwealth Games. In 2003,

Sania Mirza became the first Indian woman to win a Wimbledon title when she won at junior doubles. In 2005, the Indian women's cricket team reached the finals of the World Cup for the first time since the game was opened up to women three decades previously. In 2012, Saina Nehwal won a bronze in badminton at the London Olympics. The extraordinary boxer Mary Kom won six golds at the women's World Boxing Championships from 2002 to 2018, and a bronze at the London Olympics, 2012.

Some of these may seem minor or non-triumphs—for instance, Sania winning a junior trophy when twelve- and thirteen-year-old girls from other countries have competed and won medals at the Olympics, though in different sports. Marjorie Gestring was thirteen when she won a gold in diving at the 1936 Olympics, and Inge Sørensen was twelve when she won a bronze at the same Olympics for the 200-metre breaststroke event; Luigina Giavotti was the youngest member of a silver-winning team at gymnastics in 1928 at eleven years old; her teammates Ines Vercesi and Carla Marangoni were twelve and thirteen, respectively. But India is a country with one of the most distorted sex ratios in the world, a result of the killing of female foetuses in the womb as well as female infanticide. It is also one of the countries that records among the highest numbers of acid attacks, which is defined by many as a gender crime, because the majority of victims are women. Both foeticide and acid attacks are, to my mind, crimes of erasure. Both seek to cancel the existence of women, albeit in different ways. These 'minor' achievements in sport then bespeak a determination to be seen, to exist, and to mark that existence. They are terribly significant, if you ask me.

When I met P.T. Usha in person in 2019, thirty-five years after she became the most famous fourth-place finisher in Olympic history, it seemed to me that she had come bounding around the corner of the television set in my living room. (As it happens, the legendary

Milkha Singh also finished fourth, missing the bronze by a whisker at the finals of the 400-metre sprint at the Rome Olympics in 1960.) There was still that air of fluid motion and boundless energy about her, although she had put on a bit of weight in the middle. 'Why everybody wants to meet me, I don't know,' she said to me by way of greeting. 'But thank you for coming.' She pressed her lips together in service of something like a smile. She doesn't smile often, I realized over the next few days. Her manner is brisk and impatient—she can sometimes sound like a stern hostel warden. Her husband and manager, V. Sreenivasan, who trotted behind her most of the time, did much of the smiling on her behalf. But she is prone to short, sudden bursts of laughter.

It was easy enough to locate Usha. She runs an athletics academy for girls in Payyoli, her hometown in Kerala, and she answered my e-mail immediately, like a diligent student. But it was near impossible to actually meet her. She travelled constantly, changed her plans freely and I had to alter my tickets thrice to meet her in Payyoli. 'It is okay, no? I could have rested during this time, but I decided to meet you because you changed your ticket so many times. Now I have to give this girl some time, I thought,' she said.

I caught myself laughing in response. I know I would have ordinarily been annoyed. It's a careless, stuffed-full-of-yourself way of speaking, isn't it? But I am charmed by Usha's frankness. This is what nostalgia does, perhaps.

I have known of Usha for as long as I can remember. But it is mostly a relationship of general knowledge. When I started running regularly in my twenties, I wasn't thinking of Usha. How could I? She is an iconic sprinter, I am an amateur putting one foot after the other. But that didn't stop other people from thinking of Usha when they saw me. I had been running regularly for some months in a dusty Delhi government residential colony park when I noticed some of the walkers had started to make way for me on their own. It was an unexpected courtesy. Indians don't make way for women in public, unless they are convinced of their importance. Even women don't make way. Our tradition is to stare at women in public—we are still so unused to seeing women in public spaces.

I would thank every walker who made room for me and raise a hand in acknowledgement. And on and off, someone would say, 'Very good, beta [my child], you are our P.T. Usha.' Different people said this on different occasions. This is the legitimacy that Usha has bequeathed on every woman who runs with some discipline in India, I realized. My running had an acceptance, a meaning, a place in the universe because Usha's running had nearly won us an Olympic medal. We can run because she ran so well.

The morning of 7 August 1984 was a cool, dry day in Los Angeles, typical for that month, a comfortable twenty-something-degree centigrade. Good for sport—not too warm yet—though Usha preferred the afternoons when the weather was closer to the tropical warmth of her seaside home in Payyoli. She had prayed briefly that morning to hold her thoughts together.

She felt calm. She had run well to qualify for the 400-metre hurdles final, though it was only her third hurdle race in the year. She wasn't a hurdler, really—she was a sprinter, who thrilled at the adrenaline rush of sprinting 100, 200 or 400 metres. But the Olympic Games had added the 400-metre hurdles event for women for the 1984 edition, and her coach, O.M. Nambiar—Nambiar sir to her— had put her name down for the event. It was only in 1983 that the event had been added to the World Championships, and there had been too little time to establish standard timings yet. Athletes were still breaking down the race into its components—the ten hurdles, the distance between hurdles, the dash from the final hurdle to the finishing line. As such, standards were not benchmarked, and Nambiar felt Usha had a chance.

She trusted 'Nambiar sir' implicitly. He had trained her since she was twelve years old, when she first came to the state academy for sport in her district in Kannur, Kerala. He used to save her oranges from his share of food at the hostel and give them to her as treats if she trained well. Sometimes, he would buy her oranges with his own money. She thought of him like a father. In fact, she had spent more time with him growing up than with her own father, because she lived away from home. He was strict but not an authoritarian—a warm, stable shelter. She never hesitated to tell him if she needed a break or had to skip an event. He listened to her, though he mostly did not agree with her views on taking breaks. Even when she was a child, Nambiar sir treated her with respect. It was this that made her grow up more than anything, this trust that an adult had in her. Later, when his trust in her was gone, that bond went too.

That morning, Nambiar sir was waiting for her in the dining hall of the Olympic Village in Los Angeles with a bowl of rice that he had cooked for her in a pan. The rice in America was not like it was back home in Kerala. It looked desiccated, unlike the plump grains she had at home, so she would mix it with a little hot water to soften it. She had briefly considered carrying some rice from home, but given the starting blocks and the extra pairs of spikes and the whole sports kit, she had only managed to carry a jar of home-made mango pickle. This she used judiciously, because it had to last her the three weeks of her Olympic stay. Her mother had made it extra potent, spicier than usual, so that just a little was sufficient to eat with the rice. On non-race days, Nambiar sir permitted her ice cream after lunch and dinner. This was Usha's Olympic diet.[1] She would watch other athletes eat protein bars and supplements with their meals, but Nambiar sir had told her he would have to study the nutrients before he introduced them to her diet.

Four years ago, in her first Olympics at Moscow, she had barely eaten. At sixteen, she had been the youngest in the Indian contingent—the youngest Indian ever at the Olympics—and left to fend for herself. Nambiar sir was not included on the tour, and no one really spoke to her. She had never seen pasta, or so many confusing varieties of soup and salad. Even the bread looked nothing like the soft, white slices she had seen at home. She was, anyway, a rice eater and there was nothing that looked like rice on the menu. She survived the Moscow Games on ice cream, fruit and chocolate bars. This time before the Olympics, she took no chances. She went directly to Prime Minister Indira Gandhi's office in New Delhi to seek special permission for Nambiar sir to travel with her to Los Angeles for the Olympics. Usha told the Prime Minister's assistant, who met her in lieu of Mrs Gandhi, that it came down to eating or starving at the Olympics. If Nambiar sir did not accompany her, she would not know what to eat. The Prime Minister couldn't meet her that day, but Nambiar sir accompanied her to Los Angeles. It probably helped that she had won two individual silver medals at the 100-metre and the 200-metre sprint events at the 1982 Asian Games in New Delhi. Much of the Central government, including the Prime Minister on occasion, had been in the audience during the Asiad. Besides, she had won a gold for the 400-metre and a silver for the 200-metre sprint at the Asian Athletics Championships in Kuwait in 1983.

In the heats on 7 August, only her third international hurdling event ever, she finished first with a time of 55.54 seconds, a full stride ahead of Judy Brown (55.97 seconds), the American sprinter who was the favourite for the race. The next day, she made the front page of *The Times of India*. A couple of days earlier at the Olympics, the Indian men's hockey team, who were favourites for the gold medal, had crashed out of the semi-finals. The men's team had won eight Olympic golds in hockey until then—five of them after Independence—plus one silver and two bronzes. The travelling Indian press contingent's principal agenda, naturally, was to follow the hockey team's exploits. Freed from hockey duty, the journalists turned up to watch Usha's heats. She now carried the nation's honour on her shoulders.

She was feeling very light on her feet those days, moving and landing in rhythm with her breathing. As if her legs were moving instinctively to the quiet music of drawing breath and releasing it. Even her heartbeat, echoing in her ears, was in sync with that rhythm. It was as if her whole being was working in sync to that music, like the universe itself was moving to that music. If her breath was in beat with her heart and feet, Usha didn't need to look at anything else, not her rivals alongside, not the stands. That synchrony was enough for her.

On 8 August, a warm California evening, Usha ran even better, finishing at 55.42 seconds, but she had not thrust her torso out at the tape. Usha believed she was third. The American Judy Brown, whom she had defeated comfortably only two days ago, had won silver. The gold had gone to Morocco's Nawal El Moutawakel, who had won gold at several hurdle races in the previous couple of years. Afterwards, in the room where they were tested for dope, Usha gave her sample and watched as they replayed the finishing-line video recording again and again to ascertain who had come third—she or Romania's Cristieana Cojocaru.

Usha's foot was ahead of the bronze medallist's, but an official present told her that it did not count.[2] Cojocaru, whose country was part of the former USSR-led Communist bloc, where the culture of sport was very serious, had thrust her chest out at the finishing line, and her time was registered as 55.41 seconds. One-hundredth of a second faster than Usha.

If it had been a closer finish at the heat a day earlier, she might have learnt the trick of thrusting her chest forward at the finishing line. The term for reaching the finishing line of an athletics event is, in fact, 'breasting the tape'. It is a tiny, precise trick in a discipline that measures time by centiles—one hundredth of a second. The World Athletics rule is that any part of the torso must touch the finishing line for the runner to register her finish. Consequently, you thrust your chest out or propel your head forward. You could even dive to the finish like Shaunae Miller of the Bahamas did at the 400-metre sprint finals of the 2016 Olympics to claim the gold medal. These little tricks are legitimate, as the interpretation of Cojocaru's and Miller's victories proved, and they are part of the arsenal of athletes who have sharpened their techniques with international exposure.

Usha watched that replay again and again, transfixed by the moment she had lost her Olympic medal, one trick short of history. If this was disappointment, it did not pierce—it felt like stillness. An official from the Indian team came in to speak to her. There was a phone call from Mrs Indira Gandhi. India has lost, but you have won, Usha, the Prime Minister said. It may have been a platitude, but Usha appreciated it.

More than anything else, she noticed the body language of the Indian official who had come to summon her for the phone call from the Prime Minister—the alertness, the eye contact, the slight bending towards her while speaking. So much had changed in two days. Until that moment, the officials accompanying the Indian Olympic contingent had not spoken to anyone other than the hockey team members. It was hard not to feel special.

Nambiar sir was waiting outside, his face swollen. She hugged him and held on to him as he cried, his tears falling like raindrops on her shoulders. It did not feel odd that she comforted her coach, rather than the other way around. There was no natural order in this relationship. More than her coach, he was her collaborator, the only one who understood her journey as an athlete. What to eat on a flight, the timing of her strides, the recovery between events, wind conditions, the final acceleration, boiled rice, oranges—he was the one who lived this life with her.

Later at night in her room, as she lay without sleep, she realized that what she felt was not sadness. The lack of sleep was not new to her—this was the chemistry of hormones, as the rush of running would last several hours afterwards, keeping sleep away. In the end, it had come down to a trick, a thrust of the chest at the finish. One little move, and she would have been on that podium she had allowed herself to think about in her reveries. She knew she was good—now she realized how close she was to being the best. There was another race ahead, the 4x400-metre relay, and she would make sure India reached that Olympic final too. That night, it felt like it was only a matter of time. It felt, in fact, like the beginning.

The beach at Payyoli is a stunning expanse of clean, golden sand, dotted with parked fishing boats and fringed by a thicket of palm trees. There, it is possible even today to find that you have the beach and the melodic sea wholly to yourself. On a busy day, there may be a car coming off the highway and stopping for a picnic. It's the sort of place that has a cinematic quality to it, where the protagonist's journey begins and ends, the place of return, renewal and rest. A mythical place of power and riches.

Forty years ago, when a stick-thin girl, with her hair in a pony tail and wearing shorts, would run on this sleepy beach with a man directing her, a crowd would materialize to watch. The sea threw up many things, but nobody had ever seen anyone run up and down the beach—neither man nor woman. Why was this girl running? Why was she in shorts? Who was the man who appeared to direct her activity? What was the point of all this exertion?

In 1976, the year Usha turned twelve, Kerala became the first state in India to introduce a scheme to promote sports among young women. Kerala is an outlier among Indian states in human development indices, including in women's health and education. In 2018–20, the most recent statistics available for India, Kerala's maternal mortality rate (MMR)—the number of women who die at childbirth—was 19 per 100,000 live births, about one-fifth of the national MMR of 97 and the lowest in the country.[3] According to figures from a nationwide survey by the National Statistics Office in 2017–18, the state's female literacy rate was 95.2 per cent, well over the national average of 70.3 per cent and more than 10 percentage points over Delhi, which was in second place with 82.4 per cent.[4]

In 1976, the government set up hostels in certain districts to train women in track and field events, basketball and volleyball. Usha's maternal uncles, P.V. Sridharan and P.V. Narayanan, both schoolteachers, read about it in a circular that came to schools. They weren't thinking of a career in sport. Instead, they thought the scheme might lead to a government job for Usha—as a physical education instructor, perhaps, with decent pay, job security and the prestige of working for the state.

Usha's family was middle-class. Her father ran a popular cloth shop in Payyoli, which earned enough to feed the largish family of six children—five sisters and one brother. They were not wealthy, but there was enough to eat well. Usha was her parents' second child. Her maternal uncles taught in the local government school in Payyoli. Her mother looked after the home. It was a typical Indian middle-class family, certainly not the kind of home where young girls were encouraged to run around in shorts in front of the village. But it was unusual in one respect: It wanted the same thing for each of the girls, as it did for the boy—a solid job.

Usha's sports record in school was inauspicious, mainly on account of her sickly constitution–she was always down with a cold or a cough or a fever or whatever infectious thing was going around in the air. There was that one time in Class IV, when she had defeated a Class VII student to come first in a sprint. Other than that, she had mostly missed the annual sports day in school on account of sickness. But she did well enough at the trials to make it to the sports hostel scheme. The academy allotted Rs 20 a day for each girl selected. For this, forty girls stayed in a bare-bones building on an open ground with three squat toilets outside. The rooms had no doors, the windows had no curtains or even glass panes and the only pieces of furniture were wooden benches that served as chairs or tables for studying during the day and as beds at night—two lined up side by side per girl. The 'sports diet' included one orange, one banana and a boiled egg each day. Every morning, the girls trained for an hour and a half on the ground before going to the local government school. In the evenings, there were two more hours of training, after which the girls finished their schoolwork.

Like many things in Indian sport, it was a programme oriented not towards sporting excellence, but towards creating a cadre of government staffers. But it changed Usha's life, because she met Nambiar sir there. In time, the Usha–Nambiar relationship would become a legend in India. Nambiar sir would be one of the first three recipients of the Dronacharya Award, a government award for sports coaching instituted in 1985. And Usha remains India's best-known woman sprinter, and perhaps the most famous fourth-finisher in history.

A former Indian Air Force employee, O.M. Nambiar was a decathlon athlete who had trained in professional sports coaching at the Netaji Subhas National Institute of Sport in Patiala (NIS). He was the athletics coach at the academy, and Usha found that she enjoyed training with him. Besides the oranges he would save from his meal to give Usha after dinner, he would buy her chocolate-flavoured toffees called Eclairs as treats when she worked especially hard at training.

It turned out that Nambiar sir lived in Usha's village in Payyoli, a few minutes' walk from her home. When the academy closed for a two-month break at the end of the year, he asked Usha's father if she could train on the beach with him in the holidays. The families knew of each other in the way that families do in villages. But really, this was not the sort of thing Indian families permitted easily—a young girl training with a man in a public space. But her father didn't need persuasion. When you look in retrospect at an unusual life, like in those films that examine the minutiae of a day where one little turn puts you in a stray bullet's way, you see the little anomalies that turn away from the ordinary. Usha's father's consent was a turn like that.

It was the first time she worked one-on-one with Nambiar sir, running on the beach in Payyoli. She liked how seriously he treated her, how he pushed her hard but also listened to her. She was only twelve years old then, a child. When she felt tired, she would tell him and he wouldn't shout at her. He would tell her to try a bit more. She found in herself reserves of strength and energy she didn't know she possessed. She found herself thinking of returning the next day, even though she would be exhausted by the end of each session. It was then that she realized she could do this every day. That she wanted, in fact, to do this every day.

She picked up early medals in state and national athletics meets, paving the way to her becoming one of the youngest Indians at the

Olympics, at the age of sixteen. She featured in local newspaper stories. For someone as no-nonsense as Usha is today, the newspaper reports meant a lot, surprisingly. They built up a sense of self-worth in her that is often elusive in one's teenage years—this was she, the subject of these stories, and therefore, she mattered.

At the beach, people would gather to watch her and Nambiar sir, but Usha found she didn't mind. The gaping gave her a heady feeling, in fact. She didn't know anybody else her age who received this kind of single-minded attention from an adult as she did from her coach. Little boys ran alongside her, chirping with excitement, and Nambiar sir kept them from running into her path.

The coach–athlete relationship has the qualities of romance— the intensity of attention, the telepathic awareness of feelings, the enormous quantities of time you spend together, the sense of dependence you have on the other, the interlinked destinies. But unlike a romance, it is hard to find words for the relationship.

'Your coach is your coach, no? What is there to say?' Usha said, when I asked her about Nambiar sir.

'I mean, the things that you remember especially about him,' I said. 'If there are things he told you that you always remember. Coaches are known for saying things, or showing things that keep people going for years.'

'He was hard-working, I was hard-working. I listened. People don't listen any more. What else is there?' she said, impatiently.

Athletes dislike talking, that cliché is true—they prefer doing. Coaches are the talkers in this relationship, they ply their trade as much with sports lessons as with talk. But I was too late. Mr Nambiar was still alive, but mostly gone. At eighty-eight, he was in the last stage of Alzheimer's. His family, understandably, limited access to him. Two years later, on 19 August 2021, he passed away. Usha marked his death with a tweet containing four superb photographs, including one where her Nambiar sir is feeding her something from a cup, probably ice cream.[5]

I search for answers in the things that I sense even if Usha does not articulate them. Nambiar's greatest gift to her, possibly, was the sea. One part of it may be the science. Research in the 1970s was already aware of the harder work the human body puts in running on sand, and the strengthening of muscles as a consequence. This might explain Usha's astonishing longevity: Eighteen years on the track is astonishing by any standards, but especially by Third World standards.

But more than that, I think the sea built in her the fortitude that makes a sportsperson. It was next to the sea that she realized she loved running. It was the sea that returned her to running when she decided to give it up. And it is to the sea that she returns still, whenever she is at a loss. Ceaselessly in motion, its waters breaking on land yet coming back in again, the sea never fails to move something in Usha. In 1980, at the age of sixteen, she failed to make it past her first heat in the 100-metre sprint at the Moscow Olympics. But more than that disappointment, it was the meanness of the Indian officials, who refused to speak to her and the athletics team, that cut hard. She may have been the youngest Indian Olympian ever, but she felt like excess baggage, freeloading on a foreign trip. When she came home, the sea listened to her.

Then there was 1988, the most horrible year of her life, as she called it. She was in sensational form, having had exceptional success at the 1986 Seoul Asian Games, where she won four gold medals, and the Asian Championships in Jakarta, where she won five golds. Seoul was the venue of the 1988 Olympics, and Usha was widely expected to return with an Olympic medal. She shared in this expectation. Instead, she suffered an injury called plantar fasciitis (an inflammation of the tissue between the heel and the toes) in her left foot while training for the Olympics, and was disqualified in her first heat. 'Pathetic Show by Usha,' read the headline on a front-page story in *The Times of India*.[6] The English-language magazine *India Today* described her performance as: 'P.T. Usha finished a distant last in the heat for the 400-metre hurdles with her career's worst timing of 59.55 seconds, and collapsed in tears.'[7]

The press reports cut deeper than her own disappointment, actually. It was the first time Usha had received bad press in her life. She had been the princess of the media, the only woman who enjoyed respect on the increasingly male-dominated sports pages of the newspapers. This was the 1980s, a decade when the Indian cricket team enjoyed an inspiring, world-beating run. Yet, Usha gathered a number of much-loved monikers: Golden Girl, Sprint Queen, Payyoli Express. Now, many of the stories implied that she had been so desperate to participate in the Olympics that she had concealed her injury. Her home in Payyoli was stoned one day.

Should she quit? She had a job as a ticket checker with the Southern Railways—couldn't she disappear into routine office work? As she recovered from her injury at home, she walked often by her old familiar sea. Her anger rose and ebbed with the waves, but the sea calmed her, its vastness and ceaselessness inspiring her. Every day the waves came to the shore, broke and then returned again. So she returned to the track at the Asian Athletics Championship in New Delhi in 1989, where she was the standout athlete, winning four gold medals and one silver. At the Asian Games in Beijing in 1990, she won three silver medals. And then she retired for the first time.

'The P.T. Usha before 1988 and after 1988 are different persons,' she said to me. 'Everyone said "injury, injury", as if it was my fault, that injury. Everything changed then. People's behaviour changed. I decided to quit everything, and then my mind changed. But the person who rises from the cinders is different from the one who burnt in it. That Usha is gone, thank god.'

🌱

In 1989, she also took a second decision, an inspired one—she married a progressive feminist man, a man who was proud to be Mr P.T. Usha, although he scorned the term 'feminist'. Her parents had been requesting her for years to look at some 'good boys'. After she retired, she had the time to meet them.

Usha was expected to marry a man her parents chose. Like every girl in her village. She had had no time to date or fall in love, and she thought that an arranged match offered the most efficient means of getting married in terms of time. She had only one condition—that he be as tall as her. The practice of arranged marriage rests on the groom to be inspecting the potential bride; it is the man's approval that determines the match. In Usha's case, though, it was she who did the 'seeing'. Now that Indira Gandhi was no longer alive, Usha was the best-known woman in India, and the groom had to be sized up. The first man who came to see her was a tall, broad-shouldered policeman in Kerala, an officer of the Central Industrial Security Force, named Sreenivasan. He had played kabaddi for India, and Usha said yes to him on the first day he came to meet her.

'Why waste time?' she said, like someone who knows the value of one-hundredth of a second. 'That day only I decided.'

After her wedding, there was a nice surprise—she learnt that Sreenivasan was a good cook. He had lost his mother young and his grandmother had taught him how to cook so he could look after himself if she was gone. Usha spent the next two years enjoying her married life—she learnt cooking from her husband, she put in office hours at her job in the Railways, she watched films, she travelled to all the cities where she had gone for competitions but never had the time to see. She slept. She gave birth to her child, a boy they named Ujjwal, in 1992. She took up assignments to speak and write about sport. Usha had never wondered if she would enjoy married life. It was something everyone did, she had thought. Like breathing. It was not something one had feelings about. Now she found herself in a thrum of contentment, happy in everyday things such as shopping for groceries or signing off from office to rush home. Months slipped by like moments.

And then, one day, the spell lifted. In 1992, the Calcutta-based media group Anandabazar Patrika (ABP) invited her to write about the Barcelona Olympics. Usha took her six-month-old son and husband along to the city. She camped at the ABP office there, to watch the live telecast of the Games at night. Over the course of those two weeks, Usha's sleeplessness returned. She stayed up all night watching the Games, worked through the mornings on her columns, with her son on her lap, and played with him in the evenings. Yet, sleep didn't come, as it hadn't in the years she had been running.

The wakefulness remained even after she returned home. Young mothers typically get little sleep, but Usha sensed that her husband knew that there was something else. One night, when Sreenivasan awoke, she told him that she wanted to return to the track. He knew, he told her. And he was happy to support her. When she had met Sreenivasan the first time, one reason she had decided to say yes to him was because he had broad shoulders. Now, she felt her instinct was proved right—here was a man who was secure enough to be her lesser-known half.

Nambiar sir, however, didn't agree. She was 80 kg then. Her weight during her track days had never crossed 60 kg. She was past her prime, he said. Besides, she needed to look after her son. A woman's body changes after pregnancy—it is no longer capable of competing on the track, he implied. She had reached an Olympic final, she had made history, he said aloud. What did she have to prove now?

If it feels there are plenty of women several female athletes who have returned to competitive sport after motherhood, that is because of the events of the Noughties that the media has rightly played up. Serena Williams returned to tennis in May 2018, eight months after giving birth to her daughter Olympia, at the age of thirty-six. She has already made it to four Grand Slam finals after her return. Hurdler Nia Ali won a silver at the Rio Olympics in 2016 in the 100-metre hurdles, fifteen months after birthing her son. But in fact, almost fifty years before Serena Williams, two Australian greats—Margaret Court and Evonne Goolagong—had children and returned to winning Grand Slams.

Closer home in India, there are at least two examples. The boxer Mary Kom has won three of her six world championship titles, and her Olympic bronze in 2012, after the birth of her twins in the mid-2000s. In 2002, the first Indian woman to win an Olympic medal for weightlifting, Karnam Malleswari, was a mother. Perhaps it was Usha who inspired them to return?

But Usha was not thinking of history—she was thinking of herself when she made a comeback in 1993. She was twenty-eight years old then, still short of the threshold of thirty that seemed to mark the end of ambitions for track and field athletes at the time. Watching the athletes at the Olympic stadium through these nights in Calcutta, something had shifted within Usha. It was the first time she was not in the Olympics since Moscow in 1980. That sleepless August night of Los Angeles in 1984 came back to her. She still had time, she felt. It had only been one-hundredth of a second, hadn't it?

The months afterwards passed in a haze. Her weight made her shamefully breathless on the track—she felt uncertain in a way she never had before. She did not have Nambiar sir, but she found an anchor in Sreenivasan—he took leave from work for five years, shifted cities from Chennai to Bangalore so she could train at a good government sports facility. He took over the home and kitchen. She never had to feel guilty about being away from her son, because Sreenivasan was home with him. The absence of a mentor-coach is an orphaning of sorts, a crack in the roof over your head. But Sreenivasan offered her shade.

By her own reckoning, her comeback chances were slender. Bodies age, despite our iron discipline, despite our best intentions. She lost nearly 20 kg, but sustained a knee injury that took months to heal. She would start well off the blocks and carry it for the first hundred metres or so, but that old rhythm was gone—inhale, exhale, footstep, heartbeat. Her breath in beat with feet and heart, the rhythm that held everything together for her. Instead, she was always one beat behind now, watching others race past, 'as if I were a spectator in my own race'.

The media was cruel, describing her as a 'veteran' far past her prime, hanging on for crumbs. 'I feel everyone is looking at my face and asking how long I will go on,' she said at an event in Pune in 1996, unable to hold back tears. It was in those years that she realized that she had possessed an extraordinary talent, of which only the vestiges remained. Until then, she had never thought about her competitors, had never watched video recordings to assess their strengths and weaknesses, and to calculate her own moves accordingly. Like a dancer in a solo act, she had looked only to find that rhythm of hers where breath met feet and heart. Now she was far from the force she used to be, and she knew this. But a defiance had set in. She would run as long as she wanted to. Nobody could bully her or shame her into retiring—not the media, not her beloved Nambiar sir, not even her own disappointment.

'I was a beggar, it would seem, the way the press wrote about me. At twenty-eight, I was a "veteran". I looked up the dictionary for the meaning: "veteran" means a retired person or an old person. If you have a baby, you should retire, it seems,' Usha said.

Another sense of the word is someone with a lot of experience, I suggested.

She frowned. 'I know what it means. And I know how they meant it. I should cook food and wear a sari and pose with my son and husband on festival days. Then they will put pictures of me in the papers,' she said. 'But I am not there for your photos. I am there for myself.'

The thought of a photographer asking Usha to pose with her baby made me giggle. There is a fierceness about her in person that is hard to imagine when you see her running as a young woman—slight, serious, hair tied tightly back in a bun. Sometimes, she would smile shyly after a race was over and she had won—a tight, quick smile and a look around before dropping her gaze. In the video of hers that I saw as a child and that I now watch on YouTube, I realize how appropriate the deer running in the foreground are—there was something deer-like about her, too, then, not frightened but reserved and watchful.

Even Usha's dregs were enough to secure a number of medals for her following her comeback, in both national and international competitions. At the Asian Athletics Championships in Fukuoka in Japan in 1998, two years after she had cried in public, she won a bronze in the 200- and 400-metre sprints. She went for her last Olympics in Atlanta in 1996, where she was part of the team for the 4x400-metre relay, which failed to qualify. She finally retired in 2000, at the age of thirty-six, with a tally of 103 international medals and over a thousand medals in Indian competitions.[8]

At her home in Payyoli, these medals fill a glass case that runs the length of the longest wall of her L-shaped living room. It is a sight to behold, every inch taken up by medals or other metalware, it commands several minutes of silence to take it in. To me, it felt like a moat around a fort, designed to hold people at bay, to protect her from the inevitable question. But Usha herself brought it up when she saw me lingering by the case. 'If I had won one Olympic medal, I would not need this glass case. All of this,' she said, waving at the contents of the case, 'would be irrelevant.'

✤

In the weeks immediately after I met Usha, protests broke out all over India against a new law that offered Indian citizenship to persecuted refugees of all religions in South Asia, except Muslims. Things began slowly, with peaceful demonstrations organized by students and civil society, but gathered terrific momentum as the government controlled by Prime Minister Narendra Modi's Bhartiya Janata Party responded savagely to the protesters.[9] Police first stormed the campuses of Aligarh Muslim University and Delhi's Jamia Milia Islamia, both known as Muslim universities, and brutalized students. The images from Jamia's library were especially unsettling—spectacles and personal computers smashed, books mutilated on the floor, shelves lying like fallen trees—bringing to mind the images of Nazis burning the books of the Jews in Germany.

Resistance reared up. The video of a young woman fearlessly putting herself in front of riot police, and a photo of three women in hijabs standing atop a car speaking to gathered protesters went viral. Overnight, a thousand protests bloomed across India, a nation seemingly galvanized by the incandescent courage of the young women. It was as if citizens numbed by the authoritarianism of the Prime Minister, a Hindu nationalist with a massive democratic mandate, had awakened from their stupor. Known to be a man of decisive action, Modi and his administration had pushed through a number of dramatic policy decisions one after the other with questionable effects. We, the people, had seemingly been anaesthetized by the speed of the changes. Now something seemed to have shifted.

The most thrilling of these protests took place in Shaheen Bagh, a lower-middle-class neighbourhood in Delhi, where Muslim women, most of whom had never worked outside their homes, began a sit-in protest, where they occupied the streets day and night for months on end. Most sat with babies and children and elderly family members alongside them, setting up a community where carework, studies and feeding took place alongside protest. We are used to seeing the young protesting, mostly students and activists, and mostly male. I'd not seen a protest site like Shaheen Bagh, where protest becomes a community project, with the elderly and the very young sitting alongside the young and able-bodied. 'I am here because when my child grows up and asks me where I was when our world was being destroyed, I can say that I was out on the street protesting to stop it,' a woman with a months-old infant said in a video interview. 'And you were there with me too.'

I was unprepared for how much I would be moved by the protests, unlike any I had seen or read about. This was a movement led by the women of India, the majority of them unknown—women who said in interviews themselves that this was their first time stepping out of domesticity into the public life of the country like this, speaking politics, challenging the Prime Minister to come speak to them. Had these women ever thought that they would, one day, lead a revolution?

I hadn't thought of discussing the protests with Usha. Something told me that she would be critical of the protesters. But when I called her up to seek some clarifications on my notes, she brought up the protests herself, asking me what I thought of 'those feminists'.

I knew Usha did not like the term 'feminist'. 'No one is a feminist here,' her husband had told me when I complimented him for being a feminist husband. 'No feminism, please,' Usha had added.

I had put it down to the word's negative connotations in the minds of many. A lot of people, not only in India but also in the West, are uncomfortable with the term 'feminism'. It carries associations of angry, foul-mouthed women who burn bras. (The bra-burning image comes from a demonstration against the sexism of the Miss America beauty pageant, organized in New Jersey in September 1968. A 'freedom trash can' was kept to dump high heels, make-up, bras, girdles, fashion and lifestyle magazines—all the things women felt had oppressed them. Robin Morgan, one of the organizers of the protest, told the BBC that one of the women 'eased out her bra from her shirt and threw it in the can' and many women followed. Someone later set fire to the symbolic trash can.)

The protests against the Citizenship Amendment Act continued for weeks, and in subsequent conversations, Usha and Sreenivasan always brought them up when we spoke. He was more dismissive than she was, but Usha, too, was scornful. 'Why are they making such a fuss?' 'Why are they burning buses?' 'Why are they beating the police force?'

Sreenivasan had worked for a federal armed force, and his annoyance likely came from a personal place. It was more difficult to understand Usha's reaction. She had experienced the high-handedness with which the Indian government can behave. Her lasting achievement from the Los Angeles Olympics, she joked, was that the government officials had spoken to her. More than that, I had thought she was a supporter of women's advancement. After all, she runs a residential athletics academy solely for girls in Payyoli.

It is, perhaps, the finest athletics school in India. She painstakingly conducts trials over weeks to select girls, trains them personally, and travels constantly to fundraise for equipment, facilities and the resources to send them to national and international competitions. I saw many of her girls in the mornings when I went to visit Usha. Cheerful, bright-eyed young women with shy, easy smiles that they tried to contain so that they didn't appear too curious about me. They woke up at 5 a.m. and put in an hour-and-a-half of training before leaving for school around 9 a.m. That's when I would see them. There was no tiredness in them. What I saw was joy, energy and smiles that refused to be contained.

I could see them becoming P.T. Usha—disciplined, straight-talking, impatient with lies and excuses, and angry but never weary. But I could also see in them the women of Shaheen Bagh—confident, fearless, angry at injustice, yet burning with a calm energy. I saw them being the equals of men, claiming their place in the world without hesitation.

But Usha's perspective was different. 'I train girls because girls listen to authority,' she told me. 'They have more discipline than boys. They are easier to mould and prepare. They bring you better results, more medals. And it changes their life too. One medal, and you can get a job. Financial independence is so important. You should see their confidence, the way they talk; even their walk changes, you know?'

I know what she meant, and I see it too. There is something about sport that can intimately and powerfully shape the lives of women. There is also nothing that more clearly divides men and women into separate categories than sport. Our bodies, our biologies shape the basic differences between men and women, and the correspondingly distinct lifeworlds that make up gender. Sport takes this difference, puts men and women in separate categories, and yet gives both the opportunity to compete on the strength of their bodies. What could be more obviously liberating for a woman than to be out in the world, demonstrating the physical prowess of this body, to show that it is capable of much more than bearing a child? It can change the way a girl walks, as Usha said—the way she comes into her own.

In a way, it was the opposite of what I had thought, or hoped. Usha trained young women because they are more obedient than men, more disciplined, better medal prospects. Women are a better return on investment. The only independence she mentioned was financial. Material benefits over the independence of the mind, liberation, conviction. There is a lot to be said for this kind of thinking, of course. The Indian government supports sportspersons by offering them jobs, and the central attraction for Indians in playing a sport is the government job—well paid, secure and offering several benefits.

But the material realities are not the reason we love sport. We love it for the opposite, actually—the immaterial, unquantifiable things. The beauty, the grit, the improbable stories. Like the young woman who ate a meal of rice with smidges of mango pickle before she nearly won an Olympic medal. Who stayed awake that night, not sad at her loss but thrilled at the journey. We love it for the bloody-mindedness, for the sheer physical courage. For the woman who wanted to make a comeback for herself alone after her retirement, when she was 20 kg overweight, when her mentor told her she should stay home and look after her son.

We hear these stories, and we build up the person in our heads. We take courage from them, we construct our own experiences around them, we borrow from the resilience they narrate, we cast them in the light we want to see them in. Then, when we see that person is not the force we imagined, it diminishes us a bit, we doubt our judgement, we love with less love, we put some distance between us and the world.

The Usha in my mind saw herself in the women at Shaheen Bagh, found a reflection of her convictions in the way they fought for their ideas. The Usha I met dismissed these women as brainwashed. It was difficult for me to separate my Usha from the Usha I met. Her politics didn't take a thing away from her record on the track, from the thrill it was to watch her in action. Nor did it diminish her years of work training young women in athletics on her own, working outside of government institutions. It should not have mattered. But it did.

Then one day, sifting through my notes and research, I came across a selfie I had clicked in Calicut (Kozhikode) when I had travelled there to meet Usha. I was on the beach that evening, as were a hundred others. It was the last few minutes before the sun set, the light clean and beautiful in the way it is before it goes. I had gone running that evening, My sweaty face is at the edge of the photo, and behind me, in the distance, more than a hundred odd people enjoying the beach, many of them women in burkhas.

I knew of Calicut since school—it was a name in our history textbooks. The Portuguese explorer Vasco da Gama had docked in Calicut in 1498 in search of pepper. Thereafter, the British, the French and the Dutch were all there in pursuit of trade. It remains a place of wealth, influence and history. But to be honest, I was a little nervous here. Calicut is known to be the oldest settlement of Muslims in India with ties to West Asia. It retains a significant Muslim population—37 per cent of the city. It remains a wealthy town, and a lot of its wealth today comes from business with the Gulf countries, and because of this Arab influence, perhaps, Muslim women wear burkhas there. How would they look at me, a woman running by herself in public, without the shelter of a burkha?

There had been four of us running on the beach the evening I took the photo—a Labrador, two of his handlers, both male, and me, the only woman. All three men were graceful, sure-footed and swift—they seemed to know their way about the sand. Next to them, I must have cut a comic figure, slipping and threatening to fall over at any moment, a novice on sand. Yet, no one was looking at me. I know because I checked around in embarrassment every wobble I took. How freeing it had been! I wasn't an odd public sight—I was just another body on the beach.

Perhaps this is the legacy of P.T. Usha, I realized later. There is a road in Calicut named after her. It houses the grandest five-star hotel in a town with several other chic hotels and cafés. But this is her true mark in the city—that no one turns to look when a woman runs because Usha had made it so natural. I could run, like the Labrador pup, tongue hanging out, hair taken over by the salty ocean breeze, gloriously delirious without checking to look back on the world.

5

SANTHI SOUNDARAJAN: THE WOMAN WHO WAS ERASED

Santhi Soundarajan. Photo © Getty Images

THE 5 O'CLOCK evening light in Tamil Nadu was sharp and clean. The razor edge of the day's blinding blaze was gone, leaving behind a radiance that blesses the casual photograph taken on a phone camera with the clarity of a European summer day. I would see this later when I could look at my phone properly. At the time, the sun was forceful enough to blank out my screen even in my tree-covered refuge in the stands. The Anna Stadium is a handsome ground placed in an enclave of neat, rectangular, well-spaced government infrastructure in the chaotic old temple town of Tiruchirappalli.

At the centre was the tartan track, still crisp and granular on the surface and eye-wateringly red. The heat of the tropical day had not left, yet the track was surprisingly full with young men and women, and boys and girls in various stages of warming up—stretching, crunches, push-ups. From the distance of the stands, they looked like a mass of acrylic-clad figures warming up against an expanse of open sky. No faces were discernible—only bodies in motion, the occasional glint of acrylic and the darting shadows cast on the hard tartan track.

Even from that distance, I knew when Santhi Soundarajan entered the arena. Everyone knew. A lean figure with above-average height and a brisk, straight-backed walk, too precise and graceful to be a swagger. She moved to an unheard but unmistakeable rhythm. The bodies stretching, planking, jogging, warming up began to arrange themselves around her, standing to attention like pins around a magnet. In a couple of minutes, they gathered themselves in neat formations of specific activity—javelin, floor exercises, hurdling and running laps.

As the glorious light gradually fell away, the shadows lengthened and the stadium's wan lights came on, she moved among the various groups in training, demonstrating movements and exercises for each group, taking time trials, rarely using the coach's sports whistle and never resting. She moved slowly, but there was an unmistakeable charge in her bearing. She had turned once towards me on the stands and raised her hand, a single gesture that I understood perfectly: Wait for me. She was commander there, and I, the visiting journalist, was in attendance, like everyone else.

Earlier that evening in October 2021, when I had entered the stadium blinking in the sun, I had stopped to ask the assortment of young athletes warming up, male and female, 'I am looking for Santhi Soundarajan.'

'Coach will come,' a young man had said. 'It's almost time.'

Not 'ma'am', not 'sir', as sportspersons typically refer to their coaches. Just 'coach'.

When I saw Santhi from afar that first evening, I felt it too: Coach. Commander. Captain. The one in charge.

There is a photograph of Santhi's that the English-language news media often uses in stories about her. She is lying prone on her stomach on the track, torso slightly raised and supported by her arms, her mouth slightly open, her gaze fixed ahead. She looks like she has fallen face forward on the ground—the impression is of collapse. Another image that is also used frequently has Santhi lying prone on the track, limbs spread out, making an X with her body, her face hidden from view. Yet another has her lying prone on the track, but her face is turned towards the camera. Her gaze is spent.

The accompanying story typically recounts Santhi's humiliation at the Doha Asian Games in 2006, where she had accomplished a spectacular finish at the 800-metre event to win silver. She had stood at the podium and received her medal. Two days later, Santhi had been summoned for a medical test that took place over several hours, then put on a flight and sent back home by herself that same day. A few days later, the media broke the story that Santhi had failed a 'gender test '.[1] Today, it seems obvious that the nomenclature is incorrect. Gender is a matter of personal identity—a personal choice. How can anyone fail a test of personal choice? But at the time, everyone, from the respectable BBC to the not-very-careful Indian media, called it a gender test and not a sex test, which is what it was. A test checking a set of biological parameters set out by World Athletics to define a woman at a given point in time. Santhi was found not to possess the characteristics of a woman, and stripped of her medal. Indian sports officials informed her that she would not be allowed to compete further. She became the first athlete to 'fail' after 'sex-testing', a practice reserved for female sportspersons only, was made non-compulsory.

Competitive sport has a long and unsettling history of forcing women athletes to prove their womanhood. Compulsory sex testing was introduced at the 1966 European Athletics Championships in Budapest, which required women to walk in the nude before a group of gynaecologists. One reason for this was the suspicion that athletes from the Soviet bloc were pumped with dope. Some of these reservations were indeed borne out, as in the case of athletes from the GDR, or German Democratic Republic, administered by the Soviet Union.[2] But, in fact, the anxiety around biological sex in competitive sport goes back at least to 1936, when a German-Jewish high jumper named Gretel Bergmann was first recalled from Britain to participate in the trials for the Berlin Olympics and then not picked for the German team. Bergmann, who changed her name from Gretel to Margaret in the US and became Lambert by marriage, is the subject of a documentary by the Olympic Channel. The reason Bergmann was called back was said to be a threatened boycott by the US. In truth, it was an elaborate eyewash pulled off by Hitler's Germany to claim that Jewish athletes were given an equal chance to participate. More interestingly, the athlete who represented Germany at the high jump in the Berlin Games was Dora Ratjen, who was first outed as a man in 1938. Later evidence suggests that Ratjen had ambiguous sexual characteristics.[3]

Long hair, breasts and a vagina were considered proof of femininity. Not surprisingly, the 'nude parades' before gynaecologists were criticized and soon replaced by more sophisticated laboratory-based diagnostic tests. The 1968 Mexico Olympics saw the first of two chromosome tests, called the Body Barr Test, which required a cheek swab for a sample of cells. This was based on the notion of a clean binary difference in chromosomes between men and women—that men would test XY for the 23rd (and final pair) of chromosomes, and women XX. The problem was that a whole lot of cases fell between XX and XY.

The most serious challenge to the Body Barr Test was posed by the case of the Spanish hurdler Maria José Martinez-Patino, who passed the test the first time but failed the second time.[4] She was barred from competition and her medals were withdrawn. Her boyfriend broke up with her. But Martinez-Patino continued to subject herself to tests to seek answers for herself, and changed our understanding of sex. It emerged that she possessed testes underneath her labia, and she had no uterus or ovaries. She was diagnosed with a condition called androgen insensitivity syndrome, which meant that her body could not read her male characteristics. In 1996, a new test was devised, which claimed to detect the SRY (sex-determining region Y) gene in the male chromosome (XY), but this wasn't very effective either. In 1999, the International Olympic Committee stopped compulsory testing for women. It was decided that athletes would be tested only if suspicion arose. For this, a complaint has to be lodged against the person in question.[5]

After Santhi, another middle-distance runner named Caster Semenya from South Africa was similarly tested in 2009 and the results of her report leaked by the press, saying she lacked the characteristics of a woman. In 2014, Indian sprinter Dutee Chand was said to have failed a test measuring levels of testosterone, which is known as the male hormone in popular parlance. The South African government, however, supported Semenya and challenged the decision of World Athletics, the body governing international athletics. South Africa chose Semenya to lead the country's contingent at the 2012 Olympics in London, where she won silver at the 800-metre event.[6] In 2014, the Indian government decided to back Dutee and went to the Court of Arbitration for Sport (CAS), the supreme court of international sport, to challenge the decision that she was ineligible for competition on the basis of her failed test. In 2015, Dutee won her case.

But in 2006, the Indian government had dumped Santhi Soundarajan like a defective toy. A couple of years later, in 2009, she was found working in a brick kiln. The headline in *The Times of India*, India's largest-circulated English-language newspaper, was: 'Asiad Medallist Labours at Brick Kiln.'[7] Her parents are brickmakers; Santhi had helped them mould and bake bricks growing up, and it was the work she turned to when sports closed its doors on her. From champion to internationally disgraced athlete to manual labourer— this is the arc of every story about Santhi in the English-language press since 2009.

A handful of stories go on to note that she secured a government job as a coach with the Tamil Nadu government in 2016. But unmistakably, the tone suggests the job is a consolation prize.

The truth is, she secured this job after a media and legal campaign that culminated in an order from the Madras High Court, asking the state government to relax its job criteria for her so she could be appointed coach on a permanent basis. The government followed the order promptly. Anybody who has encountered the Indian state knows that making it review its rules for an individual case is a formidable achievement. Santhi had pulled off a major victory.

Yet, the sum of the media's reporting on her is defeat. The stories are accurate in their information, but misleading in their tone. More than anything, perhaps, the image(s) of Santhi lying spent on the track convey this impression of a person flattened by her humiliation.

When I saw her that first evening in Trichy in the sharp light of the hour before dusk, I found myself surprised, almost captivated. Straight-backed, unambiguously in charge of the ground, graceful and brisk, it was difficult to take my eyes off her. As she entered the ground, in fact, it was as if the gaze of each one of us present in the stadium collectively turned to her, like an audience drinking in the entry of a masala hero on the big screen. I found myself taken with her.

I had thought about building a rapport with her before I asked about that evening in Doha, the evening that erased her record as an athlete and her identity as a woman. But when we spoke face to face the first day, I realized it would be a waste of time. It was her gaze. Santhi Soundarajan holds your gaze throughout conversations, never aggressively but attentively. She would not abide anyone circling around a question and scratching at its surface. She is far too intelligent. She has been prised open and cut so deep that no researcher, no interviewer can make her open up unless she chooses to.

'That is what you have come to ask me here,' she said. 'That is what everybody wants to ask me. I have made you wait many months for this interview. I won't waste your time. I shall answer if I can. Sometimes, I cannot. There are some things from that evening that I can never go back to. My brain will explode if I do. But you ask.'

She was a remarkable interviewee, completely free of artifice, unlike anyone I have encountered in my years as a journalist. Several times, she would request me to move on to another question because she was unable to answer, and would answer the next one carefully, thoughtfully. Some days, tears would leak out of her eyes as she answered and she would hold her face in her hands, but make no attempt to hide the tears. And sometimes, she would answer every question I asked with detailed descriptions and wry smiles, as if she remembered it like it was a moment ago, although more than a decade and a half has passed since she ran competitively.

In December 2006, Santhi boarded the flight to Doha with her mind made up and lips sealed. She would not tell anyone. Not even coach Nikolai Snesarev, who was in charge of the Indian women's middle- and long-distance running, a man she both admired and feared deeply. She would go for silver at the Asian Games, not gold. She didn't want to risk losing her chance at a medal.

Maryam Yusuf Jamal, the Ethiopia-born middle- and long-distance runner, was Santhi's main rival at her event, the 800-metre run. Jamal had won gold at the World Athletics finals the previous year in 2005 in the 1,500-metre category, the most prestigious athletics event in the annual calendar and the third most prestigious competition after the quadrennial Olympics and the biennial World Athletics. Santhi, who also ran the 1,500 and the 3,000 metres, had watched videos of Jamal in preparation and felt her chest constrict in disappointment and simultaneous awe. Jamal was sensational at changing gear in the final lap, coming up from behind to take the lead and holding on without any apparent effort until the finish. In videos of the competition, her languid grace stood out even amid the athletes bunched up together around the narrow end of the bend as they ran the multiple laps in middle- and long-distance races. Jamal had had a phenomenal year and a half in middle-distance events, particularly the 1,500-metre run.

Santhi herself was in the form of her life. She felt light, yet full of strength; her mind felt clear, her chest seemed to fill with the breath she needed when she pushed herself to sprint to the finish. She was training harder than she ever had, under the disciplinarian coach Snesarev, who had been appointed the previous year. He came from Belarus, an East European country that had been under the so-called Iron Curtain of the Soviet Union. He carried the legacy of back-breaking Soviet-style labour and a belief in achieving podium results. Every evening, she was exhausted by the second training session, yet when she awoke every morning, she was raring to go.

In Snesarev, she found a coach who possessed a deep professional knowledge of sport and a serious commitment to performance, unlike any other coach she had worked with. Under him, India developed a respected cohort of middle- and long-distance women athletes such as O.P. Jaisha, P.U. Chitra, Lalita Babar and not least Santhi herself, who turned in medals or at least final-qualifying performances in Asian competitions. Babar became the second Indian woman, after P.T. Usha in 1984, to qualify for an Olympics track-event final when she made the final ten for the women's steeplechase in Rio 2016.

Snesarev had put Santhi in zinging form. Most importantly, he'd permitted her to focus on one event alone—the 800 metres—in which she stood the best chance of a medal. This allowed sufficient rest time, something P.T. Usha never enjoyed in her peak years in the 1980s, when she was compelled to turn out in more than four athletic events in every competition for India. It was emotional pressure in the name of national duty, and Usha, an unquestionable patriot, could never decline, even though it wrung her out. Snesarev, who came from a tradition of valuing podium finishes rather than face-saving that the Indian establishment had long clung to, believed in letting people focus on one thing.

Santhi had written in her diary in 2002 that she would win a medal in the next edition of the Asian Games. It was her first year competing at the national level, travelling to major competitions across the country, and she had felt her mind swimming. Something flared within her—awe for the competence of elite Indian athletes, some envy, desire for the respect and quality of life they had earned. There was the travel to other cities, the access to a reasonably comfortable hostel room and three proper meals a day, coaches who worked with you almost like equals, the prospect of a stable government job and the embroidered India insignia on your uniform. For a Dalit woman from a village in Tamil Nadu, who would wait outside wedding or community feasts with utensils to collect the leftovers so that she and her siblings could fill their stomachs, this looked like everything she would want from life. Perhaps this is how the other half lived, the ones who got invited to eat inside?

The Government of India recognizes medals at the Asian Games as the second rung of achievement after the Olympics.[8] In the 2000s, cheques of Rs 20 lakh were awarded for an Asiad gold, Rs 15 lakh for silver and Rs 10 lakh for bronze.[9] There was also a serious leg-up in government-job prospects. What if Santhi set herself the objective of an Asiad medal in the next five years? An Olympic promise would be too much, she felt. An Asiad was reasonable.

Now, in 2006, by her own hard labour and the happy cosmic alignment that brought her in touch with a coach such as Snesarev, she was actually on the cusp of realizing the promise she had made to herself in her diary. She had won twelve medals in South Asian and Asian competitions, travelling abroad to Korea, Thailand and Sri Lanka. She had set the national record for women's steeplechase in 2004. In training, she had already broken the 2-minute mark in the 800 metres, a threshold that was breached in the Asian Games only in 2018. The world record for the 800-metre women's time was set in 1983 in Munich by Jarmila Kratochvilova at 1 minute, 53.28 seconds.

But Jamal was a formidable threat. What if Santhi miscalculated the change of gear and ran out of wind in the final acceleration? Silver would be enough for now, she told herself. But Snesarev would be furious with her if he came to know that she planned to place second. She was still afraid of him. Somehow, that diary entry had become a talisman for her. It was unreasonable, a childlike fixation, the sort of thing that swells and swells in our mind and holds us hostage.

The 800 metres, two laps of the 400-metre oval track, is a test of strength and stamina, but most of all of strategy. It isn't only brute power like the 100-, 200- and 400-metre sprints. Neither was it a test of fortitude in the main, like the long-distance events, one foot after another and holding on to your breath. For the half-mile, you need both aerobic exercise (where the body has plentiful reserves of oxygen) and anaerobic exercise (where the body burns into a deficit of oxygen). But most of all, it is a race of judgement—choosing that precise moment to step on the gas (oxygen, in this case) from a comfortable run to take flight for the finishing line.

If you go full throttle for the lead from the start, there is a good chance you will not retain the energy and strength to meet the acceleration of your competitors, who take off in the final metres to the finish. The memory of her first attempt at the 800 metres, when she was in college in the town of Pudukottai, still surprised her. She had raced ahead of her competitors on the track, sustaining a substantial lead throughout the first lap and beginning to thrill in her dominance. By the first semicircle of lap two, she sensed a definite clicking up in the momentum of her rivals. Her lead, meanwhile, was beginning to narrow. By the time she pulled out of the fourth and last bend of the second lap of the oval track, a number of the others had drawn abreast of her, and they all seemed to be gathering momentum. But by then her breath was gone, and she found herself unable to match the acceleration of the others. She finished last that day. But she fell in love with the half-mile.

On 8 December, the day before the 800-metre final at the Asian Games, Santhi placed first in her heat with a time of 2:08.62. Jamal, who was in the second heat, also placed first in her group, finishing at 2:08.87. The third heat was the most surprising, with each of the top three doing better time than Santhi and Jamal—the first in 2:04.70, the second in 2:06.57 and the third in 2:07.34.

But Santhi knew the real race was with Jamal. Her own time in the heat was .24 seconds better than Jamal's, but she knew that her rival was saving the fireworks for the final, like all champions do. She would wait and watch. Let Jamal take the lead, set the pace and then she would see. For some reason, she kept thinking of the silver. But she would settle for bronze too. Maybe there would be another time when she would go head to head with Jamal, really race her for the gold.

The December weather in Doha is cool, 20–22 degree centigrade at the highest. The Khalifa International Stadium, with its system of refrigerating circulating air, cools the temperature inside the stadium by a further couple of degrees. For Santhi, used to the tropical weather of Tamil Nadu, it felt cold and bracing, and good. On 9 December, the day of the final, Santhi prayed like she did every day. (It wasn't until 2010 that she would stop being a believer.) The final was at 4 p.m., when the butterflies in her stomach would be nicely warmed up. She had come to discover that she enjoyed final-day nerves. She worked hard—that was her greatest gift as a sportsperson—and on the day of any final, she always knew her chances. It was a good tension she felt that day, the kind that flows into kinetic energy. And her mind felt clearer than ever.

One of the underrated sights in this world is a gallery-side view of runners emerging through the bend on an oval track. No matter what the level of competition—a subdistrict-level meet, a national championship in a country not known for athletic talent such as India or the mighty Olympics themselves—to see the adaptations and calibrations of runners as they measure up to their true positions when the track straightens out from the curve is a thing of beauty. In the 800-metre race, competitors complete seven bends of the oval track in two laps and run the final 84.39 metres as a straight line to the finish. This is typically the stretch where athletes shift to top gear.

On the evening of 9 December, the final, Santhi found Jamal holding back even after the seventh bend. A pang of anxiety flared in her stomach (or was it her chest?), but she decided to take the gamble. She would go flat out only when Jamal made the move. When there were just about 40 metres to go, Jamal's energy changed as if a lever had been clicked up one level. The flickers of anxiety in Santhi's stomach burnt to cinders as she breathed in deeply and swelled her lungs to marshal all the power at her disposal. No sensation remained, except eyes that tracked Jamal like a sniper looking through the crosshairs, and the great roar of breath that swelled and ebbed like a sea in her ears.

At the finishing line, Santhi pushed her torso forward as Snesarev had taught them all to. Physical sensation returned too—her lungs, calves, shins and stomach burnt, everything inside her chest and stomach cavity seared viciously, the result of her body blazing through the oxygen available and then running on an empty tank, melting glucose in the body to fuel movement. Yet, she also felt a fistful of warm thrill opening slowly within. She had fulfilled that scribble in her diary. She knew she had got her medal, although she did not know yet if it was silver as she had hoped for, or a bronze. Jamal was gold, of course—she was a full stride ahead. But the Kazakh athlete Viktoriya Yalovtseva, who had recorded the fastest time across all three heats the previous evening, had drawn up elbow by elbow with her.

Dizzy with exhaustion and relief, she lay on her stomach for a few moments. Ahead was the giant digital scoreboard that flashed the results. At 02:03.16, she was second after all, ahead of Yalovtseva by three-hundredths of a second. Jamal had clocked in at 2 minutes, 1.79 seconds. This is the moment captured by the photograph that is used most often in the press in India—Santhi Soundarajan on the ground, intently reading the results, the moment of vindication for the decade and more of training that had brought her to this moment.

Half an hour later, she was on the podium in her India tracksuit, holding up her medal for the photograph with Jamal and Yalovtseva, and cradling a bouquet of yellow flowers. A decade and a half later when I met her, a photograph of that moment stood on a cement shelf in her tiny, sky-blue living room in Trichy. The silver Asian Games medal is still kept carefully in a locker at her home in Kathakurichi village 50 km from Tiruchirappalli. Although the medal was withdrawn from her in 2006 and awarded to Yalovtseva, it was never physically taken back. Only her name was removed from the official records of the Asian Games and the World Athletics.

The day after she received the medal at Doha, an official from the Indian contingent summoned Santhi for tests. But he did not reveal the reason she was being tested. First, he took a blood test, and then asked her to undress. As Santhi lay undressed on an examination table, four other persons entered the room. The Indian official was the only one she was familiar with, and he left the room soon after the others came in without introducing her to them. Her English-language skills were non-existent at the time, and none of these persons spoke Tamil, her mother tongue. She guessed they were doctors, because they spent the next several minutes examining her body and probing her orifices with rubber-gloved fingers.

How does it feel to lie naked and alone with four strangers who speak a language you don't understand, who touch you, examine your body, point to it, discuss you, but make no attempt to speak or communicate with you? Santhi felt both a dead weight within her and a great distance from herself, as if she were attending her own post-mortem but they didn't know she was still there, still alive, watching all of it. The only communication they made with her was a gesture that she should get up and leave. She dressed in silence and left. When she saw the clock outside, she realized she had been there for less than thirty minutes. She did not know it then, but she would never stop revisiting those thirty minutes. Without warning, the room, those rubbery hands, that desolation still return to Santhi, filling sweltering afternoons and enervating training sessions with cold dread.

No one from the Indian contingent came to inform Santhi about the result of the examination, or even why she had been called for the test. Instead, she was handed a flight ticket back to India for the same day, while the rest of her long-distance team stayed back. At home in Kathakurichi, visitors poured into her family home every day to congratulate her and see her silver medal. One of those evenings, in a house filled with neighbours and others, she saw her face on the news with the headline that she had been 'stripped' of her Asian Games medal because she had failed the 'gender test'.[10] Another evening soon after, or perhaps it was the same one—time had congealed into a ball of anxiety by then—the secretary general of the Athletics Federation of India called her at home and informed her that they would not allow her to compete any further. Her sports career was over.

To date, Santhi told me, neither the Indian government nor the Athletics Federation of India has given her the results of the examination in Doha, and the grounds on which she 'failed'. It was like failing an exam where she did not know the syllabus, understand the questions or shown the mistakes she had made. Or rather, the 'mistakes' she was made of.

Only the Tamil Nadu state government made a gesture of support. They decided to award her a cheque for Rs 15 lakh, honouring her as the first Tamilian to win a silver at the Asian Games. Santhi would use a large part of this money to train children from her village and the neighbouring villages in athletics and field events. A couple of years later, when this money had been spent, she took up a private contractual job that paid her Rs 7,000 a month, before she quit it to work in a brick kiln. Brickwork paid more—Rs 9,000 a month. Perhaps it also reminded her less of what she had lost.

Today, no video record of the 800-metre final in the 2006 Asian Games is accessible from India. In fact, no video evidence of Santhi's athletics career is available in India any longer. You can never see Santhi in motion, never know if she ran tautly or loose-limbed, how wide her stride was, if she turned her face instinctively skywards at the end of a race or bent down towards the ground to decelerate. Athletes speak with their bodies, in kinesis. World Athletics and the Government of India took away her right to compete and, what's more, every recorded memory of her in action. As if someone wanted to erase every memory of Santhi Soundarajan, the athlete who won twelve international medals for India. What remains are the news stories, the photographs, the online archive of her competitions and times, and her own private memories.

In the Mahabharata, it was not the property dispute that finally led to the eighteen-day Kurukshetra war, although that was the start of the hostility. It was the public disrobing of Draupadi, the infamous episode in the Mahabharata that has become the cultural touchstone of arrogance and debasement in the subcontinent. When Yudhisthira, the eldest brother of the heroic Pandavas, lost a game of dice to his cousins, the Kauravas, he lost everything, including himself and his brothers. Desperate to win back what he had lost, he agreed to play again with the Pandavas' wife Draupadi as the stake. When he lost, and Draupadi was summoned from her room, she asked if Yudhisthira was a slave when he had staked her and lost. She was raising a legal point: Do slaves have ownership rights over their wives? But her question was ignored and she was compelled to appear before the Kaurava court, where Duryodhana, the eldest of the Kaurava brothers, ordered her clothes to be removed. Although Krishna foiled the actual disrobing, the entire court, including the Kauravas' blind father King Dhritarashtra, permitted the humiliation of Draupadi without objecting to it. Not even Dhritarashtra, who was the king and presided over the proceedings of the court.

Later, Santhi would come to think of the Indian official as Dhritarashtra, the man who had the responsibility and the opportunity to speak and object to what was done to her, but chose to exit the room, leaving her alone with strangers. Indeed, the entire athletics establishment of India and the Government of India behaved like Dhritarashtra in her case, abandoning their duty, instead of going to battle for her like the Pandavas did for Draupadi. Or indeed, like the Government of India would battle for Dutee Chand eight years later.

❧

Santhi Soundarajan was born to Manimegalai, a homemaker, and her husband, Soundarajan, a tailor and brickmaker. Manimegalai had been married at sixteen and had her first child, Santhi, at eighteen. The couple had hoped for a son and continued trying for one until they got their wish with their fifth and youngest child, Devendran. But Santhi was treasured because it was the first happy thing that had happened to the family in several years. Her grandfather, Muthayya, who worked and owned land in Sri Lanka, had to come away almost overnight to India in the 1970s after the Sri Lankan government declared Buddhism the official religion of the country. Thus began a long, violent process of othering Tamil-speaking non-Buddhist citizens—which did not end even with the Sri Lankan state's genocidal attack on Tamils in 2009–10. The terrorist group Liberation Tigers of Tamil Eelam (LTTE) responded to this with audacious and sustained violence, dominating headlines through the 1980s and the 1990s with news of their strikes, suicide bombings and death by cyanide pills to avoid arrest. This included the assassination of former Indian Prime Minister Rajiv Gandhi at Sriperumbudur in 1991.

Santhi's grandfather had worked as a labourer in the tea plantations in Sri Lanka and had made his way up to a reasonable level in the plantation hierarchy. Some instinct for survival made him sell his house for a fraction of its value and come away by sea to Tamil Nadu. Here, in the village of Kathakurichi in Pudukkottai district, where he managed to buy a plot of land, he started to build a life again in his fifties, this time as a labourer and a brickmaker.

Soundarajan, Santhi's father, who had just completed high school when the family had to up and leave, suffered the hardest jolt of all. Muthayya had encouraged his son to focus on schoolwork, to prepare for a white-collar career like those of the bosses he'd served. Instead, he began life as a brick-making and tailoring apprentice in a new country, where the only thing that was familiar was the language. But in fact, even the Tamil the family spoke was of a different dialect, and although there was sympathy for refugee families such as his, their tongue immediately set them apart. As a young man entering his twenties, Soundarajan was naturally expected to shoulder the responsibility of his family to a greater extent than his elderly father. After a full day's work in the brick kiln assisting his father, he would cut cloth late into the evening for his tailoring practice.

Unlike many south Asian families, the family distributed sweets when their daughter Santhi was born. Her grandmother made traditional rice-flour sweets at home, and they shared it with their neighbours in the village. It was all the family could afford. As the eldest child, Santhi would spend many hours lining up at temples, weddings and community feasts to collect the leftovers they gave away. At feasts, she would wait with a large vessel until the guests were fed. When the organizers came to give away the leftovers, they would ask those waiting to put their vessels on the ground so they would not have to touch the vessels. Those lining up for the food were often Dalits like herself. At the temple, she would keep a cloth below the plantain leaf on which she was served, and keep taking helpings until she had enough to feed her siblings in the cloth bundle.

On Deepavali, when their schoolmates and other children of the village wore new clothes, Santhi and her siblings wore their school uniforms, because those were the best, least-torn clothes they owned. That day, they would eat real coconut chutney with their idlis to mark the festival, but Manimegalai, who ate last, would often go without. When she first started running in competitions, Santhi remembered the pang she had felt at the realization that her mother ate idlis without anything. It kept her focused, she found.

In Class VII, Santhi won her first prize for sports—a set of four teacups—and her grandfather promised her a pair of sports shoes by the next year if she kept winning. Sure enough, the next year she received a pair of canvas 'Keds', the most basic sports shoes that came with rubber soles.

Muthayya enjoyed sport and encouraged her. It was largely because of him that the family was indulgent with Santhi. She was his favourite grandchild. In impoverished households, time and labour are especially vital resources, and children contribute significantly to household work. Even after Santhi reached adolescence, when girls were expected to contribute to household labour, they let her play in the evenings after she came home from school. She helped with some things, such as going around the village requesting leftovers from sympathetic neighbours when food fell short—which was not an infrequent occurrence—so that the siblings could eat. But for the most part, Santhi was permitted to do as she pleased.

The neighbours in Kathakurichi were annoyed, unsurprisingly. Santhi was a bad influence on their daughters. Some of them had also started asking for free time now. What if they, too, ran around outside? What was the point? What good would it do a girl like Santhi to take part in sport? Why couldn't she help at home?

For many years, their scepticism seemed valid. Even by the middling standards of competitive sport in India (with the exception of men's cricket and men's hockey in the main), Santhi was an especially late bloomer and received no structured support until she was in her twenties. Although she did well at school, subdistrict and district competitions, she was not awarded any state-funded sports scheme or hostel. She trained pretty much freestyle under her high school physical training instructor Loganathan, who coached her in athletics and throws, along with a handful of sports enthusiasts in a community club with a patch of ground. But mainly, she practised by herself under the keen eye of her grandfather Muthayya. This training lacked focus and was a bit of everything in track and field. In fact, she first represented her state Tamil Nadu in hammer and discus throws in 2001, not athletics.[11] It was 2002 when she represented Tamil Nadu in athletics the first time.

Thereafter, her ascent was swift. In 2003, she placed third in the 800 metres and the 1,500 metres. She was twenty-two years old then. Performance at the national level is what makes athletes eligible for the coveted national camps, where the Government of India provides training and support. Until then, she had done everything on her own. She put herself through college, earning an undergraduate degree in history in the nearby town of Pudukkottai, where she fed herself by gardening and cleaning for a wealthy advocate. She lived in a shed on an open ground in Pudukkottai that functioned as a sports ground. The shed was used as the office of a local sports club. In return for staying, Santhi cleaned the shed and took care of the grounds.

Effectively, Santhi got four years at the national level until her career came to an end with the Asian Games in 2006. In the brief window from 2003 to 2006, she put up a pretty good show, winning twelve international medals at Asian competitions for India as well as countless national medals. In the process, she travelled overseas to South Korea, Thailand and Sri Lanka, and criss-crossed the country for competitions. The Asian Games medal, her dream, was her thirteenth international medal for India, the one that would eventually end her career.

When the hordes of journalists would descend in Kathakurichi in 2006, the village community, annoyed by Santhi in general, was certain of one thing—she was not a boy in disguise. Why would any family hide the good fortune of a son? Neither was Santhi a child of indeterminate sexual identity. These things can't stay hidden in a village. People know. Rural life in the subcontinent is cruel in its certainties and exclusions, but it is also comfortable with certain ambiguities and amorphousness in a way that Western modernity, with its definition and precision, is not. They knew Santhi was a girl. A boyish, foolish, irresponsible girl, but a girl, nonetheless. They also knew another thing from the countless times they had argued with her about wasting time and not helping her family: Santhi didn't lie. She was what she was—an obstinate girl.

Amid all the questions about her identity and the flood of journalists arriving in her village to unearth the 'truth', it was nice to know that some people in the world believed that she was truthful. Yet one day, Santhi chopped off her long hair herself, taking the help of a friend to wear it close-cropped like a man. She had always thought of herself as a woman, and she still does. But she was tired of people staring at her face, trying to ascertain her identity. She was tired of the face that was flashed all over the press. She wanted a new face to prepare to meet the world again.

Sometime in 2013, Santhi received a phone call she was unprepared for, that made her throat catch embarrassingly before she could gather herself again. Nothing would surprise her again, she had thought, not after that phone call in the winter of 2006 that ended her career. Santhi does not cry easily. It wasn't just the events of 2006—she has never been that way. She saw herself as a realist. Sport makes you practical. You work hard. Sometimes you do well, mostly you don't. What was the point of crying? Yet here she was, startled by how moved she felt by a stranger's call.

'Akka, you don't know me, but I am your greatest fan. I am your greatest fan in the world without even having met you,' the stranger said, by way of introduction.

It was actually a time when her phone rang all the time. On 24 July 2012, *The Times of India* published a front-page story on her, reporting that the Asian Games medallist was working as a labourer in a brick kiln.[12] It was accompanied by a serious-looking photograph at the site. The story triggered a storm of follow-up stories across all forms of media. Television channels made short documentaries on her life and interviewed her at length. Seven years after she had been disgraced in public, the media returned to Santhi's story—this time not with suspicion, but with pity. There were calls from filmmakers and writers who wanted to tell her story.

Santhi was grateful for the attention, but also bemused by it. She was not embarrassed about working in a brick kiln. The journalists in the media seemed more ashamed on her behalf. Why would she ashamed of the work her family did? She had known this work from girlhood. It was the termination of her sports career that had left her in shock. But by then, even that shock had dried up. Where she had once felt cleaved into pieces, she now felt a tiredness. An unending tiredness.

The Union government made an overture of help. Or was it of guilt? It was the Government of India that had abandoned Santhi in her moment of crisis, and seven years later, the media underlined this. Santhi would get financial help and some admission concessions to study for a coaching diploma at the government-run National Institute of Sports in a campus of her choice. She chose the Bangalore campus because it was closer to her home in Tamil Nadu than the main campus in Patiala would be.

Yet, even at the NIS, there was an unpleasant question about accommodation: Should Santhi be allotted a place in the men's hostel or the women's one? Once again, she was summoned for a sex-verification test, and this time she refused to present herself for it. Someone in the bureaucracy realized the indecency of submitting Santhi to the same traumatic process that had ended her athletics career abruptly. Eventually, the sports ministry arranged an independent room outside the campus for her. But to her, the sequence of events underlined what she had felt since Doha—that she did not belong, so she must be kept apart from other people.

It infected her time at the institute, although it was not a time without hope or joy. She found she loved studying, and would eventually graduate with distinction. She loved the track so much that she loved anything that brought her close to it again. But she often felt like she was in an antibiotic stupor, locked out of the world around her by the memory of humiliation that would not leave her.

Perhaps this was why she was so moved by that phone call in those dazed Bangalore days, the stranger who addressed her as 'Akka', elder sister, right away. No one called her Akka any more, except her siblings and those neighbours in the village who had known her since she was a child. Who was this person who still thought of her as a woman? That part of her identity had gone, erased by the test, even though many people had expressed support for her, especially after *The Times of India* report. In fact, the only identity that remained was that of a wronged athlete. Santhi Soundarajan, the Victim.

The caller was Gopi Shankar Madurai, who identifies as an intersex individual. The intersex identity constitutes those individuals born with indeterminate sexual characteristics comprising genitalia, hormones and chromosomes. When I called Santhi to seek permission to interview her in 2020, it was Madurai who first interviewed and vetted me, a process that took almost a year before I was approved. Among several other things, Madurai informed me about the existence of gender-neutral pronouns such as ze/zir and they, and the importance of using these for people who are uncomfortable with 'he' or 'she'. I found I didn't mind being instructed. Madurai is a strikingly confident individual with a big mop of curly hair, big charm and a big, warm energy that make it hard to dislike the assertiveness.

Madurai was in high school when Santhi competed in the 2006 Asian Games, a time the adolescent was viciously bullied by classmates for zir androgynous appearance and slightly effeminate manner. Santhi's story gave Madurai the courage to run away from home, something ze had been toying with for a couple of years. Although it was frightening, Santhi's Doha story told Madurai that there were other people like zir, people who suffered for not inhabiting precisely defined sexual characteristics. Ze was not alone in the world. Perhaps ze could try to meet some of them.

Madurai, whose parentage is half Bengali, travelled to Calcutta and found refuge at the Ramakrishna Math in Belur. There, under the guidance of monks, ze followed zir interest in Hindu philosophy and mythology, and came to realize that there exists a spectrum of sexual anatomies far broader than the male–female binary dominant in our perception.

By the age of eighteen, Madurai had identified as an intersex individual, left Ramakrishna Mission, worked as a sex worker and then given it up to enrol in university. At twenty, while still a student at the American College in Madurai, Madurai organized zir first pride march in 2011 and informed journalists reporting on it on the use of gender-neutral pronouns 'ze' or 'them', and why they were preferable to the gender-specific 'he' and 'she'. In 2016, Madurai became the first intersex-identity candidate to contest state legislative elections in India. Three years later, in 2019, Justice G.R. Swaminathan of the Madurai bench of the Madras High Court thanked Gopi Shankar Madurai for zir work in an order in favour of a transwoman named Srija, who had petitioned the court because the marriage registrar had refused to register her marriage to her husband.[13] Justice Swaminathan noted that Madurai's work had delineated fifty-eight variants that fall between the man–woman binary. Madurai is articulate, charismatic, deeply knowledgeable on sexual minorities and Hindu philosophy, and carries the conviction that comes from years of fending for yourself. In many ways, Santhi's opposite.

From the day they spoke for the first time, Santhi felt some of the loneliness she had known all her life ebb away. Though she had always thought of herself as a girl, a woman, there was something that had changed in the adolescent years. Or some things, perhaps. As the years went by, the girls in her class, her neighbourhood, didn't say anything. The boys said a lot. But Santhi herself knew there was something that kept her apart from both.

For many years, she had kept her awareness of the difference she sensed in herself closed like a fist. And after Doha, she had secured herself like a fortress. Now it felt like someone had swum across the moat, not to attack but to listen to her. Her life had changed after Doha in 2006, now it changed for a second time in 2013.

Their relationship is as intense as a romance, except that it isn't one. Madurai is an intellectual and emotional mentor to Santhi, although she is older by at least a decade. Santhi holds an unmistakeable sense of awe for Madurai's activism and advocacy, a world where she feels both uncertain of herself, yet grateful for the window it has opened inside her mind. She learnt, for instance, that the global statistic for intersex individuals is 1.7 per cent. This means nearly two out of a hundred babies born are intersex, an incidence as high as that of natural redheads, according to the United Nations.[14] Two out of a hundred people were something like her. Santhi would not become a believer again, but the rage she had felt against the gods she had once prayed to every day started to ebb.

On Madurai's urging, Santhi wrote to the sports ministry, asking for her 'failed test' report and an explanation for being barred from competitive sport. Neither has been furnished so far. Nor has the Government of India helped Santhi with a job. However, Madurai's push bore fruit elsewhere. The Tamil Nadu state government relaxed its criteria for the position of coach in its sports department and offered Santhi the position of an athletics coach with full tenure benefits in 2016.

'The track is my identity,' Santhi told me one evening at the Anna Stadium in Trichy. 'Gopi Shankar told me to say this at a newspaper interview, and I realized that I had always known this, but, somehow, not so clearly. I am an athlete, but they took that away from me. But they can't take the ground away from me. Even when I was not a coach, I trained students with whatever money I had. My students are my legacy. They will make my identity on the ground.'

⚘

If you watch video interviews of Santhi, which have been quite frequent since *The Times of India* report from the brick kiln, you will notice a transformation. Her short hair has got more and more close-cropped and confident, the shoulders have loosened, the gaze has become more expressive and less glassy, she smiles more easily. With Madurai's presence in her life and the support expressed by most sections of the media, Santhi has visibly gained in confidence.

But the precariousness of her situation has not changed much. By abandoning Santhi the way it did in 2006, the Government of India left her unprotected on a minefield. She remains susceptible to nasty name-calling—freak, cheat, defective maal—and charges of sexual perversion. Consequently, the shadow of violent physical assault never leaves her.

Some weeks after I met her in Trichy, a popular Tamil gossip magazine called *Kumudam* published a story on Santhi based on the allegations of a man named Abraham Rajan. A colleague of Santhi's in the sports department, Rajan claimed that Santhi was a man pretending to be a woman, using her physical proximity to the young boys and girls coaching with her to sexually prey on them. Santhi, the freak *and* paedophile.

When I called Santhi after hearing about the magazine story, she picked up immediately. 'Yes, Sohini … Tell me?'

How are you feeling, I asked, aware of how trite I sounded.

'Not good, Sohini,' she said, and her voice cracked. 'A bomb has blasted inside my head. I can't lift my head. I will speak to you later, okay?' she said, and disconnected. Over the next few days, I practised what I could say to her, but I didn't have the courage to call again.

When *Kumudam* reached out to Santhi for her comments, she asked them to direct their questions to her employers, the sports department, first. But the published story carried no comment from the sports department. The entire story rests solely on one allegation, but what makes this single voice potent is that it comes from a colleague Abraham Rajan is also a former India athlete who has represented the country at 800 metres. In 2018, Santhi had in fact complained against Rajan to the National Commission for Scheduled Castes for humiliating her because she used the women's bathroom in the office, and for scorning her Dalit status. He retaliated by calling her a man in drag in an interview to the same *Kumudam* magazine in October that year.[15]

As journalism, however, the *Kumudam* story on Santhi's alleged predation fails the basic test—the person charged with the serious offence of sexual predation goes unrepresented in the story, presumably because the publication did not bother to wait for the official response from the sports department. They rushed a titillating story into print on allegation alone. But why did Santhi not speak to the magazine, you may ask. Think of how much weight her word would have carried—a woman who was banned from sport in a massively public manner for failing a sex test denies a colleague's allegation that she is sexually abusing her training wards. Add to it the general unease with gender-non-conforming identities.

In fact, every story speculating about her biology puts Santhi at a real risk of physical violence. An alarming 47 per cent transpeople and gender-non-conforming individuals reported sexual assault in the 2015 US Transgender Survey.[16] In India, data on such violence is unavailable in the public domain, but a 2014 Central government report on transpeople contains seventy-two mentions of the word 'violence' as against fourteen mentions of 'poverty'.[17]

Five young women and a young man, aged from eighteen to the mid-twenties, training under Santhi live with her in her matchbox of an apartment in Trichy. One is an orphan; two sisters are the daughters of a street vendor; another is the child of a manual labourer in Singapore; another's father is a barber. The young man's father is a driver. Santhi permits them to live with her, feeding and housing them at her own expense, because they are promising athletes from backgrounds similar to her own. What would their parents feel when they read this story? What would any parent feel?

You could argue she has the option of filing a defamation case against the magazine. Indeed, she does. But from the time she secured this government job in 2016, she has faced this kind of gossipy, speculative story about her anatomy nearly every year. Santhi does not have the financial or social resources to challenge every such story with a legal case.

In fact, the public understanding of atypical sexual anatomies is so limited that high-quality, responsible reportage also has harmful consequences. In 2015, when *Caravan*, one of the most respected and esteemed English-language news magazines in India, published a deeply reported, empathetic story on Santhi and suggested a likely prognosis of her unusual sexual identity, her younger sister's wedding ceremony was halted and her family was told at the ceremony that a favour was being bestowed upon them. 'We're marrying our son to the sister of a freak. To the family of a freak. We can still call the wedding off.'

Santhi had kept quiet, watching her frail father bend over with apologies and appeal to the groom's side to not leave his daughter unwed. If the wedding had fallen through, perhaps her sister would never be able to get married. When the paedophile allegation story was published in *Kumudam*, this sister's husband beat her, Santhi told me. 'Although I have helped my sisters find jobs and get married, and supported my brother and parents, and bought land for the family, they all suffer because of me,' she said on the phone a few days later. Then she corrected herself: 'Because of what happened to me.'

Some days after the disgusting paedophile story was published, I went to Trichy to meet Santhi again. The first day we spoke one-on-one, she appeared to be back to her usual self—cheerfully resigned. And somehow even more frank, holding her face between her hands when tears rolled down, yet making no attempt to hide them. Even aside from the ever-present threat of crisis, there was something else in the story. Her high school physical training teacher, Loganathan, had also been quoted briefly there, she told me. He'd called her an ungrateful student, who had not given him credit for coaching her. This is manifestly untrue—in a number of interviews available online, you can see that Santhi has mentioned Loganathan and her grandfather right after Nikolai Snesarev. When we drove to her home in Kathakurichi, she pointed out the ground where she had trained under Loganathan. More than her colleague Rajan's nasty allegations, it was this that had wounded her, the words of a person she still held gratitude for. Why did so many people she loved disown her?

Yet that evening when I watched her from the gallery at the stadium, training her students, I saw it again—her squared shoulders, her poise and precisely measured movements, her sure-footed confidence, the way the young men and women in training seemed to hang on to her every word. The light was at first radiant, and then it turned gentle and slightly melancholic. Then the shadows started to lengthen, and the dogs that lived in the stadium complex crept out to the steps on the galleries, and the birds were no longer visible as they flew home. The lights in the stadium didn't come on that day. In the gloaming, as Santhi and her students trained, I could still tell her apart by the way she held herself. I thought of the ceaseless struggle she carried within her, and how proudly, precisely, proprietarily she moved. The woman who had been erased on the official record. But here, in this ground, in this little piece of the world she had reclaimed for herself inch by inch over the past ten years, she made sure that you didn't miss her. This is me, she seemed to be saying. And you have to acknowledge me.

the driver sidled away from the window. I had never seen anyone like them. They had the square jaws and muscular bodies of men, but wore lipstick and bindis, and dressed like women. There were three of them outside our car window. They asked for money and promised a house full of children for my mother, vast riches and long, shining lives for us. Their voices, too, were those of men. In the cars around us, several windows were hurriedly rolled up.

I turned to my mother to ask, but she was staring fixedly ahead, avoiding eye contact with me or the people at the window. When the light turned green, we hurried away with a terrific growl of speed. My mother relaxed a little. 'Hijre,' she said through her teeth, still shaken but allowing herself a tiny smile. She wouldn't look at me. Later that day, when we were out of earshot of the driver, she told me that they were neither men nor women. They have the *things* ... of both.

Although 'hijras' are a public sight in the subcontinent, I carried the incorrect impression that the term referred to intersex individuals who had indeterminate genital organs. It's only now when I research it that I learn that the term 'hijra' encompasses a number of identities—intersex individuals or individuals born with ambiguous genitalia, hormones and chromosomes; transgendered men who do not subscribe to the sex they are assigned at birth; and men who have been castrated. Hijras are documented in our history, our epics (the Mahabharata), the *Kama Sutra* and our folklore, but despite this scriptural acknowledgement, they live severely marginalized lives. They are both feared and loathed, and excluded from any form of employment. Their main form of livelihood is sex work. Other means of income for the community are dancing at weddings and childbirth ceremonies, and begging.

That day, my mother's explanation lobbed a ticking bomb into my heart. Another memory—of a white-hot afternoon in Delhi.

I was perhaps five years old, and my parents were not around. I sat on the bed, in the privacy of a blanket and a rare solitude. I had just discovered my vulva, and I was thrilled by the dark, silk skin that pleated and wrapped and yielded to my fingers. I rubbed my fingers along the skin and likely found pleasure without recognizing the electric charge of the erotic sensation. Like an explorer, I pulled and probed at the skin, delighted at how much there was, excited by the prospect of what lay beyond, when the raw pink skin surfaced. Like a wound without skin. I panicked and looked for blood—I thought I had torn my skin.

Some days later, I dreamt of wandering around gardens and gurgling brooks and mist inside the body. When I awoke, I was heavy with the realization that it was a dream. Why couldn't my body be made of flowers and trees and fragrant, beautiful things? Why was there flesh and blood, and folds of skin that could break and wound, and uncomfortable orifices? The truth is, I was revolted by the pink between my legs. I was terrified of what lay beyond. When I saw the hijras that first time, a collective revulsion fused with a private terror. Were they male or female? Did they, too, have that horrid raw pink between their legs? Was it like mine? Was I one of *them*?

At the heart of the Pinki Pramanik story, and our ravening interest in it, was her sexual anatomy. Between the police and the media, her story unfolded like a ceaseless freak show, where the curtains were never drawn. There was the suggestion of 'unnatural' sex (which is the legal term for non-penetrative sex in India, typically used to refer to homosexual sex), there was a woman who was allegedly a man, there was the leaked MMS of a confidential sex test, there was the privacy of a life undone.

I found myself unsettled by Pinki's story when it broke in 2012, decades away from my uneasy adolescence and the fearful dreams of my childhood. I wore my hair in a very short, chic crop at the time—a lovely gamine style. I loved how I looked in that hair. I smiled instinctively when I caught my eye in a reflection. But as I looked at Pinki's photo, I remembered how people stared when I went running, their eyes boring into me until I drew close enough for them to notice that my cheeks were smooth and hairless. I started thinking about questions that I thought were long settled, at least in my own mind. Hadn't my body and choices made it clear that I saw myself as a woman?

Pinki's story, like Santhi's, underlines the central anxiety of being a woman athlete at this moment—a question that has come up again and again, and increasingly in connection with athletes of colour in the past twenty years. Are they female enough? Do their bodies align with the precise measures of hormones, chromosomes and anatomy that World Athletics has laid down for that specific moment in time?

Unlike Santhi, Pinki was validated by the Calcutta High Court and received a measure of public acknowledgement that she had been wronged. I wanted to understand what it was like to pick up the pieces after such a horrific scandal. I also thought that I could understand something of myself through her story, although my humiliations were experienced far less publicly than hers and were far less severe.

✤

When I first called Pinki, it had been more than three years since she was arrested, and ten months since she was cleared of rape by the Calcutta High Court. That first time, she picked up immediately. Her voice was unexpected—the just-broken pitch of an adolescent boy. But it was many, many calls before she took my call again, and gave me a time to meet. Late one afternoon, I took a taxi to the Sealdah station in Kolkata, the city's second-busiest train junction. There is that smell in the air—so characteristic of railway stations in India—of men and women who have travelled packed tight in compartments, sweating for several hours, wafts of urine and faeces, and that particular scent of tiredness and great hurry. Inside the station, it felt like I had entered a giant beehive—there were swarms of people moving in all directions and a constant deafening buzz punctuated by announcements of departures and arrivals, and great blasts let out by the train whistles.

I found Pinki surrounded by a clump of colleagues, who nodded at me perfunctorily when she introduced me, then melted away. They were used to Pinki being interviewed, I realized. She was dressed in her ticket checker's blazer over a shirt and a pair of straight-fit jeans. A cap lidded her face. After a brief glance at me when I said hello, she avoided eye contact. Instead, she kept her gaze fixed ahead on the crowds boarding and disembarking from trains. She was a ticket checker at the time—her job was to keep an eye on potential ticketless travellers. She was working, yet the lack of direct eye contact was intentional. In the sea of people around us, I noticed a number of persons who gawked at her and some stopping to look properly, but Pinki kept looking into the distance impassively. Sometimes, she stared back at them dispassionately. Occasionally, she would summon a passing person and ask for a ticket. One time when two men failed to produce their tickets, she made them follow her to a policeman, who pushed them inside an enclosure with collapsible gates and locked them in. This continued for an hour.

I asked if she had a break coming up when we could speak. 'No, this is it—the breaks between work,' Pinki told me, still without making eye contact. 'You can do your interview.'

I was taken aback. The station was a terrible place for an interview—noisy, chaotic. And Pinki's eyes were constantly scanning the crowds to identify potential ticketless travellers. I asked if we could set up an interview in her free time. 'I have no free time,' she said. 'This is it.'

'I can barely hear you speak, and the recorder will catch all the ambient noise,' I said.

She shrugged, and said, 'This is how I give all my interviews.'

A railway station in a metropolis in India is the last place for an interview—the noise is ceaselessly overwhelming and there is no time when you are not jostled by arrivals and departures. Because of the nature of her work as a ticket checker, we stood in the thick of the comings and goings of trains. Still, a station regular like her would know its quieter spots. She could, I thought, have taken me to such a corner during a break. I realized later that she saw me as one of the media—the ravening news hunters—who had fed on her arrest, sex test and court trial with insatiable greed. Who ran after the police cars to capture photographs of her handcuffed, her face framed against the cage-like grille of the van, or waited for the moment when she lifted the towel covering her face to step out. Now she had decided that she would deal with us reporters on the terms that she set. Perhaps not just the media, but the public at large.

She also wanted me to see her in a place where she is a figure of authority, in a blazer and trousers with the power to lock people up, to see her being stared at and staring back sometimes, to see her colleagues who know she had to be left alone for an interview. She wanted, too, for her colleagues to see her being interviewed. If the public gaze had devoured her during her bizarre case, she was now unmistakably staring back at us all. The public, and in particular the media, people like me who came to interview her.

So we spoke there in a mix of Bengali and Hindi, amid announcements of arrivals and departures, piercing whistles and the deafening echo of thousands of human voices speaking at the same time and magnified by the enclosed space. The noise gave me a throbbing, persistent headache that remained with me for the rest of the day, long after I was gone from the station.

The case against her was a neighbour's personal grudge, which weaponized her androgynous appearance—her deep voice, boyish looks and masculine attire. Her story embodied the central argument of the trans community—that society attacks them viciously, and sometimes violently, because they look different, because they cannot be boxed neatly into the familiar binary of male and female. I had experienced only the tip of it. Pinki had felt the full force of this prejudice through the police and the administrative machinery of the Indian state.

Three years before she was arrested in June 2012, Pinki had started sharing her home with a woman named Anamika. They were not lovers, she told me, but neighbours who were now roommates. The media referred to her as Pinki's partner, but I chose to go with what Pinki told me. When Anamika's husband separated from her, Pinki let her and her child stay in her home in return for keeping house for her. After three years of this arrangement, Pinki and Anamika had found themselves getting on each other's nerves.

On the morning of 14 June 2012, the day Pinki was arrested, Anamika called her at work to say that she wanted to leave and needed to return the house keys. Pinki was relieved. When she arrived on her bike to pick up the keys, she saw Anamika standing with a policeman and some other men. Later, she would learn that they were all cops. When she reached the spot, the cop in uniform informed her that she had been charged with rape and cheating, on account of pretending to be a woman. She would be 'tested' for her sex first. Pinki felt the ground lurch beneath her feet.

The next thing she remembered was a nurse or a white-clad health worker looming over her, trying to unclothe her. But she could not resist because her limbs were tied. Unfamiliar faces floated above her in the harsh white light of a medical facility. The place was too crowded, the light too much, the faces too close. Who were these people? How had she got there? Why wasn't she in a proper room? The words in her mouth drowned in her throat. She gathered what she could of herself and screamed, 'Take me inside! Give me a room! Close the door!!'

The faces drew back a little. She was wheeled into a room. Perhaps she had been really loud.

In that room she noticed the face of the policeman who had informed her about her arrest. She signalled to him and said, 'Call my father.'

'Yes, yes, you just relax,' the policeman said. 'You need to rest. We'll give you saline.'

Her next memory was of harsh white light again. She was flat on her back, they were taking her somewhere. She was still tied. There was a terrible drowsiness hanging over her. In a flare of clarity before she slipped back into sludge-like sleep, she realized that they had given her a sedative, not saline. They had 'tranquillized' her like an animal for capture.

The initial part of Pinki's arrest was a blur—moments in flashes, like the fragmented illuminations of a torch in a dark room—most likely because she was deceptively sedated. But she retained a clear, linear memory of events from the time she was taken to Dum Dum Central Jail. She was told that she had been remanded to police custody for fourteen days, although the report of her 'test' had not come in. She was not offered the services of a lawyer, in violation of Article 22(1) of the Indian Constitution, which guarantees every citizen under arrest a legal practitioner of their choice.[2] At the time, she did not know the law well enough to demand one. She was escorted to jail by a squad of all-male policemen and placed in a solitary cell in the male ward.

A couple of days later, her father was permitted to visit her. He had brought along a lawyer, who instructed her to ask the jailer why she had been put in the men's ward. He would also petition the court, but the jailer's answer was important to the subject, he told her. Somewhat emboldened by the visit, Pinki put the question to the officer-in-charge. He responded by asking her if she was 'one of those who clapped their hands in trains to ask for money'. He stopped just short of making the clapping gesture with his hands; a colleague beside him laughed aloud in amusement.

Nevertheless, three days later, the men in the ward were led out, leaving Pinki the sole prisoner in the ward. What was curious was that she was not allowed to live in the women's section, although she identified as a woman. Instead, a new, separate space had to be created for her.

On 19 June, a week after her arrest, she was taken to the Barasat General Hospital for a second sex-determination 'test'. The first test was inconclusive. It was conducted at a private facility called Uma Medical in blatant violation of the law that requires medical testing of those under arrest at public hospitals only. She spent three hours there, subjected to various diagnostic and clinical examinations. But this test, too, did not provide a definitive answer.

On 25 June 2012 she was taken to one of Kolkata's largest public hospitals, the Institute of Postgraduate Medical Education and Research (formerly known as SSKM), for a sex-determination test for the third time. An inmate in jail showed her a newspaper the next day. There was a report about her in the paper, along with a photograph of a massive crowd—people had climbed walls and made their way to adjoining terraces to watch. It was the sort of crowd you see at an India-Pakistan cricket match, Pinki would write in an essay titled 'This Past Year of Mine'. Had all those people gathered only to watch her being escorted in and out of the police van? Was she an animal in a cage?

This set of tests, too, provided unclear answers, which would take time to analyse. The results were sent to a laboratory in Hyderabad for karyotyping, or chromosomal analysis. An eleven-member medical board was formed to analyse the results. In fact, the case rested on medical *opinion* rather than *evidence*.

Though it was the state that was unable to make sense of her test reports, Pinki was not given bail after the assigned two weeks. Instead, her remand in police custody was extended for a further two weeks. She stayed in jail one day short of a full month. Most nights, she lay without sleep. The heat and the mosquitoes and the memories of her deep humiliation kept her awake.

But she also found unexpected companions in jail. An elderly prisoner, whom she called 'Kaku', the Bengali term for father's younger brother, ran the water pump through the night for her so that some water would drip on to the floor of her cell and cool it. He introduced her to a young prisoner named Hussain, another prisoner, whose job was to serve breakfast to the prisoners. Hussain would give her an extra piece of fruit every morning and afternoon. He also helped her wash her clothes. In return, she taught Kaku and Hussain floor exercises so they could work out in jail. Sleep was still elusive, but her nights were a little less lonely.

On 3 July, a twenty-nine-second clip of Pinki lying face down and naked with the camera zooming in on her genital area made its way around the internet and went viral. A neighbour from her Kolkata residence came to meet her in jail to inform her about it in person, so that she wasn't taken by surprise. In her essay, Pinki wrote that she had thought of killing herself that day and pulled out the laces from her shoes and tied them together to fashion a noose. But it was too short to hang herself from anywhere. The thought of suicide did not leave her, but she found Kaka and Hussain sticking to her side over the next few days. Perhaps they had sensed her distress, or they simply did not want to leave her alone, knowing that the nasty clip had made its way all over the jail.

When she secured bail on 11 July 2012, her father came to pick her up. With him was a woman named Payoshni Mitra and a host of prominent local sportspersons. Outside, there was a crush of media waiting to speak to Pinki, whom Mitra handled authoritatively. A researcher on gender in sport, she would lead the challenge against World Athletics and the Athletics Federation of India on behalf of Dutee Chand in 2014–15. Mitra had reached out to Pinki's family and had come along to tell her in person about the support for Pinki in civil society, the meetings she had organized and the various newspaper op-eds published to protest her mistreatment by the police.

Later that day, Pinki learnt that she had been granted bail because the medical board at the hospital had released a statement saying she was incapable of rape but that she had 'prominently' male features.[3]

✤

Unlike the South African middle-distance runner Caster Semenya in 2009 and her Indian 400-metre colleague Dutee Chand in 2014, Pinki was not called out in competition. She faced a criminal charge of rape from a flatmate. The police took seven months to file the charge sheet against Pinki and listed six charges under the Indian Penal Code—Sections 376 (rape), 417 (impersonation), 420 (cheating), 325 (assault), 506 (intimidation) and 493 (when a man deceives a woman who is not legally married to him to cohabit with him or have sex with him under the belief that they are married). Pinki appealed for the charge sheet to be dismissed, but the lower court rejected it on the basis of the medical opinion that she was 'not a female in the ordinary sense of the term'. It was a curious interpretation, given that her bail was secured on the strength of a medical opinion that held she was 'incapable of sexual intercourse like an ordinary male'. It was on the basis of this point that Pinki would eventually win her case in the Calcutta High Court.

But one fortuitous development made things move quickly. One evening Mitra found herself on a TV discussion with Anand Grover, one of the most high-profile lawyers in India. Grover and his wife Indira Jaising have led the fight for the rights of the HIV-positive community and sexual minorities in the country since the late 1980s. On that particular television programme, Mitra, speaking from Calcutta, and Grover, speaking from Delhi, found themselves in agreement. At the end of the show, Mitra asked to speak to Grover off-camera. She asked him if he would take on Pinki's case. He agreed. On his advice, Pinki's team took steps that enabled the case to come up quickly for hearing before the Calcutta High Court.

It was a sui generis case—the only one of its kind—and involved, even by the standards of courtrooms, an unsavoury emphasis on sexual anatomy. Grover carries with him the unmistakable glamour of the Supreme Court. He has a brisk manner, speaks warmly and has the gift of remembering faces. He also has years of experience campaigning for uncomfortable, 'disreputable' causes, often before judges of what would be called conservative sensibility. When he flew to Calcutta for appearances in the high court, he often spoke about the food in the city—that evergreen friendly overture that seems to work wonders in India.

Rape is a physical crime. Until 2013, the legal definition of rape rested on a specifically male sexual act—penal penetration of a woman by a man. Following the gang rape and killing of the twenty-three-year-old paramedical student in Delhi in 2012, the Criminal Law Amendment Act, 2013 included non-penal non-consensual sex within the purview of rape. But Pinki's case was heard in 2012. In Indian law, the 'rapist' can only be a man and the 'raped' a woman. Grover and his team focused on proving that Pinki was not a man. The medical opinion that she was 'incapable of sexual intercourse like an ordinary male', he submitted, means she was incapable of committing rape. And the finding that 'she is not a female in the ordinary sense of the term', Grover argued in court, does not imply that she is a man either.

The eleven-member medical board had concluded that Pinki had a disorder of sexual development (DSD), as a result of which she had an intersex anatomy. Pinki was born with the primary characteristics of the male anatomy, but developed the features of the female anatomy over time. Her male 'anatomy' was rudimentary and underdeveloped. In the words of the medical board, it made her 'incapable of sexual intercourse'.

Pinki is most likely an intersex individual. The word 'intersex' is an umbrella term that includes several conditions. There may be as many as thirty-eight variations on the spectrum between male and female, the Indian intersex rights activist Gopi Shankar Madurai has said. According to the UN, 1.7 per cent babies, nearly two in one hundred, are born with intersex anatomy.[4]

When you subject a person incapable of sexual intercourse to a rape trial, is it not an act of perversity, asked Grover.

Justice Subrata Talukdar in the Calcutta High Court listened intently to Grover's arguments without much interruption—usually a sign that the argument is going well. Other things mattered too. Justice Subrata Talukdar was younger than the star advocate and was newly appointed to the Calcutta High Court when he heard the arguments in the case over February and April 2014. Grover's team crossed their fingers. On 12 September 2014, Justice Talukdar gave his order: All six charges against Pinki Pramanik were dismissed. The charge sheet was quashed.

Pinki was on duty at the Sealdah station when she got the news on the phone. The day's heat had still not broken, but the evening rush had begun. The city swirled around her. She had attended some hearings in court, but had found that she was unable to hear herself being discussed in front of an audience, like she were a specimen in an anatomy lesson. She had preferred, instead, to report to work even if it meant standing before a railway station bursting with crowds who often stopped to gape at her. Many took photographs of her, without asking of course. But she needed this job. Although she was certain to be dismissed from service if she lost the case in court, she would do everything she could to keep the job.

'It is better for me to face people. If I did not come, they would say I ran away. Even now [after the court victory], people stare at me. Where will I go?' Pinki told me one day. Like everything else she said, she avoided eye contact as she spoke, giving the impression of an incomplete performance. An act where she had still not learnt all the cues. Even though it was true that people have always stared at her.

Pinki was born in 1986 in a village called Tilakdih in the district of Purulia, to Durgacharan Pramanik, a heavy-vehicle driver, and Pushparani, a homemaker. Electricity arrived there only in 1997, half a century after Independence, and eleven years after Pinki's birth. In 2015, when I travelled to Tilakdih, it was wrapped in paddy fields, where men and women squatted on their haunches in ankle-deep water to tend to their rice crop. Some residents had moved to cash crops such as corn. Almost everyone still lived off the land. Life there was agricultural, governed by the seasons of sowing and harvest. The village is bordered on one side by the river Subarnarekha.

Durgacharan Pramanik, Pinki's father, owned and drove a goods carrier, perhaps the only one in their block of villages in the 1980s. Sometime in 1997, when electricity arrived, Durgacharan brought a television home and the family sat it on one of their few chairs, like an important guest. When the TV was set up, the village gathered for the inaugural viewing. The images were snowy, as if they had travelled from distant lands, and the set crackled with voltage fluctuations.

In 1991, India liberalized her economy and in the next couple of years, a plethora of private broadcasters, including international companies such as Rupert Murdoch's STAR network, offered their channels in India. The 1990s is sometimes known as the MTV decade, when the American cola brands Pepsi and Coca-Cola launched with huge campaigns and the Hindi film industry visibly Westernized its aesthetic with blockbusters such as *Dilwale Dulhania Le Jayenge* and *Kuch Kuch Hota Hai*. Both starred the poster boy of India's liberalization Shah Rukh Khan. The English-language news media upgraded to spot video reports, live conversations and American-style studios on news broadcasts.

But Tilakdih received only the state broadcaster Doordarshan's stations—boring, staid programmes, where people talked endlessly in a studio. Still, television was a novelty there, and some of the Pramaniks' neighbours would come to watch in the evenings.

'Sometimes they showed sport,' said Pinki. 'I still remember the first time I saw a race on a beautiful red track. I had never seen a track like that, so clean and neat and nice. The runners looked so good—the way they ran, their bodies, the rhythm! I thought this was something I could do. I could run. Then I could also be on television! Then these people could see me too.'

A couple of years before this, when there was a race in the district hosted by Tunturi High School, Pinki had competed against older, much bigger boys. When they reached the finishing line near the high school, the principal of the hosting school scooped her up and hoisted her up on his shoulders. She hadn't placed in the top three, but at eight years of age, she was the youngest runner and among the best finishers. The principal asked her to join his school, the Tunturi Higher Secondary School, after she passed Class V.

He kept his word when she came for admission. But as she stepped into the new high school, she found herself in a very lonely place. Puberty is difficult for everyone, but it took her to a stranger, harder place—her chest didn't swell into breasts, her voice dropped to a lower pitch like an adolescent boy's, the hair on her face felt more prominent than the other girls'. But Pinki had always thought of herself as a girl. She thought her long, curly hair was enough evidence of girlhood. But the girls in school didn't. There was quite a bit of sport at the large, government-funded Tunturi High School—kho-kho, kabaddi, football, athletics and gymnastics. The girls complained to the physical training teacher, Shyamal Chandra Mahato, that Pinki was too strong for them, her temper was unpredictable—not like a girl really. 'A half-half thing', someone said. Sports involves physical contact, and they didn't want to be touched by her.

Mahato was Pinki's first coach in sport. Amiable and easy to talk to, he was empathetic to her isolation. But he was also a practical man. He sensed that if he made it compulsory for the girls to play with Pinki, it would not solve the problem. So he encouraged Pinki to focus on athletics, something she could do on her own. Soak some gram overnight, he told her, and eat the sprouts. If you can afford it, buy a pair of spikes. Run on sand. She could not afford the spikes and the gram, but the sand was free. The broad, beautiful Subarnarekha river, which gave its name to Ritwik Ghatak's celebrated film, curved around Tilakdih like a bracket, and its banks are filled with clean, white sand.

Every evening after school, she started running down to the river bank. She ran like the athletes she had seen on TV, taking what she hoped were handsome, loping strides. You had to run like that if you wanted to be on TV, she had thought.

Her mother Pushparani didn't like it at all. How could she run in front of the whole village like that, shamelessly? Her neighbours complained that it was obscene, 'a girl running around like a boy'. Pinki was the fourth of Pushparani's six children, and she had little patience left to manage Pinki. When she threatened Pinki with no meals, she kept her word. At the annual Durga Puja, the biggest festival in the Bengali calendar, when all her siblings got to select nice new clothes, Pinki received a set of her school uniform. The family would not allow her to choose 'those boy clothes'.

'I started running at night instead. It was surprisingly easy. I would eat dinner and fall asleep—the easy sleep that rice brings. And I would wake up a few hours later on my own. As if someone had called me and said it was time. It was quiet and dark outside, the heat of the day gone, perfect for running. And the river, how black and beautiful it looked at night. At that time I didn't feel the loneliness I did otherwise. I had a door of my own that I could open to a place where I could be myself. I thought I was running on that red track I saw on TV and that all the students in the school and the people in the village were watching me.'

One night near the village, she saw a figure running towards her. But she felt unafraid. 'Who are you?' she asked him.

'Shilet,' he replied.

Shilet was a boy about her own age. In fact, Pinki had seen him at school. But she didn't speak to anyone in high school, wary of being rebuffed. Shilet was a cook at her high school. They made a plan to run together. He would come by her house at night and tap lightly with his shoe outside her door. *Thuk thuk thuk.* Pinki would come out then. They would go down to the river together. The sand was cool at night, soft and deep, and their feet drowned in it. It was hard work running on it—it ate up the breath quick and challenged them to hold out longer. She hadn't thought about it, but she liked having a running companion. Shilet was a loner like her. He was an orphan—he lived with his elder brother and sister-in-law; he missed his parents. He was sometimes filled with a sadness that he could not articulate, and his elder brother was impatient with his moods.

One day, Pinki saw posters announcing a sport meet in Jharkhand, the neighbouring state across the Subarnarekha. It was not a district or state sports competition, but it promised big prizes—a Jersey cow, a pair of oxen and a motorbike. Shilet agreed to go with her. A large number of people showed up to compete, including state-level athletes, attracted by the prizes. Pinki came home with the cow, the bike and the oxen.

These prizes were valuable things, and the Pramaniks softened towards Pinki. Durgacharan agreed to take his daughter for the West Bengal state trials. In 2000, at the age of fourteen, she travelled to Kolkata for the first time to compete in the state athletics meet. Almost all the runners had spikes. She had basic canvas shoes, yet even these got stolen. She ran anyway. She did not place among the top finishers.

Yet, something changed after that trip. Perhaps it was the fact that Durgacharan saw her run without shoes, seemingly unaffected, as if nothing could taint her determination to compete. Pushparani dropped the criticism. Durgacharan bought her a pair of spikes. Pinki's own mind was clearer than ever—she had to become a competitive athlete.

She had a breakout year in 2002. She won the 100-, 200- and 400-metre events in West Bengal state, and was chosen for the national athletics meet. A scholarship from the Sports Authority of India enabled her to move to Kolkata to the hostel there. Over the next five years, she stayed at the SAI complex in Kolkata and represented India at several international competitions in the 400-metre, 800-metre and 400-metre relays. She was part of the gold-medal-winning 4x400-metre relay teams at the 2006 Asian Games in Doha and the Commonwealth Games in Melbourne. In 2004, she represented Asia at the Athletics World Cup in the 800-metre sprint.

In 2006, when she came home for the first time in three years, she twisted her leg running on the sandy bank of the river. She returned to the Sports Authority of India complex after her break, but her recovery was not simple. It was the first in a series of injuries and accidents over the next three years that would end her career abruptly.

'Those were the best years of my life. I was earning money from running. I was winning. I was a star. I went on foreign trips. I lived with people who were like me—athletes, sportsmen. No one judged me except for my performance. We were all playing for India there. Even when we went in a train or a bus, it was like India players were going. People would come to see how we looked. That was the thing, you know—that respect for India players. You become an important person.'

When I met Pinki in 2015, she told me she had again started training seriously for the track. She wanted to run competitively again. That would be her true validation before the public, she believed—proof that she was a champion who had overcome the horrible scandal that had befallen her. I requested to watch her train, but she refused, saying she would not be able to focus with me present.

Instead, she took me bean-bag shopping at a desolate suburban mall one day. That is to say, she paid for a bean bag, I sat on it to try it out on her behalf, and the man at the cavernous furniture store in the mall gaped at her.

'How much?' she said, pointing with her thumb to a too-bright blue bean bag.

'Rs 2,700,' answered the man, staring at her.

'How shall I carry it?' she asked, returning the stare, her voice as flat as earlier.

'It'll fit in the dickey of your car,' he said, seemingly transfixed by her. She returned the stare for several seconds.

Then she turned abruptly, stood in front of a glass cabinet and dipped her hands into the front pockets of her jeans.

The man now turned his attention to her reflection.

'Can I get it in red?' she asked, examining her reflection.

'No,' he told the reflection. 'Meaning, yes.'

'Meaning?' the reflection asked.

'I mean yes,' he said again, 'but you can only collect it in a couple of days. We don't have it in stock now.'

'Okay,' said the reflection. 'Take down my address.'

All the three people in the room were staring at Pinki's reflection—the storekeeper, Pinki and I. I giggled. It was a bit like being at the cinema, an audience of three staring at an image on a screen.

Then Pinki turned and walked towards the storekeeper. 'I'll pay by card.'

'Okay,' he agreed, fascinated, transferring his stare from the reflection to Pinki's person.

It was among the strangest human interactions I have witnessed, one from which I was eliminated. You know those films in which a character wanders around as a ghost or as an invisible person? I felt like that, as if I were present but no one could see me. Every second, every centimetre of Pinki's presence was devoured. The man may or may not have recognized who she was, but what he stared at was a person whose gender identity was not easy to determine—a person with the just-broken voice of an adolescent boy, the defined pectoral muscles of an avid gym-going man framed in a tight T-shirt, the swagger of a young man about town, and the smooth, mostly hairless face of a young girl.

It gave me a sense of what Pinki encountered every day, though oddly enough, I thought she had enjoyed the storekeeper's discomfiture. 'I am grafting myself anew,' she wrote in the essay she published a year after her arrest for rape. 'What people say, how they laugh—I try not to think about these things. Man, woman—these are labels given by people. I am Pinki Pramanik—this is my only identity … I know I am unusual, that is why people are so curious about me.'

I got the feeling she was trying to return the public gaze that ravens on her. Once, she had felt like a caged animal, imprisoned by the staring. Now she sometimes locks her eyes on a particularly insatiable starer, like that man in the furniture store. Defiantly, as if she is daring them to confront her. *Yes, I am here. I'm not embarrassed. What about you?*

After her release from jail, she had started participating in rallies in support of rape victims, queer rights, and conferences on gender and sexuality. She was something of a local celebrity, invited to inaugurate blood donation camps, local sports clubs and Durga Puja pandals. She was met with terrific crowds, particularly in small towns and rural areas. They took selfies with her and made videos. 'I know that many of them come to stare,' she told me, showing me photos on her phone.

I had become Facebook friends with Pinki a couple of months before I called her. She does not engage much with other people on the site. Her only activity is uploading photographs of herself every week or ten days. In these, she is dressed most often in a sleeveless T-shirt and jeans, or track pants. Her arms are muscular and defined. Her chest looks flat and her shirt stretches taut over her torso. She poses alone, occasionally with her pet dogs.

She always smiles in these pictures, with her lips pressed together. She's not a natural before the camera, but she seems to enjoy being photographed, in particular, to show off her physique. Walking in the mall with her, I noticed how she always glanced at herself in the long shop mirrors as she passed by. I sensed that she had a fascination with looking, and being looked at.

Soon after the bean-bag outing, Pinki sent me a voice note, telling me she wouldn't speak any further, that I had enough material to write with. It came as a surprise as she had asked me to come home to see her dogs at our last meeting. But I knew even then that I had struggled to strike a rapport with her. Every interaction left me second-guessing myself. Was she annoyed with me? Why hadn't she taken my calls the last several times? The interviews I did with her may well be the weakest in this book.

I decided to travel to her village in Purulia by myself. Tilakdih is six hours from Kolkata by car, a drive leavened by the gentle paddy green of the Bengal countryside and the malty tea brewed in roadside stalls. Somewhere along the way, the soil turned reddish brown; and after five hours, the road began to curve gently upwards. The landscape changed, and with it the season. The oppressive heat of Kolkata slipped away, and my skin felt clean and cool, the film of sweat gone. Inwardly as well, the season changed. Some of my annoyance abated.

Once we entered the district of Purulia, the taxi driver stopped at the first gram panchayat (village council) office we encountered. Everyone appeared to know Pinki there; several heads nodded among the many people standing in queue to get work done. Several came up to our car to show us how to get to her home. She was a local landmark, and we were pilgrims on her trail.

Her village retains the cinematic beauty of rural Bengal—gentle green paddy, winding dirt roads, placid hillocks in the distance, thickets of the white kaash flowers, so familiar to anyone who has seen Satyajit Ray's films. Almost everybody here still works the land, women walk with pots and there is little farm machinery on view. The afternoons are still long, shimmering, ceaseless here. Except for the local government school, some TV antennas and electricity poles, it is the late-nineteenth-century pastoral landscape that Tagore and Bibhutibhushan Bandyopadhyay wrote so unforgettably about.

I saw that lovely Indian cliché come to life—a line of delighted children trailed our car, while older, more demure heads peered out of homes to trail our progress. The first person we stopped to ask for directions in the village showed us how to get there, smiled and asked, 'You are from the press?' Another person we asked right before we reached, nodded at Pinki's name. '*Cinema thhekey* [You're from the film business]?' Everyone here knew where the star lived. Everyone wanted to say she was theirs. In the natural course of things, we are identified with the places we come from. But Tilakdih was now Pinki's village, like Payyoli was Usha's. The place derived its identity from her.

Villages can be cruel places, radiating prejudice, superstition, discrimination, abuse—perhaps even more than big cities. If Kolkata, one of India's biggest and oldest cities, could take such an insatiable interest in Pinki's anatomy, the narrow-mindedness of this impoverished, remote village is far more understandable. But whatever it was that the people of Tilakdih once felt for Pinki, it was gone by the time I travelled there. She was no longer the 'half-half thing'. She was their identity in the world. Such are the dividends of wearing the national colours.

The Pramaniks lived in a house with a red metal gate and a peacock-design grille. They welcomed me warmly when I mentioned Pinki. Tiny rooms were arranged around a large, dusty courtyard with two charpoys. A small dog was tied in the corner next to a stack of paddy. The house itself was a small structure with a slanting roof, but it was one of a handful of pucca houses I saw in the area. The awkwardness I had felt about visiting her home in her absence thawed a bit. Her family were seasoned welcomers of journalists. And perhaps, many others had travelled on their own like me.

Durgacharan showed me a bike with the name Pinki Pramanik spelt out on the number plate. 'This is for when the police stop us. They let us go when they realize we are related to her,' he said, laughing.

The next afternoon in Tilakdih, I went looking for her friend Shilet in the next village. He was a serious-looking young man with the slight frame of an adolescent boy. He was dressed in a vest and a lungi. He invited me inside his thatched one-room mud hut and hurriedly pulled on a torn T-shirt over his sleeveless vest. He insisted that I sit on the bed, while he sat on a chair that a neighbour brought running on account of my visit. His wife, a shy young woman who nodded at me in welcome, made tea for us.

'We were inseparable, Pinki and I. What is there between you and that half-half thing, people would say. When I got married, I had to tell my wife that Pinki and I had nothing going on. But I was the only friend she had, and I didn't want her to be alone,' he said. There is a gentleness in his manner that tells you this is a man who knows what it is like to be lonely.

'Are you still friends with Pinki?' I asked.

'Yes,' he answers after a pause. 'We speak if we meet.'

He is quiet for a few moments. 'But I don't have her phone number, so we are not in touch. At least, I don't know if it is her number. When I called the number I have, no one picked up.'

Then he added, 'Do you want to see our river?'

His discomfort was palpable. Friends drift away from each other, of course. The contemporary term 'ghosting', which refers to a complete severing of ties, is used both for romantic relationships and friendships. But being cast aside by a friend is still an experience that is hard to speak about. In a sense, Pinki has ghosted me as well, ending our communication abruptly as she did. My association with her was far more ephemeral than his, yet I, too, had felt the unmistakable prick of shame.

It took us ten minutes in the taxi to reach the river, through narrow dirt tracks, mired in the deep mud of the monsoon. And then suddenly it was before us—the river, broader and more beautiful than I had imagined. The Subarnarekha, whose name translates to 'Line of Gold', is one of eastern India's most significant rivers, with its own entry in the Encyclopaedia Britannica. I was unprepared for its majestic beauty and wind it sent roaring inside my ears.

Smoke arose from one point on the bank. From the people standing around and the distant sound of their chants, I gathered it was a funeral pyre. I had read that it was the practice in villages to cremate the dead near a body of water. This was the first time I had witnessed it, the chants of the mourners near the water echoing in the open space. It was almost evening, and a man walking a herd of cows by the bank suddenly pushed one into the water. It looked like an act of violence, but to my surprise, the large cow started swimming gracefully, if leggily, and the rest of the herd followed. It was a curiously magical thing to witness. Who would have thought cows could swim so beautifully? Far ahead, at the farthest point of my sight, stood a temple that appeared to be in the middle of the river, underlining the otherworldly sense of that evening.

I took off my shoes, kept my bag aside and ran for a bit. I had not been able to watch Pinki run, nor would I, but I could run where she had. The white sand was cool at that hour of dusk, silky to the touch, but it slipped away from my feet at the last moment, making it hard work to land a foot and raise the other. I stopped when I noticed small black heads of rocks peeping out from the sand. Pinki and Shilet would run up to the point of the temple and turn back, unfazed by the rocks the river had left on the bank. I washed my face in the river, tasted the water on Shilet's recommendation and returned to the village with him.

Some days later, back home in my apartment, that memory of sand slipping away from my feet at the last moment returned. I was walking barefoot in my flat, as I often do in the long summer. Something about the tactile memory of things just slipping out of grasp made me realize what I had been grappling with in my mind. It was not her moderately successful athletics career that was Pinki's triumph. Nor was it her court victory, brave as it was. It was that Pinki Pramanik had held on to her sense of self—one that had brought social ostracism from childhood, and shame and criminal charges later—and decided to own that identity, whatever it took.

7

DUTEE CHAND:
THE WOMAN WHO CHALLENGED
THE OLYMPIC RULES

Dutee Chand. Photo © Getty Images

ASHISH SHAH IS a fashion and fine art photographer with a distinctive style. When you look at his work, his imprint is evident. The way his subjects look at you, without artifice, the distance between you and the subject dissolves in the frankness and vulnerability of their gaze.

It's hard to look away from a Shah image. His subjects are what he calls 'ordinary people'—people waiting at the railway station, drinking tea on the streets, cycling somewhere, dozing in public parks, sitting in a bus, going someplace. Faces in the crowd. Except that Shah makes them singular—individuals, rather than faces. There is a painterly quality to his images, that ability to hold time and fold us in its embrace, in the way that certain canvases in galleries can make you stand still before them, fading out the things around you. Once you see Shah's people, you come away with something of them. He makes them people you know, because you've seen what's in their eyes. Long after you look away, their eyes hold you.

This is why he prefers to not shoot with 'celebrities'. They have a certain practised ease before the camera that takes away from the secrets he likes to unlock in unpractised eyes. But for Dutee Chand, Shah felt differently. In May 2019, the sprinter became the first Indian sportsperson to come out as gay. A couple of months later, when *Vogue* India approached Shah to shoot images of Dutee, he agreed at once.

Less than a year earlier, in September 2018, the Supreme Court had struck down part of the infamous Section 377 of the Indian Penal Code, which criminalized sex between consenting men. This homophobic legacy of Victorian England survives in many of

Britain's former colonies. Unsurprisingly, in 1967, Britain herself removed the provisions of the deeply wounding Criminal Law Amendment Act, 1885, which deemed any male homosexual act, including those conducted in private, illegal. The law contains no mention of gay women, presumably because the citizen, in the public imagination of that time, was male. The first country in the modern age to allow women the right to vote, arguably, was Australia in 1902, thereby recognizing the woman as an equal citizen. In Britain, all women without qualification received the right to vote by the Equal Franchise Act of 1928. Besides, the thinking at the time of the Criminal Law Amendment Act, 1885 was that very few women showed homosexual tendencies, and any mention of this would only encourage the practice.

The 2018 Supreme Court judgment in India was momentous. India became one of the first former British colonies in the Global South to remove the provisions of this law, and among a handful of developing countries to do so.[1] Singapore—which is far wealthier, far more developed and outperforms India in every human development indicator—continues to maintain the criminal provisions of Section 377. Within India, Dutee is probably the first public figure outside the world of the arts, which is typically seen as more liberal, to come out. Even the prominent Hindi-film director, producer and talk-show host Karan Johar was less forthright, writing in his memoir *An Unsuitable Boy* in 2017, 'Everybody knows what my sexual orientation is. I don't need to scream it out. If I need to spell it out, I won't only because I live in a country where I could possibly be jailed for saying this. Which is why I Karan Johar will not say the three words that possibly everybody knows about me.'[2]

On May 2019, Dutee said, 'I am having a relationship with a nineteen-year-old woman from my village [Chaka Gopalpur] for the past five years ... I have found someone who is my soulmate. I have always believed that everyone should have the freedom to love.'[3] Her statement was greeted with rapture by the national press in India and by sections of the international press. She is the first sportsperson in India, and indeed the first female public figure in the country, to openly acknowledge she is gay.

In July 2019, Dutee secured gold at the 100 metres at the FISU World University Games, formerly known as the Universiade, in Naples, Italy. The Indian press reported it as a historic first—the first time an Indian woman had secured a gold at the Universiade.[4] In the scheme of athletics, even for a lightweight such as India, this is a minor competition. The Indian government ranks this competition at the lowest level of international achievement, offering Rs 3.5 lakh for securing a gold medal at these games, as against Rs 30 lakh for a gold at the Asian Games or the Commonwealth Games.[5] But Dutee's statement about homosexuality had arguably set her up for a different level of attention. She was everywhere after she returned from the Universiade—on the popular TV quiz show *Kaun Banega Crorepati* with the Hindi-film legend Amitabh Bachchan; in an hour-long prime-time interview on the English-language news channel NDTV; in a live talk show with one of the most prominent female journalists in India, Barkha Dutt.

To those who follow track and field athletics, Dutee became a known figure in 2014 when she challenged World Athletics, which sets the rules of all track and field competitions, including the Olympics. That year she had been declared ineligible for competition because her testosterone levels were found higher than permitted. In the news, this was bluntly and incorrectly described as her failing the 'gender test'. Several athletes in the Global South have been charged with high testosterone counts, the South African Olympic medallist Caster Semenya being the most prominent. Dutee was the first to successfully challenge this regulation and ask for the right to compete without undergoing a change in her hormones.

In 2015 she won her case at the Court of Arbitration for Sport (CAS) in Lausanne, Switzerland, the highest court in sport. This was a landmark verdict that underlined that the World Athletics rules for female athletes discriminated against women by setting a threshold for testosterone. Such a ceiling on natural testosterone does not exist for male athletes. Testosterone is popularly identified as the male hormone and oestrogen the female hormone, although human beings typically produce both. Men typically produce much more testosterone and women much more oestrogen. Testosterone is perceived as the hormone that powers strength and stamina. In other words, those with higher levels of testosterone are at an advantage in activities such as physical sport.

The question of testosterone cracks open the fundamental division in sport—the separation of men and women. Competitive sport is perhaps the last major domain where the strict differentiation of men and women is maintained to promote equality and fairness. In every other domain, including armed combat in defence forces, the opening up of previously male worlds to women is celebrated. But in sport, the separation of women and men is deemed necessary to maintain fairness in competition.

Like Santhi Soundarajan and Pinki Pramanik, Dutee's case takes us deep inside the question of what it means to be a woman in competitive sport. But unlike Santhi and Pinki, Dutee's experience gives us a precise, even if too precise, answer about womanhood and its measurement in competitive sport. Santhi and Pinki, on the other hand, widen our understanding of what womanhood includes without telling us what it means for competing in sport.

The CAS verdict, followed by Dutee's articulation of her gay identity, has made her among the most discussed personalities in

India. Although the two things are separate, the media's simplistic reporting on hyperandrogenism testing as a 'gender test' likely made the two appear related in public understanding—a young woman who had once failed a 'gender test' was now identifying as a lesbian. In fact, her gay identity may actually suggest to some that the hyperandrogenism result had got something right—Dutee Chand is not quite a woman. As I see it, it takes quite some conviction to own an identity so prone to be misunderstood.

Perhaps this is why the photographer Ashish Shah had been impressed when she stepped out of the closet. To be honest, even for those of us who think of ourselves as non-conservative, who would have thought that the first Indian sportsperson who self-identified as gay would be from a village in Odisha and not a big city, an athlete and not someone from cricket, badminton, tennis or one of the more high-profile sports? In the three hours that Shah shot with her, Dutee's confidence was evident. From her body language, Shah could see that she had become accustomed to facing the camera. His style is that of a therapist's—he likes to work at eliminating the distance between himself and his subject until he finds the moment of truth when appearances fall away. The face his subject has prepared to show to others slips away, leaving behind the face that shows itself when no one else is in the room. That is the moment of intimacy Shah's camera seeks.

With Dutee, he said, that moment never come.

The images of Dutee that Shah made are, without a doubt, striking. The magazine's brief was to capture her strength. And in the three images he published, she holds imperious, masculine poses of authority. Her defined muscles gleam. Her direct gaze exudes defiance. There is the stillness that confidence typically brings along with it.

What I find missing in these images of hers is that intimacy that Shah is a master at invoking. There is a guardedness about Dutee, although she is looking directly at us, the viewers. It is as if there is a layer of clingwrap that Shah was not able to peel away. This is a woman who had opened up about her private choices—her sexual preference—to the public in a society where the lives of women—and indeed anyone who does not identify as a man—are constantly examined and judged. This is a woman of magnificent courage.

Yet, what I see in Dutee's photos is circumspection. Something untouchable, unreachable, removed from us by an invisible layer. Striking as she is, Dutee's gaze does not invite you to see her. Instead, you realize she is watching you, and you look away.

Still, her image made the October 2019 cover (digital) of *Vogue*, a space this high priest of mainstream magazines exclusively reserves for the 1 per cent of Indian society—superstars of the Hindi-film industry, their children and occasionally the business elite. Only a couple of times in the twelve years of *Vogue* India's existence has the cover made room for one of the 99 per cent. Dutee is one of those exceptions.

※

When Dutee Chand burst on to prime-time news in July 2014 for being dropped from the Commonwealth Games contingent for hyperandrogenism, the media's reporting of the matter was unprofessional and prurient to begin with, resting on 'sources', lacking direct attribution and employing innuendo. It did, however, improve with time, largely thanks to the response of the Government of India, which took a different stance from the one it had taken for Santhi Soundarajan.

The previous month in June, Dutee had won two gold medals, for the 200-metre sprint and the 4x400-metre relay at the Asian

Junior Athletics Championships held in Taipei from 12 to 15 June 2014. At these championships, coaches from other countries had reportedly complained to the AFI chief M.L. Dogra about Dutee's 'stride and musculature', Dr Arun Kumar Mendiratta, chairman of the AFI's medical committee would submit to the CAS hearing in Lausanne in 2015.[6] Mendiratta would add that female athletes in India had also complained to Dogra about Dutee's masculine physique that very month. At the end of June 2014, Dogra communicated to Dr Mendiratta that Dutee and another female athlete were experiencing intense pain in their lower abdomen, and requested a medical check-up. Additionally, he asked Dr Mendiratta to conduct blood and urine tests as part of anti-doping checks.

On 30 June, the AFI sent the Sports Authority of India (SAI) a letter, it is reported on the CAS order, stating that there were 'definite doubts regarding the gender of an athlete, Dutee Chand'. But Dutee was not informed about this. The next she heard about her tests was on 13 July, when an official informed her that she had been dropped from the Indian team because her 'male hormone' levels were too high. On 15 July 2014, when she still hadn't received her medical reports herself, a story headlined 'Athletics Team for CWG Pruned Down to 32, Dutee Chand Dropped' appeared in *The Times of India*. 'Dutee Chand has reportedly been under the scanner, with the Sports Authority of India having ordered a gender test on her. SAI Director General Jiji Thomson confirmed that a woman athlete underwent a gender test in Bangalore but refused to name her,' the story reported.[7] Over the next week, several newspapers and television channels carried a version of the story with the same prurient and inaccurate phrasing: Dutee had failed the 'gender test'.

The Times of India published the story on Dutee without checking with her or asking for her version of events—essential procedure in journalism. Consequently, the report had the effect of making Dutee's medical test results public. In India, there is no specific law yet to safeguard the confidentiality of medical information, although the government is said to be working on such protection in the proposed Digital Information Security in Healthcare Act.[8] But evidence-based medical practitioners and hospitals often indicate that patient records are confidential information.

Moreover, the term 'gender test' is incorrect and harmful, as I have written in Chapter 5. To write that Dutee had failed a gender test implied that she had failed to fulfil the social identity of a woman, a psychologically and socially damaging suggestion. What Dutee had failed was a test of hyperandrogenism—her test results showed high levels of testosterone in her body, outside the limits specified for women by World Athletics. Think of how common a thyroid imbalance is. Testosterone, like thyroid, is a hormone. Her body produced a high level of a hormone.

Presumably, the media took their cue from the AFI, whose letter to SAI used the words 'definite doubts regarding the gender of an athlete, Dutee Chand'. The AFI is the official body for athletics in India and was acquainted with the terminology of hormone testing. Moreover, *The Times of India* and the media as a whole are in the professional business of communication. It is unprofessional to use words so carelessly. Besides, both the AFI and the media were familiar with the cases of Santhi Soundarajan and Caster Semenya. They were well aware of the scandal and damage that the language of gender testing causes. But in fact the media gains substantive readership/viewership from the prurient interest that this language gives rise to.

There was, in fact, an admission of sorts that there was a mistake. On 16 July 2014, to contain the damage done, SAI issued a clarification and *The Times of India* carried an 'updated' online report with quotes from the SAI statement: 'IOC [International Olympic Committee] and the IAAF have banned gender-verification tests.

We are therefore simply trying to find out if the athlete has excess androgen in her body.'[9]

On the other side of the world, in Stanford, California, the medical anthropologist Dr Katrina Karkazis woke up on 17 July to an inbox full of news stories about Dutee's disqualification. She was in the midst of researching her book *Testosterone: An Unauthorized Biography*, and had set up a news alert for the term 'hyperandrogenism policies'. She was interested in studying how these policies had been shaped since Caster Semenya's case in 2009.

Karkazis e-mailed the Indian researcher Dr Payoshni Mitra in India, who had been in contact with her. Mitra had been studying intersexuality since 2010 as part of her academic research and advocacy work. In 2012, she was the prime mover in securing Pinki Pramanik justice from the court, articulating the human rights violations by the police and state administration, mobilizing support for Pinki and organizing a powerful defence team for her led by the influential Supreme Court lawyer Anand Grover. Indeed, through her work on this case, Mitra showed that it was possible to shape a compelling narrative of rights and protocol for women athletes questioned on the parameters of biological sex. She had also made a documentary on Pinki with the queer rights collective Sappho and consulted with the Government of India in an official capacity to create a standard operative procedure (SOP) for testing female athletes for hyperandrogenism.

Karkazis and Mitra are like minds. Both view testing for hyperandrogenism as an ethical, social and human rights issue, rather than simply as a matter of science and sport. Perhaps unsurprisingly, none of Mitra's recommendations had been accepted in the final document of the SOP. Over a series of e-mails, the two researchers discussed whether it made sense to lobby the Government of India to challenge the decision to suspend Dutee from competition, like the South African government had challenged Semenya's disqualification. What were the legal options available? Would the science on testosterone get due weightage in a court of law? Encouraged by Karkazis's interest, Mitra approached the sports authorities with a proposal. Like Caster Semenya, Dutee Chand was from an impoverished rural family. South Africa had protected their athlete. Would India?

There was nothing to suggest it, but this time, everything would go right. The government agreed to go to court to challenge the rules of hyperandrogenism. This meant going to the CAS. More interestingly, it meant going up against part of the Indian sports administration itself—the AFI, which is a member of the World Athletics. In fact it was the AFI that had conducted the tests on Dutee to check for hyperandrogenism without informing her what they were doing.

This is how it stacked up. On one side stood Dutee Chand, the appellant. On the opposite side stood the AFI, named first respondent, and World Athletics, named second respondent. The costs of Dutee's case were borne by the Government of India. Dutee travelled to Lausanne with Mitra for the hearing held over three days, from 23 to 26 March 2015, at the CAS. Eight persons, including Dutee herself, testified in her support. Dutee spoke with the help of an interpreter, who translated her words to English, the language of the case proceedings. World Athletics and the AFI lined up ten persons. Their witnesses included, interestingly, the former Spanish athlete Maria José Martinez-Patino, who was barred from competition in 1985 for testing male in a chromosome test and then thrown out of the Spanish team in 1986. Martinez-Patino suffered from a medical condition called androgen insensitivity, which made her body insensitive to the testosterone it produced. She would find this out on her own expense and initiative after her disqualification.

In 1988, World Athletics (then IAAF) permitted her to compete again, taking note of her medical condition. In this case, however, she argued in favour of hyperandrogenism testing.

World Athletics's definition of hyperandrogenism is that it is a condition where a female athlete tests in excess of 10 nanomoles of testosterone per litre of blood. The 'normal' female range is 0.3–2.4 nmol/l, and the male range is 9.2–31.8 nmol/l with minor variations.[10] But hyperandrogenism is solely a female condition. There is no upper limit defined for testosterone levels in men, and hence men cannot be deemed hyperandrogenic. Naturally, the levels found by such tests on athletes are confidential. All we know is that Dutee's results had showed hyperandrogenism by the World Athletics definition. Dutee put forth three arguments. First, the definition that a female athlete with a natural testosterone level above 10 nanomole per litre is hyperandrogenic is discriminatory, her lawyers argued, because male athletes have no ceiling or maximum level defined for endogenous testosterone. Second, why is the naturally produced level of testosterone considered an unfair advantage but not the height of an exceptionally tall athlete, or the prosperity and superior facilities that an athlete from a wealthy country trains in vis-a-vis an athlete from the Global South? Why are those not disqualifiers? Third, high levels of testosterone are not sufficient for winning performances; her side argued that scientific evidence does not back the importance World Athletics has attached to testosterone.

World Athletics (and the AFI) failed to answer why male athletes do not have a ceiling cut-off for testosterone. Consequently, the CAS panel agreed with Dutee that the hyperandrogenism category for women was discriminatory.

The central argument, which takes up much of the 161-page ruling, however, concerns the science that looks at testosterone. Do we have the evidence to say that testosterone alone powers champion performances? Elite sport requires supreme strength, remarkable stamina, extraordinary physique and astonishing levels of training, not to speak of mental strength. Is a naturally high level of testosterone a bigger factor than a tall athlete's large stride in her sprint or the cutting-edge training facilities of a wealthy country? Can the strength and stamina that track and field sports require be zeroed down to just this one hormone? If we are singling out testosterone in a competition of extraordinariness, do we know how extraordinary it is in numerical terms?

To a certain extent, we do. The CAS panel agreed with World Athletics that naturally occurring testosterone was a significant factor in athletic performance because higher levels of testosterone in men led to higher lean body mass (LBM). High LBM is crucial for excellence in athletic performance and explains the substantive difference in athletic performance between elite male and female athletes. This difference is in the order of 10–12 per cent, meaning that male elite performance in an event is 10–12 per cent better than female elite performance. It is on the basis of this marked difference in athletic performance that men and women compete in two separate categories in sport.

The hyperandrogenism regulations are clear and strict. A woman testing as hyperandrogenic cannot compete in the female category unless she undergoes hormone treatment or surgery to reduce the level of natural testosterone produced by her body. Otherwise, she can only compete in the male category.

But the evidence for hyperandrogenic athletes—women with testosterone levels touching the male range—does not demonstrate that their performance, too, might be elevated by 10–12 per cent like that of elite males. If the equation on the basis of which the regulations are framed is that naturally high testosterone + elite female athlete = remarkable outcomes that rival elite male performance, then the CAS panel found evidence for only a part of this equation. Not the whole of it. There was evidence that a small percentage of elite female athletes who performed superbly possessed naturally high testosterone levels. (It is also worth noting that we do not know what percentage of women in the general population are hyperandrogenic, since only the subset of athletes are tested for testosterone.)

But how superbly did the hyperandrogenic athletes perform? Did they rival elite male performance? Were their performances 10–12 per cent better than other women, thus necessitating their disqualification from the female category? This quantification of exactly how well they performed was missing from the scientific evidence presented to the CAS panel over the three days of the hearing, and the written submissions made beforehand. Without this precise knowledge, was it fair to bar such female athletes from competing with women? If naturally higher levels of testosterone are found to elevate hyperandrogenic athletes' performance by, say, 1–3 per cent, is that then enough to merit disqualification from the female category?

Moreover, is testosterone the only biological attribute that is sought to be controlled in this manner? A taller athlete, for instance, is not asked to reduce her height by surgery. In basketball, large hands are known to be an advantage. But there is no rule requiring players to undergo hand surgery above a certain threshold of size.

The CAS ruled that, without this evidence, the disqualification of Dutee Chand appeared to be based on speculation. Dutee was free to compete without any hormone therapy or surgery. The panel provided a window of two years to World Athletics to provide the evidence to substantiate the hyperandrogenic regulations.[11]

The 161-page verdict arrived via e-mail at the close of July 2015, four months after Dutee had travelled to Lausanne to appear before the CAS in March. She had made history. She was the second athlete after Caster Semenya to push back against the biggest international athletic federation's rules and win the right to run unaltered by surgery or hormone therapy. She was, in fact, the first athlete to take the most powerful organization in athletics to court and win. For the first time in many decades, female athletes faced no testing specific to women for the 2016 Rio Olympics.

In the newspapers, the momentousness of her win felt muted. If this had transpired in India, perhaps, with costumed judges delivering a verdict with all the ceremony of India's colonial-style courts, the significance of the moment might have registered more effectively. Instead, 'CAS Clears Dutee' was the lead story on the second page of the sports section of *The Times of India* on 28 July 2015. For the moment of history that it unambiguously was, it was not splashed across the front page of a leading newspaper or broadcast on prime-time TV.

Sportspersons thrill in physicality. They dream of the records they will set to the roar of their heart and racing breath. They feel the pleasure of pushing their bodies to defy gravity and other natural forces. Dutee had likely not dreamt of making history in a 161-page legal document. But the verdict left a very physical impact on her. In 2014, when she was disqualified for hyperandrogenism, she was averaging a time of 11.8 seconds in the 100-metre sprint. In 2015, six weeks after her win, she broke an Indian national record with a timing of 11.68 seconds in the 100 metres. And in June 2016, barely two weeks before the Rio Olympics, she qualified for the Olympics with a timing of 11.24 seconds in Almaty, Kazakhstan. In nine months, she had shaved off nearly half a second, 0.44 second, to be precise, in her timing. It was as if she had let go of a weight that was holding her down.

Dutee's village, Chaka Gopalpur, is 90 kilometres from Bhubaneswar, the capital of Odisha, long considered to be one of India's poorer states, pockets of which have been persistently stalked by hunger.[12] Malnutrition was rumoured to run so deep in the districts of Kalahandi-Bolangir-Koraput there that residents would sometimes die because they had a diet of mango kernels, wild roots and mushrooms. This is not that old outsider's error of mistaking a local staple for a food foraged in desperation. Recipes with mango kernels may well be eaten by choice. But when you read reports of children being fed mango kernels when they are sick with measles in 1987,[13] and people dying after eating mango kernels in 2009[14] and 2018,[15] it is an indication of food scarcity. In each one of these reports, the government version denies the possibility of starvation in these deaths. Over the past ten years, there have also been sporadic reports of an encouraging increase in rice production in the area alongside the stories of deaths by eating mango kernels.[16]

Chaka Gopalpur lies on the route of National Highway 16, which connects the coastal states on the east of India, from Bengal to Tamil Nadu. In a car, it takes about two hours to reach the village from the well-behaved, quiet, neatly organized capital city. There is in Bhubaneswar a distinctly sarkari aesthetic—the look and feel of a city designed by unsmiling officials of the Central government in Delhi, people who sit in chairs with towels at their backs and never open their e-mails themselves. There are square blocks of apartments with clear lettering, and roads with broad, people-free footpaths that meet at radials like in Lutyens' Delhi. There are few food hawkers, but they have patrons who look eminently respectable, who stay nicely on the footpaths without spilling on to the roads, like they do in Kolkata, Mumbai or Chennai. It is a city of cars, like Delhi. Here, too, the broad roads are not easy to cross quickly on foot; the footpaths are high and require healthy, pain-free knees, and a certain intrepidity to be comfortable about the visible lack of people in the city.

What I noticed most in my week in Bhubaneshwar was that there were very few women visible on the streets—women walking or waiting by themselves for public transport to take them someplace. The women I saw were invariably accompanied by men, stepping in and out of shops, or cars, or the many majestic temples that dotted the landscape. Perhaps this was on account of Covid. Indeed, schools and universities were still shut when I visited at the close of 2020 and many offices operated with reduced staff. I saw a handful of working-class women—women who likely served as domestic workers or performed manual labour at construction sites. But other kinds of women—office-goers, vendors, retail workers or even college-going women or teenagers—were not visible. In my week and a half there, I saw only one bunch of women on foot, dressed in jeans and sneakers and backpacks, who looked like they knew their way across the city. They emerged from the massive multisport Kalinga Stadium complex in the city. They were sportswomen, likely stepping out after their morning round of training, relaxed but also purposeful, confident and energetic. Young women of the sort you'd see everywhere in Mumbai, Kolkata, Chennai and Bengaluru. But here, they were a striking presence.

The drive to Chaka Gopalpur from Bhubaneswar is almost entirely along the creamy smooth national highway, magically pothole-free. National highway work is undertaken by the relatively wealthy Union government, and perhaps this explains why these are different from the cratered non-national roads of India. There are large hoardings on either side of the highway featuring Naveen Patnaik, the chief minister of Odisha who is in his fifth five-year term. The state has benefited substantively from Delhi's largesse during his reign. Odisha, rich in natural resources, was for long sucked dry by a postcolonial Central government hungry for minerals and heavy infrastructure development. The state and its people remained impoverished. But Patnaik, son of career politician Biju Patnaik, after whom Bhubaneswar's airport is named, proved to be adept at securing resources from the Union government in exchange for a non-confrontational attitude on critical, contentious issues, particularly those that are put to the vote in Parliament. Under him, the state has visibly grown more prosperous in its urban parts, with air-conditioned offices, stores, cafés and restaurants, neat blocks of flats or gated complexes, and the road and highway network.

The Odisha section of this national highway was completed by 2003, when Dutee Chand was eight years old. Her village, which lies barely a mile off the highway, must have gained from the proximity to the big city that this enabled. She is a child of the visible development that the new millennium brought. Before the highway was ready, the trip to Bhubaneswar would have been far longer and more cumbersome. But when she began training as an athlete on a state government scheme, she could take one of the many buses that plied between Chaka Gopalpur and Bhubaneswar, a journey of approximately three hours.

When you take a right turn off the highway, a paved but pockmarked road goes right up to the Chand home. Every person we stopped to ask for directions, from the nearby town of Jajpur onwards, knew the way. The closer we got to Dutee's home, however, the more impassive the faces grew and the more awkward I felt about my grin and thank you. Even the children looked unimpressed, their gazes pitying at my wave. They had probably seen this too many times by now: an urban journalist or researcher arriving in a car with questions about the star of their village.

When I visited, only two homes in Chaka Gopalpur were cement-and-concrete structures. One was Dutee's two-storey family home and the other, directly opposite to hers, was her paternal uncle's home. The rest were what we call kachcha houses—single-storey structures built with bricks, mud, straw and readily available natural material, unfortified by factory-made material such as cement and mortar. Beyond the rows of homes, a large body of water glinted in the November sun. This was the Brahmani river, which flooded the village at least twice a year. It was on the banks of this river that Dutee ran for many years, at first trailing her sister Saraswati, who practised here.

I met Saraswati, the eldest of the seven Chand siblings, who was fifteen when Dutee was born in 1996. The likeness with Dutee is startling—she, too, is diminutive, lean, with raven-black hair pulled back from her face in a tight ponytail. Dutee was twenty-four at the time and Saraswati touching forty, but you wouldn't be able to tell this from looking at them. They had the same slight, taut physique. Saraswati spoke to me in too-fast Hindi, words crashing into one another and some crumbling with the impact.

Neither of us is a natural Hindi speaker, but her impatient accident-prone Hindi is better than mine, which is Bengali in disguise. But it turned out to be useful—my Bengali-strewn Hindi had the effect of loosening up Saraswati. It warmed her confidence, and I noticed the corners of her mouth folding into a slight smile. We sat in a small drawing room, where every showcase, shelf, corner and free surface was adorned with trophies and medals won by Saraswati and Dutee. The latter had moved out of this home, taking her major prizes with her, so these were Dutee's minor triumphs.

In the entrance way outside, their mother Akhuji sat weaving a gamchha-style handkerchief on the loom. The Chands are weavers by caste. The village of Chaka Gopalpur is a settlement of weavers.

Within the village sits an outlet of a tussar and silk textile house registered under the government. Villagers, including Dutee's parents Akhuji and Chakradhar, sell their work here. A handkerchief fetches Rs 10, a gamchha (traditional towel) Rs 50 and a sari Rs 500. It takes approximately one day to make ten kerchiefs, half a day to weave a gamchha and five days to make a sari. Going by this, the earning for eight to nine hours of work a day is approximately Rs 100. When both senior Chands work, the earnings of a good day can touch Rs 200–250. In a month, where they work all thirty days without a break, they stand to earn a maximum of Rs 7,500 by the current rate of payment. Now there is also Saraswati's police officer's salary.

But until Saraswati got a job with the Odisha Police in 2004, a household of seven children and two adults survived on Akhuji and Chakradhar's weaving income alone, which rarely crossed Rs 3,000 a month at the time. On good days, they ate rice and potatoes, most often rice and salt. The first time the family purchased eggs was when Saraswati bought them with her first salary at the age of twenty-three, along with a pair of canvas shoes for Dutee. As a constable, she earned Rs 7,000 a month and sent Rs 5,000 home to her mother, with instructions to feed eggs to her siblings every day.

In 2003 Saraswati had won medals at a district sports meet in Jabalpur, running barefoot, and secured a spot in a state government sports-hostel scheme. She was a 400-metre sprinter and relay athlete, who represented India in second-rung international events such as the World Police Games. She came to sports late, only at the age of nineteen, when she was in college, the time by which competitive athletes start to peak. That year, she had taken part in a district sports meet in Jajpur and placed in a couple of events. The physical training instructor of her college, Ranjan Sautar, was present in the audience and told Saraswati to keep practising. The college didn't have the facilities—in fact, Saraswati did not even know her college had a

PT instructor—but the government had a sports quota for jobs, Sautar told her, and she could try for it.

The most minimal sport in terms of equipment and rules, without even the need for a team, is running. So Saraswati began jogging, then running, on the sand banks of the Brahmani river. Dutee was four years old then, and there was an even younger sibling who was a toddler. Saraswati took Dutee and the toddler to the river because she felt odd running by herself. How strange, neighbours would say—people played football, cricket, why would anybody run by herself? Taking her siblings along gave her a licence of sorts—she was on an outing with the kids. Dutee would sit with the toddler while she ran.

'After some time, Dutee also started running behind me,' Saraswati said. 'I encouraged it. I told her she would get a good government job if she did well in sports. She was really good. I could see that, so I pushed her. At that time, she ran barefoot. I also ran barefoot. But I told my parents to organize vegetables for her so she could get some nutrition. My mother would ask the neighbours for vegetables. Sometimes, Dutee and the younger siblings would go to the highway to pick up vegetables that fell out of trucks and tempos. Some days the vendors on the highway mandi would give them a couple of tomatoes and carrots that had spoilt a bit.'

In 2008, when Dutee was twelve, she was selected for a sports-hostel scheme run by the state government of Odisha, thanks to her own talent and Saraswati's keen ear for opportunities. Saraswati herself was peaking as a runner then. By 2010 Saraswati had made her way into the national camps meant for elite athletes representing India in international competitions. In the Indian framework, the national camps allow access to the best training, facilities and nutrition possible in the country. In 2012, the senior women's coach, Nagapuri Ramesh, saw Dutee perform at a junior meet and asked Saraswati about her. Saraswati, who trained under Ramesh too, thought this was her chance to set things up for her sister. She called Dutee to the Netaji Subhas National Institute of Sports in Patiala, India's oldest sports institute, where a national camp was under way, and organized a paying-guest room for Dutee outside the campus. For meals, she would save some food from her own meals at the camp to give her younger sibling.

Her bet paid off. By 2013, at the age of seventeen, Dutee made it to the national camp herself with a breakout year, becoming the national champion in the 100- and 200-metre sprints. She also picked up a bronze in the 200 metres at the Asian Athletic Championships.

That same year, Saraswati developed a calf injury, which didn't heal in time for the athletics season in India, beginning January and continuing through the summer. In fact, it didn't heal for a long time and Saraswati returned to her family in Chaka Gopalpur. She was thirty-two years old then and sensed that this might be the end of her national time in athletics. Yet she found she wasn't as depressed as she thought she would be. Her career had begun late, but Saraswati knew how providential even this brief period was. She was not a sportsperson until college, yet something had clicked into place for that conversation with the PT teacher, which had set her on this path.

'I had started late, but Dutee was doing so well. I thought this was how it was meant to be—I was the start and she would be the real athlete. There was some sadness, I suppose, but it wasn't so much.'

In 2014, when the news of Dutee's hyperandrogenism broke, Saraswati was overwhelmed with the support they received from neighbours. It took her by surprise because she knew what had happened to Santhi Soundarajan, one of the finest middle-distance sprinters India had produced. When Saraswati was starting to participate in state competitions, Santhi was among India's brightest stars in athletics, a marquee presence at national meets and a multiple medal winner in Asian competitions. A young woman from an impoverished rural background, like almost all women in Indian athletics, Santhi was what many like Saraswati wished they could be. And then, when Saraswati was still at the threshold of breaking on to the national level, it all changed so suddenly for Santhi. There was news of Santhi's disqualification for failing a 'gender test'—that phrasing was ubiquitous in the media then.[17] The Asian Games medal was withdrawn, and the Indian government and athletics authorities abandoned Santhi like a defective toy.

Saraswati had watched from the fringes of Indian athletics how Santhi had been abandoned by the sports establishment, and seen her own feelings shift—from aspiring to be Santhi to gratitude that she wasn't Santhi. Perhaps this was why she was pleasantly surprised by the way her community rallied around the family, very much like how Santhi's neighbours had come to her support. They had seen Dutee from girlhood, neighbours told Saraswati. Some of them had fed her; she had played with their kids. They knew her better than the medical tests did, they told the Chands. Their support took a lot of Saraswati's anxiety away, although she wished Dutee had secured a government job.

Five years later, when Dutee came out of the closet, some members of the community were less sympathetic. Many of them knew Dutee had 'relations with a girl' and that was fine, but why did she have to tell the world? And Saraswati found herself agreeing with them.

'There are many things people accept if you do well for India, but it stops somewhere. This is where,' Saraswati said.

The world outside Chaka Gopalpur, however, reacted very differently to Dutee's statement. She was invited to television studios across India, including the quiz show *Kaun Banega Crorepati* hosted by Amitabh Bachchan. She secured major endorsement deals, including one with the global sportswear giant Puma. *Vogue* put her on its cover. In fact, she received much more attention with this one declaration than she had with her athletics triumphs. Naturally, her family found themselves unheeded. Sometime afterwards, Dutee stopped visiting home on her breaks from the national camps, preferring to stay in Bhubaneswar.

Saraswati, who had made Dutee's career her life, has tried to shift her focus to training other young athletes. She earned an athletics coaching diploma from the Sports Authority of India's Kolkata campus in 2018, thanks to an opportunity she received as part of her police job. Now a sub-inspector in the police, she is responsible for training sportspersons in the police for competitions. She has also secured permission to use the grounds at a local stadium near Chaka Gopalpur, where she holds daily morning and evening training sessions with a bunch of boys and girls from the villages nearby. I got the impression that she was looking to train the next big thing, perhaps to prove a point to Dutee.

The Kalpataru Das Stadium, named after a local MLA, surprised me. The approach was through narrow alleyways left potholed by groaning tempos carrying cement from a nearby factory. The stadium itself is the cement company's gesture towards community support. It is a ground with basic stands, a bust of Kalpataru Das and an imposing black grille gate. As I entered, I saw distant low hills rising in the backdrop of the ground. The grass was mown, and the ground levelled and looked after. As the afternoon gave way to an early winter evening's fading light, the beauty of the place grew on me.

A handful of young women and a couple of boys had turned up for Saraswati's practice session. Some other boys, unconnected to her, played cricket in the nets. The kids stared at me and quickly looked away when I looked. Saraswati's students were naturally awkward around me. They told me things that Saraswati had already said—

that they wanted to do well in sport, that they hoped it would fetch them a government job, that no one in their families had a good job yet. That they had read about Saraswati's training at their school/college noticeboards or heard from friends.

I know the general contours of this story. It is the general story of track and field athletics in India—impoverishment and the hope of respectable employment. But it was hard for me to draw out these children's private ambitions and hopes. Dusk arrived abruptly and mosquitoes arrived swiftly in battalions. My time was up, the mosquitoes informed me.

Later, when I looked at the photographs I had shot that evening—images of five girls and two boys sprinting and resting under Saraswati's regimen—one image in particular made me return to it again and again. A girl is sprinting, and a tall boy is recording her run on his phone. But in that instant, when my camera captured them, he is looking over his phone at her as she blurs past him. In the gloaming, his face is lit slightly by the smartphone in his hand and I think I see in it a look that says what most spoken words are unable to express—that he is seeing her as something he hasn't thought of before. A person who has possibilities no different than those he has.

I have had to write about Dutee from a distance. I did not have a choice. When I called her to request time for a conversation, she said that her story had been documented in several interviews in the public domain. 'I have nothing to add. In fact, I feel bored of my own story now,' she said with a dry chuckle. 'But speak to my manager. We can have a small interview. I will not waste my time and you will not waste your time. Best for both.'

I was taken aback by her frankness. I was at a disadvantage, in any case—we spoke in Hindi, a language that both of us communicated in but neither of us was comfortable with. In this unfamiliar language, she sounded distant, although polite and professional.

I was disappointed, of course, but I could also see her rationale. Dutee is arguably the most interviewed Indian athlete, even more than P.T. Usha, perhaps. She is also an active athlete who spends up to six hours a day training. The time she has is limited, not only in her everyday life, but also as an athlete. In 2020, when I sought to interview her, she was twenty-four, the age at which track athletes peak. By thirty, typically, they are done. She probably had two more attempts at the Olympics left in her. Some continue running well into their thirties, like P.T. Usha, but usually in less prestigious competitions. Olympic aspirations are packed away; the circumference of the competition becomes smaller.

Instead, I watched her on her many television and video interviews. There is a documentary about her on the Olympics website, titled *Dutee*. There was her appearance on *Kaun Banega Crorepati*. There are about half a dozen longish interviews with Hindi- and English-language journalists. She speaks rapidly, her discomfort with Hindi evident, but she always appears confident. The story is consistent—of an impoverished childhood in a weavers' village, rescued by running; the shame of the androgyny scandal and the betrayal by the press that leaked her name; the unexpected support from researchers and her village and the subsequent coming around of the same press; the vindication from the court and how that changed everything. More than anything, the court verdict gave her the scientific evidence to show the world that she was not a fraud. Nor a freak because there were many others like her. And that changed the way she saw herself.

It was as if her entire life had been examined and granted a giant tick mark. The further we are from privilege and power, the less sure we are of ourselves. Dutee Chand, impoverished, rural,

female and then challenged about her biological sex, had likely felt
hollowed out to a shell. But the court's answer gave her a mineful
of confidence.

In all these interviews, I notice her gaze. Dutee makes direct eye
contact, and yet there is that thing I saw in Shah's portraits of her—
directness without intimacy. Confidence without ease. A wariness
that never leaves her. I watch her tell her story on several interviews,
yet I never get the sense of being part of a sharing. The only time I see
her shining with happiness is in the episode of *Kaun Banega Crorepati*,
but this is not an interview, after all. It is a meeting with Amitabh
Bachchan, and her thrill is palpable, her excitement infectious. It is
perhaps the only time I glimpse the person she may be.

Athletes are generally not articulate. They speak with their bodies.
I know this from the many conversations I have had with athletes in
the course of writing this book. When I asked them to explain what
they liked about running, they scoffed. What is there to like? You run
because you are good, because you want a job, because it is the one
path that will get you some money. They often found my questions
silly, because my upper-class privilege made me blind to many things.
And they were probably right, that it was a waste of their time.

She speaks a lot about herself. Watching her is like looking at
a building from outside its gates. You can see the form and the
facade, some detail, but not the inside, the minutiae. Off-camera,
she has a manager. This is the person whose number she gave me
to fix an appointment. He offered me the option of a single thirty–
forty-minute interview, saying long interviews were not possible on
account of Dutee's intensive training schedule for the 2021 Tokyo
Olympics. It was far from the time I had hoped for, but I agreed.
But he rarely picked up my calls at the times he had appointed.
Naturally, my conversations with him were strained. Eventually,

I secured a twenty-minute interview with her through Puma, the brand that had signed her on as ambassador.

I searched for the manager on social media and found that he was a large, muscular man in the shape of the American cartoon character Popeye—enormous chest, bonsai legs. His profiles were filled with images of Dutee and him working out in gym-like settings. Next to the diminutive Dutee, he looked like a small vehicle. I imagined him swelling over her like an umbrella. What was Dutee afraid of that she needed a bodyguard who looked like he could swat people away like flies?

In the weeks and months I tried to contact Dutee and failed, a traumatic assault was playing on loop on the news. A thirty-four-year-old Bollywood star, Sushant Singh Rajput, had died by suicide in Mumbai on 14 June 2020. The news coverage departed rather soon from coverage of mental health and suicide in India—a country that has among the highest suicide rates in the world—to alight on Rajput's girlfriend Rhea Chakraborty.

Chakraborty, then twenty-eight years old, works as a model and actress in the Hindi film industry. She has acted, albeit in the smaller productions, of one of India's most prestigious production companies, Yash Raj Films. She was not married to Rajput, but acknowledged herself as his girlfriend in a tweet a little more than a month after his death, on 16 July.[18]

She was known to be living in with Rajput, and news reports noted this fact copiously, in the tone of prurient relatives. Although live-in relationships feature often in Bollywood films, and the widespread internet access of Modi's Digital India project streams contemporary Western society into millions of smartphones, such relationships are a tiny urban phenomenon in India. India is still a conservative society, clearly uncomfortable with a sexually active woman who was not married.

The commentary on Chakraborty gathered momentum after she identified her status in the relationship with Rajput in the tweet. Within days, on 25 July, Rajput's father had lodged an FIR with the police in Patna, naming Chakraborty culpable for the death of his son and for siphoning off money from his accounts.[19] With this, the mainstream media's thrill at a sordid family scandal reached a sickening crescendo, with a handful of honourable exceptions. On 30 July 2020, journalist Aman Sharma tweeted an image from a segment on the Hindi TV news channel Aaj Tak, headlined 'Sushant par Rhea kaa kaala jaadu [Rhea's black magic on Sushant]'.[20] The accompanying visual showed the young Chakraborty, long tresses left open, her hands framing an orb with Rajput's face inside. It is a cleverly morphed image, combining real photographs of Chakraborty and Rajput, and to uninformed viewers those photos may indeed have carried the impression of being real. On 28 August 2020, the day after Chakraborty appeared in an almost-hour-long interview on the English-language news channel NDTV,[21] the writer and social commentator Shobhaa De wrote a column drenched in scorn, 'For nearly two hours on a humid Thursday night, a 28-year-old woman nobody had really heard of till her 34-year-old high-profile boyfriend died, made minced meat of seasoned star anchors. At the end of the tepid grilling, it was the anchors who looked like they needed whichever drops Rhea was allegedly adding to Sushant Singh Rajput's tea to keep him calm.'[22]

Through August 2020, when India registered the highest number of Covid cases in the world, the Indian mainstream news media's prime-time focus was Rhea Chakraborty. She was described as a woman who had performed black magic on Rajput, given him drugs and diverted funds from his bank accounts—for which no evidence was found by the Enforcement Directorate. On 6 September 2020, a Sunday, *The Indian Express* published an extraordinary photograph on their front page: rows and rows of cameras arranged like a battalion of guns around the slight figure of Rhea Chakraborty, who appeared to be shrinking from their glare. It captured the frenzy of the weeks in July and August, and the metastasis of voyeurism and savage misogyny through the technology of the media.

On 8 September, Chakraborty was arrested by the Narcotics Control Bureau on amorphous charges. She was arrested, rather, on the suspicion of procuring 43 grams of marijuana for her late boyfriend. Not a single news report in September could spell out the specific drug charge Chakrabarty was booked under. It was only in March 2021, seven months after her arrest, that the Narcotics Control Bureau filed a charge sheet naming Chakraborty for being part of a 'drug syndicate' along with thirty-two others named.[23]

The media lost interest in Chakraborty a couple of days after she was sent to jail, when the courts kept denying her bail and it appeared that she had been safely put away behind bars. On 3 October, the country's premier medical institute, the All India Institute of Medical Sciences (AIIMS), tasked with the post-mortem investigation of Rajput's death by the Central Bureau of Investigation, ruled out 'foul play' in Rajput's death. But this did not seem to matter to much of the television media. When she got bail on 7 October, the story was a small news clip in the media, almost unnoticeable. Chakraborty had been put behind bars—their job was done. The focus had changed.

During these weeks of ceaseless prurience on the media, a young woman named Panchali Ray wrote about her own experience of being hunted by the media two decades earlier. She was then a student who had completed a brief but successful stint at modelling, lived with a single mother and enjoyed an occasional smoke. 'City-based local newspapers (no, tabloids) screamed headlines about us (my mother and I) being suspects, which soon turned into a free-for-all accusation of us being "prostitutes" and running "sex rackets",' she wrote. 'The fact that I was once a model supposedly gave weight to all these accusations. My pictures, pulled out from my modelling days, were printed on front pages ...'[24]

She added, 'I spent my 20s and a large part of my 30s battling depression, guilt, shame and low self-worth, stemming from a sense of violation that nothing could get rid of, but I also worked with a trade union of agricultural workers in rural Bengal and was active in people's movements against land acquisition as well as the women's movement. Though I must admit, I slipped away every time the media showed up.'

In 2014 it was Dutee who was the hunted. It was the media that leaked the results of Dutee's 'gender test' in 2014 and all but named her. By the rules of World Athletics, the results of testosterone testing must remain confidential. The news that an 'athlete' had failed the 'gender test' appeared before Dutee received her test results on paper, and several weeks before the Sports Authority of India communicated this to her in person. 'No one bothered to call me before publishing this. No one informed me. I learnt I had failed the test in the news, publicly,' she said, in the brief phone interview I had with her. 'I have to be very careful with the media. I have learnt that now.'

The South African Olympic silver medallist Caster Semenya's test was leaked in the media after she won gold in the 800-metre event at the World Championships in Berlin in 2009, and published before she was informed she had 'failed'. Santhi Soundarajan, the first athlete to be tested after compulsory 'sex tests' were stopped, learnt she had failed her test in 2006 on television news before anyone told her what she had been tested for. Martinez-Patino, the first athlete to challenge testing for 'gender' after her karyotyping result said she was male, found her story published in the press when she resisted her team's order to quit sport.

The technologies of mass media are relatively new, beginning with the devising of the moveable type printing press by Gutenberg in the fifteenth century. But the public hunting of women is neither new nor confined to the subcontinent. The term 'witch hunt' originates from the historical practice of burning women alive, branded as witches, from the fourteenth to the seventeenth centuries across Europe. In certain German cities, there were two women burnt every day, 'leaving alone Sundays', as Barbara Ehrenreich and Deirdre English write in their influential essay, 'Witches, Midwives, and Nurses'. 'Witch hunt', 'burnt at the stake'—these are not metaphors, but refer to actual events that took place repeatedly over centuries.

There was no mass media at the time as we know it. The size of 'public opinion', too, the philosopher Jurgen Habermas has written, was far smaller than what it has grown to be with the technologies of modernity. The witch burnings were authorized by the church and the state, but their decisions coalesced from the public opinion of that time—the opinions of men in inns and taverns and guilds and the marketplace.

There were three reasons that certain women attracted the anger of this 'public', Ehrenreich and English write. First, these women were influential in the community because they were successful healers. Second, the healers were organized as groups of women and met regularly, signifying their collective power. Third, and arguably the most misogynist and unsettling, was their sexuality—the witches were women. That these healers helped women with abortion or contraception was further cause for sexual anxiety.

'In the eyes of the Church, all the witch's power was ultimately derived from her sexuality,' write Ehrenreich and English.

'Her career began with sexual intercourse with the devil. Each witch was confirmed at a general meeting (the witches' Sabbath) at which the devil presided, often in the form of a goat, and had intercourse with the neophytes. In return for her powers, the witch promised to serve him faithfully ... As the [text by] Malleus [Maleficarum] makes clear, the devil almost always acts through the female, just as he did in Eden: *"All witchcraft comes from carnal lust, which in women is insatiable ... Wherefore for the sake of fulfilling their lusts they consort with devils ... it is sufficiently clear that it is no matter for wonder that there are more women than men found infected with the heresy of witchcraft .... And blessed be the Highest Who has so far preserved the male sex from so great a crime ..."*'

The womb itself was seen as a powerful, phantasmal thing. The sexuality and sexual functions and activities of women induced fear and loathing. Has modern Western science been able to dissolve this ball of dread and disgust in the public imagination? Or does it remain lodged deep in us somewhere? Has the omnipresence of contemporary technology actually magnified this unease by broadcasting the prurient gaze on women into millions of personal devices? A giant mutant camera eye surveilling women ceaselessly.

There is also the episode from the Ramayana where Sita is desired by the powerful king Ravan of Lanka, setting off a battle between her husband Ram, the exiled prince of Ayodhya, and Ravan. Lanka was set on fire in the course of the bid to rescue Sita. But on Ram and Sita's return to Ayodhya, Ram overheard 'public opinion' in the bazar that a woman captured by another man was sexually impure. And so he put his wife through a trial by fire.

Think about it. The Ramayana is an epic with outsize influence on life in South and Southeast Asia. The witch burnings in Europe are a historical reality, many centuries and a continent apart. Yet how similar they are. The lives of sexually active adult women have long been the subject of surveillance, anxiety, scandal and horrific violence.

Imagine, then, how it plays out with Dutee Chand, and Caster Semenya, and Santhi Soundarajan and Pinki Pramanik—women whose sexual anatomies do not fit into the comfortable binary of male and female. Women whose anatomies are dissected in public. An image arises in my mind—a figure being taken out of a van and a thousand people gathered to watch, some of them standing on top of walls and cars. It could be the scene of a beloved star's public reception, except that no one is clapping or smiling. 'There was silence,' Pinki Pramanik had told me. 'I have never seen so many people in so much silence. I felt like my body, my everything, was ripped out, and there was nothing left.'

I look at the photographs of Dutee Chand again, the ones taken by Shah for *Vogue*. The ones that pop up first on my computer when I search for her. In the absence of access to her, I have often searched for her on the net and looked at these. Chin down, gaze direct, hands in her pockets as if she is sizing you up. Her eyes look straight at you, but it is not an invitation to look back. You can see so far, but no further. There is a lock, a gate, a shield.

'There was something in her that just didn't give,' Shah had said. And I think I can understand why.

Speakers at the Court of Arbitration in Sport Hearing

For Dutee:

Prof. Richard Holt

Dr Sari van Anders

Katrina Karkazise

Payoshni Mitra

Natasha Singh

Dutee Chand

Paul Melia

Madeline Pape

For Athletics Federation of India (first respondent) and World Athletics (second respondent):

Prof. Martin Ritzen

Prof. Angelica Linden Hirschberg

Dr Stephane Bermon

Prof. Arne Ljungqvist

Prof. Thomas Murray

Maria Jose Martinez-Patino

Joanna Harper

Paula Radcliff MBE

Nick Davies

Dr Arun Kumar Mendiratta

8

LALITA BABAR: THE WOMAN WHO TOOK THE LONG ROAD

Lalita Babar. Photo © Getty Images

THE SIGNS WERE auspicious. On the morning of 13 August 2016, he temperature touched 49 degrees Celsius at the Olympic e in Rio de Janeiro, Brazil. It was the kind of weather that Lalita had grown up in, in her rain-starved village in Maharashtra. illed off a terrific performance in the second heat of the chase event, remaining in third place for the most part of en-lap race before slipping to fourth position in the closing its. She was adjudged the 'fastest loser' of the race.

lio, there were three heats for the women's 3,000-metre hase event. The top three in each heat automatically made it ial. The remaining six positions went to the two best losers in t, those who placed fourth and fifth in other words, making a fteen. At 9 minutes 19.76 seconds, Lalita had placed fourth ond heat, and ranked as the best loser in it. Her timing was n Hyvin Kiyeng, who placed first in the third heat. Overall, he seventh-fastest of the fifteen women who qualified for In addition, she had bettered the Indian national record 7 seconds.

al of the women's steeplechase was on 15 August. Lalita was dian woman in thirty-two years to qualify for the final of a ield event at the Olympics. Who could miss the climactic of a possible Olympic medal on Independence Day for a rved of sports achievements? And there was the uncanny . Usha's performance at Los Angeles in 1984. Usha had ough to first place in her heat, but missed a trick at the e to end fourth in the final. Here, Lalita had been overtaken from a well-maintained third place to finish fourth. that she would reverse the order of things in the final?

219

It looked doable. The coach of the Indian women's middle- and long-distance team, Nikolai Snesarev, asked her to aim for a time of 9 minutes 10 seconds, 9.76 seconds or almost ten seconds faster than her performance in the heat. When Lalita had slipped back to fourth, she had ample breath left. As a long-distance runner, she was still learning how to time the flat-out acceleration to the finishing line. Now Snesarev had given her a new target time. The high summer in Rio was a plus, a close relative of the burn of the bone-dry summers in her village in Satara, legendary for its droughts. She was used to this kind of weather.

But there was one thing—the orb of pain in her right thigh, above the knee. That day in her heat, as she had reared up to clear the fourth hurdle in the second lap, Lalita had slammed her right knee into the obstruction, grazing skin, the blood in her capillaries contusing into a large bruise just above the knee. Though the impact snapped her rhythm for a moment, and in the water jump that came next she landed almost on all fours as a shockwave of pain flamed out from the site of the injury, she recovered in a blink and finished a superb heat. But the real damage from such injuries typically manifests only hours afterwards. She spent the forty-odd hours between her heat and the final ice-packing the bruise and sealing off news of her injury from the press. Snesarev and his wife had taken turns to hold the ice pack, mainly to sit with her as she kept her leg up and stayed put in one place.

Would the pain flare up when she ran again? Could she ice it out of her leg? Was she making too much of it?

As soon as she got off the mark on 15 August, she felt the pain radiate out from the knot, as if someone had turned on a switch. Could she complete the 3,000 metres like this? Would her knee be able to take the impact of landing after she had jumped across a hurdle? When she lifted off the ground for the first hurdle, the pain ceased for that half a moment, until it burst aflame and ricocheted up through her torso as she landed. But she landed her left foot after her right, pulled into a stride and found that she was still standing. She would survive the hurdles, she realized, but what about the water pit? It was 12 feet long and 0.7 metre at its deepest, the ground sloping downwards like in a swimming pool. It was the hardest part of the event—the most attention-grabbing and with the maximum potential for embarrassment. Steeplers have been known to fall belly first into the water, swim in it, slip in it, stumble in it. The water pit gives the event its reputation of being one of the toughest in the Olympics.

When Lalita touched ground after the water jump, her right leg combusted in white hot pain. But her left leg managed to absorb the weight her right leg could not, and she found she was still standing. There was still some breath left in her. One foot on the track, then another, and she was out of the water. She would take it stride by stride, she thought—7 laps, 28 hurdles, 7 water jumps and 3,000 metres. One foot after the other. She would run till she could, notwithstanding the white hot pain in her leg. If she had to stop, it would be when foot failed to follow foot. There were degrees of not finishing—she would at least be the best non-finisher.

This was familiar territory. Lalita had the marathoner's intimate understanding of endurance. It was a matter of bargaining with herself. She knew that every intake of breath would bring a lick of relief. If she pushed herself from exhale to inhale, there would be a small reprieve every time she breathed in. Her knee throbbed with pain when she landed her right foot on the ground, then let up as the left foot landed. She slowly grew familiar with the intensity and shape of the pain, its coming and going. Her mind stilled, her anxiety dried up, the world receded, rhythm settled. Lalita breathed in and breathed out.

She had landed in Rio on 11 August, a day and a half before her heat, and missed the opening ceremony on 5 August. It was her first time at the Olympics, but she did not mind. Her coach Snesarev had decided that the excitement of being present at the grand opening of the Games would lead to a loss of time and precious emotional energy, and Lalita found herself agreeing. She was Maharashtrian and had her people's fabled austere, pragmatic approach to life. They could, instead, use a couple of days' extra training.

When Snesarev and the long-distance team landed on 11 August, the Games were in their second week and the cutting-edge business of competitive sport was in full flow. Lalita slept off her jet lag for a day and a half, and saw the Olympic stadium for the first time on 13 August, the day of her heat. After it was over, with the happy knowledge of her qualifying time, she had allowed herself to soak in the Olympic arena before heading to her room. Over the next day and a half, she remained in her room, sealing herself off from the media after one brief press interface and getting her right calf ice-packed at careful intervals. She had decided not to tell the media about the hit to her calf.

Now, past the second lap in the final, she felt able to work with the pain. A medal was out of the question, but she would use this race to see how she apprehended pain and performed with it. It was a first-rate synthetic track, the weather was hot and familiar, and she thought she could hold out till the finish. Ruth Jebet of Bahrain ran exquisitely, leading throughout, to finish with gold. Jebet's 8-minute-59.75-second finish was a league ahead of the second- and third-place finishers. Defending gold medallist Hyvin Jepkemoi of Ethiopia finished at 9 minutes 7.12 seconds for silver and American Emma Coburn at 9 minutes 7.63 seconds for bronze. Lalita finished at 9 minutes 22.74 seconds at tenth position, only three seconds slower than her superb heat performance. She felt utterly spent, almost doubling up and unable to stand. Then, as the remaining finalists crowded the finishing line, she hurried off to the side—ever the professional. A terrific exhaustion descended on her. Her work was done.

At home in Mohi village, Satara, her parents had visited the local temple that morning before going to work, her mother cutting corn on the family land and her father tending their cows and buffaloes. It would have been 7.30 p.m. in the evening when they saw her on TV at home, at the end of a long day at work. But Lalita had no energy to speak to them and to be honest, what was there to say? She turned off her phone. There would be time enough to talk later.

Rio 2016 was a remarkable outing for the women in the Indian contingent. Sakshi Mallik, a wrestler, won bronze in the 58-kg category for women. P.V. Sindhu made it to the women's badminton final and came away with silver. Dipa Karmakar, a gymnast from Tripura, became the first Indian woman to make the gymnastics final, and finished fourth. And there was Lalita Babar, whose completing the steeplechase despite her injury was a feat in itself. For the first time India's medals at the Games were all won by women.

In her remaining days at the Olympics, Lalita watched, cheered and tucked in at the Village buffet table—the variety of food was as stunning as the sports on offer. She felt a strange disconnect with the action around her, as if she were watching it on television. 'It becomes hard to grasp the world. You haven't eaten rice and roti and the food you know for months on end,' she told me four years later in 2020, when I met her at her apartment in Navi Mumbai. 'You have woken up at 3 a.m. to train at 3.45 a.m. and gone to sleep at 6.30 p.m. You do your stretches and warm-ups, and everything you are told to do to avoid an injury. You have missed your own sister's wedding. You think you've found the person you want to marry, but you have to wait because … You are considered to be one of the best athletes in the world. You've finished eighth in the world in the World Championships, the top competition after the Olympics. You want to see for yourself how far you can go. You run the best you can and suffer a crushing blow just above the knee. You run with that sharp pain to finish tenth among the best in the world.'

She went quiet for several seconds before she spoke again. 'It occurred to me, of course, that I may simply not be good enough for the best. I'm not a fool, you know! But how long can you go on thinking about that?'

She returned home to a rapturous welcome at Mumbai's international airport after the Olympics, and a boisterous, joyous rally in her home district of Satara, accompanied by television crews. The village had never seen a reception like the one she got. In fact, she hadn't imagined it herself. She had long known that she had done things that no one in her village had, not even the handful of men who had landed jobs in the Indian Army. She knew she was permitted freedoms other women were denied. At twenty-seven, she was the oldest unmarried woman in her village, perhaps even older than all the unmarried men.

Now she had made up her mind. It was time to get married. She didn't need approval from anyone any more, not even her parents. That relationship had changed. They could disagree, but they could no longer decide. Her parents would accept the man she had chosen.

There would be time to run again. There would be time to find out how good she really was. Or perhaps there would not be. For now, it was time to move on, try normal life. One foot after another. She would breathe in and breathe out, and let the world recede.

I first heard of Lalita Babar in August 2016, when the sports pages of English newspapers in India started their quadrennial Olympic round-up. For this one month every Olympic year, cricket receded to one page out of the three or four allotted sports pages in the daily newspapers, and every other sport came to the fore. Coverage was dominated by medal prospects—foremost among them was Mary Kom, the then five-time world boxing champion (45-kg pinweight division) and bronze medallist at the London Olympics, and Saina Nehwal, the badminton player who had also won bronze at the London Games. The men's hockey team always gets a decent amount of Olympic coverage by virtue of its past triumphs—out of the thirty Olympic medals won by independent India, nine are for men's hockey. P.V. Sindhu, another badminton player, was seeded ninth out of forty competitors in the women's singles. She was billed as a medal prospect, and she delivered.

A couple of veteran sportswriters had listed Lalita as a dark horse in India's chances. On 14 August, the day after her smashing heat, the dark horse was on page one of most English newspapers in India. She had made history—the first Indian woman to qualify for an Olympic track final since P.T. Usha in 1984. In academic terms, a time period of twenty-five to thirty-three years is considered to constitute a generation, as per the measures of different disciplines. Thirty-two years after Usha ran the 400-metre hurdles in the women's final of the Los Angeles Olympics, Lalita had reached the finals at the Rio Olympics.

I watched the women's steeplechase final on the internet—Lalita appeared at the start, lining up for the race with the fourteen other runners, and fell out of view within a couple of seconds as the eventual gold medallist Ruth Jebet seized a lead from the start and the camera naturally followed her. Jebet was magnificent, finishing more than a lap ahead of the silver and bronze medallists, and when she ran, the camera remained on her, tracking her mesmerizing, ballerina-like performance. In the end, it felt like she was in her own separate time zone, because when she finished, the camera tracked back to the second- and third-place finishers, who were still in the middle of running the final lap.

Lalita reappeared briefly towards the end, when she reached the finishing line, knelt forward and bent double, and then as she saw the remaining finishers drawing up, walked off the track. There was no way to tell that she was injured. It looked like a bad day at work, no more.

There was no mention of her injury in the press. In fact, there was little about her at all in the press in the days after her final. She was seemingly eclipsed by the silver medal of P.V. Sindhu the day after, and Sakshi Mallik three days later. Lalita told me that she wanted it that way. To speak of her injury after the final, especially after she had decided to keep it to herself, felt like a cheap move, an excuse for not performing. And she felt she was too good for that. Besides, these things were part of competitive sport—injuries, falls, a sudden cramp. Why should she make so much of it?

In the thirty-two years between P.T. Usha in the 1984 Los Angeles Games and Lalita Babar in 2016 Rio, no Indian woman had made it to the final of a track and field event at the Olympics. Not even Usha herself, though she was widely expected to bring home a medal in the 1988 Seoul Olympics after a sensational showing in the 1986 Asian Games in Seoul, where she picked up four golds, including three individual medals for the 200- and 400-metre sprints and the 400-metre hurdles. But an ankle injury meant she was far from her best in 1988.

Lalita comes from the quiet, gritty, unglamorous cousin of sprinting—long-distance running. Here's a test: Do you know the current world-record holder in the marathon? Male or female?

Most of you reading would be able to name the 100-metre sprint record holder right off the bat—certainly Usain Bolt has had that kind of outsize reputation. Besides, it is the men's record that becomes *the* record in our minds. Many of you would also be able to hazard a guess on the women's record—Florence Griffith-Joyner's time is unbeaten since 1988.

But the marathon?

I'm going to be honest: I didn't know the answer, even though I was working on this book. In fact, I couldn't name even one legendary marathon runner. The answer is Eliud Kipchoge for men, the only person to run a full marathon in under two hours. For women, it is Brigid Kosgei, who clocked a time of 2 hours 14.04 minutes in 2019. She broke a record held for sixteen years by Paula Radcliffe, who set a time of 2 hours 15.25 minutes in 2003.

This privilege that sprinting enjoys over long-distance running is primarily a matter of optics. Perhaps no sport can match sprinting in sheer viewing pleasure—watching chiselled human bodies in full stride propelled by a terrific burst of kinetic force. The skill and strength on display in gymnastics and diving also provide stunning spectacles, but these are performed individually by turn. The suspense of simultaneous competition is missing.

Consider, also, the visual design of athletic competitions, and the factor of time. Short- and middle-distance events are held on the 400-metre oval track, designed specifically to optimize stadium spectatorship with stands around the track. The 100-metre, 200-metre and 400-metre sprints and hurdles take place on one lap of the oval track. The 800-metre sprint, which comprises two laps of the 400-metre oval track, is also easy to follow. But from 1,500 metres to 10,000 metres, which involve multiple laps of the oval, there is a repetitiveness to the action despite the frequently glorious athleticism on display. How long can you watch people circling the same track? In the case of the steeplechase, there is the formidable water jump that offers the perhaps amusing prospect of athletes tumbling and crash-landing, but beyond the occasional embarrassment, there is a sameness to the action.

Races longer than 10,000 metres take place off the oval track, on the road. So do the 20- and 50-kilometre walks, although these are not technically running competitions. They have many more competitors than in track competitions and the lack of an enclosed stadium space makes camera placement far more tricky. Typically, the cameras follow the leaders. But how long can you watch legs moving? The flagship long-distance event, the 42.2-kilometre full marathon is supposed to be run in three hours. Three hours of watching legs moving? This is probably why many more people are interested in running marathons than in viewing them. Sprint events, which comprise distances of 400 metres and under, finish in less than two minutes.

In the tiny corner of the public imagination that athletics occupies in India, the two stars who have dominated for decades are sprinters Milkha Singh and P.T. Usha, both fourth-place finishers in Olympic finals. Both loom large in the public imagination, aided by popular culture and the advertising industry.

When Lalita Babar qualified for the final of the women's steeplechase at the Rio Olympics, she was already India's finest woman marathoner, the reason a couple of veteran sports journalists anointed her a dark horse. From 2014 to 2016, she won the Indian competition at the prestigious Mumbai marathon, India's most prominent marathon event, and its wealthiest.[1] The Mumbai marathon has, for years, been dominated by Kenyans, considered to be unbeatable long-distance runners. In other words, Lalita had been up against the best in the business for a while. But outside of a niche circle of sports professionals—coaches, journalists, talent-management companies and athletes—she was largely unnoticed.

Since 2014, she had also been making attempts at the steeplechase with growing gains. At the 2014 Asian Games, she won silver at the 3,000-metre steeplechase. In 2015, she became the first Indian runner to qualify for the finals of the biennial World Athletics Championships in Beijing in the steeplechase event—before her, there was Anju Bobby George in women's long jump, Inderjit Singh in men's shot-put and Vikas Gowda in men's discus throw.[2] She took a wide lead in the final and maintained it for the first five of the race's seven laps, but lost ground in the all-out acceleration in the last two laps to finish eighth. Among the athletes competing against her in the 2015 race was Ruth Jebet, who would go on to win won the Olympic gold in Rio three years later. But in Beijing, Jebet did not medal.

Lalita came into the national spotlight with the Rio Olympics and reaped richly deserved rewards in the immediate aftermath. The Government of India and the state government of Maharashtra showered her with prize money. She was earlier a junior-level Central-government employee in the Indian Railways. The Maharashtra government offered her a senior officer's role. She was signed up as brand ambassador by the global automobile tyre brand Bridgestone as well as the Indian steel and power conglomerate Jindal.

When I met her in 2021, it was two and a half years since she had seriously competed on the track. In the interim, she had settled into the rhythms of marriage and a mid-level government job in Mumbai, had a child and completed her graduation degree through a correspondence course.

Her son was two years old at the time, a charming full-time handful with an aptitude for throws. Lalita was a model of patience and agility as she caught and retrieved and removed objects like smartphones, air-conditioner remotes, government IDS and cups of hot tea from his grasp and restored them to safety. Until he found them again. Her husband, Sandeep Bhosale, came home from work around 9.30 p.m., three hours after she had returned from office, and although he was a hands-on father, it was clear that Lalita undertook most of the childcare in the household. From the few days I spent with her, it looked like she enjoyed it too, proud of her child and content in the identity of wife and mother.

Our conversation, though, was mostly about her career in sport and she was frank about her feelings in a way that elite athletes in India, indeed the subcontinent, are typically not. Weakness and uncertainty are rarely acknowledged, especially by persons in the public eye. The business of acknowledging weakness has become prominent in the West—swimmer Michael Phelps, gymnast Simon Biles and tennis player Naomi Osaka are among the prominent ones to have spoken of their mental-health concerns. In the subcontinent, this is typically viewed as 'seeking sympathy' or 'playing the victim card', despite stars celebrities such as the Hindi-film actor Deepika Padukone talking about their experience of depression. A somewhat predictable turn of events took place in 2022, when cricketer Virat Kohli spoke of what was perceived to be depression in a newspaper interview. 'I personally have experienced times when even in a room full of people who support and love me, I felt alone, and I am sure that this is a feeling that a lot of people can relate to. It is definitely a serious issue and as much as we try to be strong at all times, it can tear you apart,' he was quoted as saying.[3] Within hours of the interview being published, *The Times of India* carried a comment from Kohli's manager Bunty Sajdeh, 'Every top athlete has gone through mental challenges of dealing with pressures and expectations that come with the positions they are at. Depression is too big and significant a term to be used so loosely,' said Sajdeh, the CEO of Cornerstone, the company that manages Kohli.[4]

Four and a half years after she kept quiet about her injury in Rio, Lalita spoke about it at length to me. 'Everything was gone—the pain was gone, the swelling … All that was gone within a few days. It looked normal, but I knew my knee was not the same. Even after taking a break of six months, I could feel it. That old ease was gone.'

Diagnostic machines were unable to pick up any contours of damage. But she could sense a hint of slippage where earlier there was none—a whisper of a wobble in her knee when her weight shifted from the left to the right foot, a tiny lurch as she adjusted to the wobble and an infinitesimal wrench, no matter how much she calculated the adjustment. The pain was nothing like it had been in Rio. It wasn't pain, in fact. It was a spectre of it.

She believed she could adjust to this new development, and in a way she did. One of Lalita's strengths as a steepler was that she did not have a particular hurdling leg—she could lift into a jump with whichever leg was in front. That meant she could withstand landing on either leg. This is an important point, because the leg you land on holds your entire weight for that fraction of a second before your other leg lands. Lalita never had to break stride to hurdle earlier. Now she did, to avoid landing on her right leg. So her left leg became her main hurdling leg. With practice, she did this well. But occasionally, she would go wrong in her stride calculation and then there would be that wobble, that lurch, that wrench.

In 2018, when she returned to competition at the national athletics championships in Guwahati, the first big event after a break of almost two years, her husband was in attendance. He had only watched her run on television before this. The thought of him watching her stand on the podium, bending her head to accept her medal, kissing the medal and holding it aloft sent a buzz of anticipation through her. The anxiety of her unhealing injury slipped away a little then. All her life she had wanted to win because she had calculated the returns from the medal for her sport, for her team, for her job, for her prize earnings. But this was a different kind of aspiration. The practical Lalita found herself smiling at her thoughts. It was one of the things that made her look forward to her return, a feeling distinct from the other reason—matching up to her form before Rio. That was anxiety—a heavy, throbbing feeling. This was a warm, pleasurable buzz.

But right from the time she did a training run at the Sarusajai Stadium in Guwahati, she knew she was no longer the runner she had been. Faced with her old competitors on the track, she realized that the constant calculation to land on her left foot at every hurdle was wearing her down. More than anything, it was the worry—the way she tensed to prepare for the momentary discomfort in case she got the calculation wrong.

When she told Sandeep how she felt, it was the first time she acknowledged the thought that had been waiting at the back of her mind. That the x-factor that made her the runner she was—the agility and strength to hurdle on either leg—was gone. And gone with it, most likely, was the athlete who was among the best steeplers in the world, waiting to break through to the top. What remained was a fine, disciplined athlete, the sort who made the best in the middling athletic talent pool that was India, but not the potential game-changing wild card she had been. Even with that injury, she had finished tenth at the Olympics; the year before at the World Championships, she had been eighth. It hadn't been unreasonable to think she could have been a contender for bronze in the next edition of the Olympics. At least the World Championships, the second most prestigious event after the Olympics.

Sandeep, a gentle, mild-mannered, studious man, whose only brush with competitive sport was watching Lalita, was supportive. Let's have a short holiday instead, he told her. Once she had said it out loud, Lalita found the tightness inside of her loosening a little. She ran her steeplechase event without finishing, perhaps the only time in her life that she left a race without running till the end. She found it hard to shake off the sense that she was filling in for the real Lalita Babar.

Training as an elite athlete at the top levels of international competition is always severe, but what do you do when the moments of exhilaration are gone? The times she pulled off a superb burst of flat-out speed, the times she cleared a hurdle and landed with such perfect balance that she even gained momentum in her run—those were becoming rarer. What remained was the anxiety of avoiding that pain—the ceaseless vigilance. The joy had leaked out. Now there was only exhaustion.

'I thought, why am I doing this? I was dragging myself to training day after day. It was the only life I had known since school. It was my routine. But now I had a husband, a marriage ... I thought I would try for a baby, then see. I would take time off. I was tired of preparing for pain,' she said.

'It's always there in my head, you know—I had gotten tenth place even with an injury, competing with the best in the world. There were five people after me,' she said. 'I am an achiever from childhood. I always felt that I have to achieve something. When you have stood in an Olympic final and not got a medal, you know how much you want to go back there again. Is there a day when I don't remember that?' She fell quiet.

At the same time, Lalita seemed unsentimental and slightly distanced from the questions, as if she had left that life behind. One day when I was interviewing her at Navi Mumbai home, the doorbell rang. It was a new neighbour, a woman with her daughters. She apologized for the inconvenience as she was moving into her new home, and then introduced herself. When Lalita introduced herself in response, there was no flicker of recognition in the other woman. She did not know of her at all. They exchanged pleasantries, then Lalita shut the door and went to the dining table to check on a dessert she had made.

'I am surprised that your neighbour did not recognize you when you told her your name,' I said.

'That is how it is with athletes,' she said. 'I got a lot of support from the media when I did well. But I am not playing now, not performing, so why should people remember?' she said without dropping her gaze.

Then she excused herself and went to call her husband out to eat. She had not changed the topic hurriedly, I thought. She really did not care how the world saw her. For now, she was a mother, a wife, a partner in a marriage that seemed to define her. For now, this seemed enough.

'One of the first things I learnt in sports is to take a defeat and forget it the next day,' she told me. 'You do badly in a race, you are upset—it is natural. Go to your room, cry, sleep, stare. The next day return to training. If not, the day after. But return like it is the beginning. You are no one. Talent, discipline, all those are necessary. But most important is that when you return after a bad race, you have to start like new.'

Perhaps this was the pragmatism of the hardy drought-fed Maharashtrian in her, measured in her expectations of the world, tempered with the stoicism born of years of living with water scarcity, of seeing people, animals, lands, rivers shrivelling and drying. It does something to you, doesn't it, this realization that the world can withhold so much from you, even its water? That you have yourself, and not much else to draw on.

In 2002, the administrative taluka of Man, where Lalita's family lived, saw a dry spell so savage that the government declared it an official drought. She was thirteen years old then, and she and her siblings and cousins spent all the hours of the day that remained after school looking for water in the wells of the area. More than the cooking, which could be restricted, and their ablutions, which they could skip on alternate days, they needed the water for their animals.

Like many families in the area, Lalita's family owned no land. Even those who did could grow little on it because of the absence of water. Animals were the chief source of sustenance, not only for the Babars but for the villages in the Man taluka at large. Milk from the cattle provided nutrition for the families and served as a source of income as well. The other source of income was agricultural labour. But the opportunity to work on other people's land arose only when there was a crop to be sown or harvested—at the most, it was a couple of days of paid work at a time.

In many households in the Mohi village, the men had travelled out in search of paid work. Lalita's father, Shivaji, was one of them. He was a truck driver in Mumbai, and this increased the burden of household labour on those who had remained behind, mainly women and children. Even if the men were home, they would work outside. This makes economic sense. Agricultural labour and any form of manual labour usually pays men at a rate that is double of what is paid to women. For instance, today, the daily wage for agricultural labour for a man in Maharashtra is Rs 300 and for a woman Rs 150. The market incentivizes men to not participate in household work.

Maharashtra is the wealthiest state in of India in terms of GDP, but it is also a state that reports the highest number of farmer suicides in the country.[5] Much like the nation itself, it is a state of extremes— the incredible wealth of coastal Maharashtra sits alongside the brutal impoverishment of the Marathwada[6] and Vidarbha[7] regions, which include nineteen of its thirty-six districts. The district of Satara, where the Man taluka is located, is not in either of these regions. It is actually a reasonably prosperous district dotted with picturesque hills and rugged forts, and was once the capital of the Maratha kingdom that mounted a serious political challenge to the Mughal empire. The celebrated Maratha warrior king Shivaji's dynasty ruled from Satara. On a spectrum of low, medium, high and very high, the human-development index of the district was marked 'high' as per the figures of 2011 in Maharashtra.[8] By a sleight of geography, the village of Mohi and the Man taluka fall in a rain-shadow area—the side of the mountain that faces away from rain-bearing winds, where the clouds carry no water because the outward face of the mountain that meets them first receives all the rain.

A declaration of drought meant that the government would provide relief supplies—tankers of water from which every family would get rationed amounts, a collective shelter for the cattle to be fed and housed in, and some guaranteed work for government projects paid at the more generous official rates that the government offered vis-a-vis private individuals and contractors. This relief freed up substantial chunks of time for residents—the many hours they would have spent searching for water, tending to their animals and cooking their own meals. Instead, many families such as Lalita's camped near the government cattle relief shelter so they could watch over their animals, cook meals collectively and go back to their individual homes for brief intervals to store water and other chores.

To Lalita in particular, it came as a huge relief. As the eldest child in the household and an unusually tall thirteen-year-old, she had been assigned the responsibility of checking the wells and other sources of water and filling at least two containers. In fact, the drought officially continued for two years, from 2002 to 2004, and changed the course of her life, freeing up several hours in the day that she put into the training that shaped her into a gifted cross-country runner in her teenage years. It was in these two years that she shifted from kho-kho to running.

In her high school Mohi Kanya Vidyalaya, Lalita had started to gain a reputation for being a star player at kho-kho, the popular south Asian game originating in Maharashtra. Lalita stood out with her speed and her seemingly endless stamina. In 2002, the first year of the drought, the physical training instructor at school, Bharat Chavan, started to make her train before school with some others to improve her stamina. When I met him in 2022, seventeen years after Lalita had graduated from that school, Chavan proudly showed me a thick stack of albums filled with photographs of Lalita and her exploits from school right up to Rio, her kho-kho teammates and younger athletes he had trained in subsequent years. When he trained Lalita, he had secured his first full-time job, but he seemed to have still retained the same enthusiasm for it. Earlier that day at the school, he requested me to give away prizes and certificates to every child who had won something in sport in the past five years or more. No competitions had taken place in the pandemic, so these were victories that were more than two years old. Later, at his home, I would recognize the faces of some of the children I had met in the photos in his albums.

The story of Indian women in sport is, in part, undeniably the story of men such as Bharat Chavan, and Usha's 'Nambiar sir' and Dutee Chand's coach Nagapuri Ramesh—PT teachers, and individual coaches and state-appointed coaches who took on the training of young women like personal missions. Men who had somehow escaped the endemic patriarchy of the subcontinent. Who saved oranges and dessert for their students from their own lunch, and arranged the photographs of their school prizes and district competitions in big plastic photo albums that they shared with visitors, and went to work a couple of hours earlier and stayed back afterwards to train the young women they took on. For whatever reason, they felt that the young women who came under their supervision had the same promise as the young men under them. The accidental feminists.

Lalita would show up sharp at 6 a.m. for practice every day, typically the first to report, as Chavan remembered it. She would come running the 2 miles from her village to the school in the dark. Located near the western coast of India, dawn breaks late in Mohi, close to 7 a.m. After the declaration of drought, Chavan started a second practice session after school, and Lalita gladly stayed back. She had hit a terrific growth spurt around this time, suddenly standing a head or two above her classmates, a striking lanky young woman. Besides, she had a natural athleticism. Coupled with her height, this made her a formidable kho-kho player.

More than the kho-kho, perhaps, it was the sense of importance that she enjoyed—having Chavan ask her mother and uncles for permission to let her travel outside the village for a school match, the thrill of being among the chosen few travelling outside the village as they set off, that sense of standing out from the others in the village.

'Some of the other girls complained about waking up so early. I never had that problem,' Lalita told me. 'The evening before a match, I would keep my sports clothes and shoes ready. I would get up before 5 a.m., quickly wash my face and get ready and leave. Everyone else in the house would still be asleep then, even my mother and aunts who worked the hardest in the house. I used to love that feeling, as if I was doing something special, something important. Not everyone was called for practice. I used to feel that I was different and I have to do something with my life.'

It was in these years of double practice hours that Chavan asked her to try athletics. He had noticed that she would often be running throughout the nine-minute duration of a kho-kho innings, seemingly effortlessly. Perhaps the better nutrition, thanks to the drought relief, helped as well. She enjoyed the change. Running was not a team effort like kho-kho was. It was individual, and it made her stand out even more.

Apart from Chavan, Lalita had another prominent band of supporters in her village. Mohi and its neighbouring villages have a number of residents working in the Indian Army. In 1961, the district of Satara got the first Sainik school in the country, part of a nationwide programme of schools to orient schoolchildren to join the armed forces. The then chief minister of Maharashtra, Yashwantrao Chavan, was the prime mover of the project. In 1962, Chavan would become the Union defence minister, an appointment that likely aided the Sainik school scheme. These schools employ personnel from armed forces in select positions to orient young minds to join the Indian Army. When Lalita was growing up, a handful of men in her village had joined the lower ranks of the army. These were the undisputed heroes of the village—Central-government job holders with smart uniforms and the palpable importance of 'doing something for the nation'. They had travelled outside their district, they had seen the world, they were men whose views carried the weight of the Indian state in them.

Lalita's armed-forces neighbours were among her earliest champions. When she travelled outside the village, some of them accompanied her to cheer for her and keep an eye on her. The Indian Army has a strong culture of sport and a superb record of Olympic performances—many of India's best male sportspersons had jobs in the army, from hockey legend Dhyan Chand (and so many other hockey stars) to the country's first sprinting hero Milkha Singh; from the double trap shooting silver medallist Rajyavardhan Singh Rathore to the first track and field Olympic gold medallist Neeraj Chopra.

Lalita's family was easy-going, but the visible support from their army neighbours was a crucial factor in her high school days. The onset of adolescence is when girls are increasingly domesticated, told to return straight home from school and get to work on household jobs. It's the time when they start to disappear from public view. Their movements are policed, and their dress and manner are made more modest. They have to account for every activity that takes them out of the home. And more than that, this is the time they are trained in cooking and other household chores to prepare them to be good wives.

Lalita, on the other hand, became more and more publicly visible, physically and figuratively. She started travelling in the district, and gradually the state, for athletics competitions. By the time the drought was officially over and the village had returned to its old rhythms of searching for water, Lalita was a star at local meets, attracting a band of supporters who cheered for her. Her family largely left her alone, and she was permitted to practise and not assigned much housework. Sometimes, she won small cash prizes worth a few hundred rupees. It was enough to take care of her own expenses and chip in for occasional household things—treatment for a sick cow or medicines for a family member. In subcontinental households, dowry expectations and wedding expenditure mean girls are viewed as financial liabilities. Boys, on the other hand, bring in money through the dowries they receive as well as inherit property.

Lalita, with her own pocket money and occasional contribution to the family, was different from the other girls in the village right from her teenage years. 'I had this thing, that I have to achieve something in my life. My schoolteachers called me an achiever. My army neighbours too,' she said.

It was a fairly conflict-free adolescence, but one incident stands out. Her father Shivaji had come home from Mumbai for the Diwali holidays. One day he scolded her in front of the joint household of uncles, aunts, cousins and her grandfather. Perhaps she had been speaking of her competitions ahead, she doesn't remember. What she remembers is her father's unexpected vehemence. No more sports! Enough! You're a girl, behave like a girl—go to school, come back home, study quietly, help your mother.

'That was the first time I properly thought about running, I think,' Lalita said. 'I had never had to make a choice. I was good at it, and I just did it. For the next ten or twelve days, I was in a daze. I didn't talk or go out. Everybody thought I was sulking, but I was just thinking. I hated studying. I didn't want a life like my mother's or aunts' or the other women in the village. I wanted to get out of the village. I had learnt [from coaches and district sports officials] about jobs given for the sports quota. That was my chance. What else could I do other than running?'

Do you think you realized how much you love running then, I asked her.

'I wouldn't call it love,' she said categorically. 'It was not a hobby either. I don't know if I thought I loved it then. I was a child, really. I hadn't seen how much it takes out of you to be an international athlete. It was the only thing I knew I could do,' she replied. 'It was the only thing that could give me a different sort of life.'

In 2006, the year after her Class X board exams, Lalita cracked a job in the Indian Railways based on her performance in cross-country running. She became a ticket checker on a monthly salary of Rs 5,000. She was the first woman in her family and her village to get a job, a government job at that. 'At that time, that was my dream. I was not thinking of Olympics. I just wanted to have a different sort of life. I didn't want to be married after school—I wanted to have my own money, and I wanted to see the world outside [the village] a little.'

For the next couple of years, in fact, Lalita stopped running. She found herself adrift in Mumbai, missing her home, although she had wanted so much to live in the big city. But how vast it was, and how expensive and dirty! She sent most of the Rs 5,000 back home, keeping only a few hundred rupees for herself. She skipped meals, and survived on vada pao and juice, and found herself feeling lonely and bereft.

☙

One criticism of Indian sportspersons is that they are uninterested in sport. All they want is a government job. The sports quota is a means to this banal end. My family says this, the officials I met researching this book—not only government clerks at the Sports Authority of India, but also those at private coaching academies—said this, the movies say this, the pundits in the press say this—India doesn't make sportspersons, only potential babus.

This is true, and it is understandable. Isn't it? Arguably, there is nothing more prestigious than a government job in India. The obvious reason is that the government offers substantial benefits, particularly healthcare, leaves and job security, relative to the private sector. But there may be more to it. My sense is that it comes from our colonized past. The British Raj established the apparatus of the modern state and its governance mechanism in the nineteenth century. When the bureaucracy was opened up to Indians, communities that had been receptive to the Western model of public education imparted by the colonial state took the exams, joined the government and enjoyed a terrific boost to their already prestigious status. These were largely Bengali and Tamil upper-caste elites and some Parsis, as the three major colonial cities in the nineteenth century with institutions of Western education were Calcutta (now Kolkata), Madras (now Chennai) and Bombay (now Mumbai).

As these privileged elites dominated government jobs for decades, the marginalized castes and communities viewed these jobs as ladders of social mobility and markers of unquestionable social status in a society navigating modernity. To my mind, a government job offers a solid, authoritative jump in social status. This is what explains the peculiarly inflated appeal of government jobs in India.

Perhaps it was natural, then, that with a government job in Bombay, Lalita's enthusiasm for sport waned. She had already gone farther than any girl in her village, hadn't she? Sport is a ceaselessly demanding career. You train, you watch your food, you miss out on celebrations because you must wake up early, you suffer injury and recover and injure yourself again, you learn to live with the weight of disappointing yourself most of the time. The Bollywood template of the sports hero gets this absolutely right—there is no respite.

Two things snapped Lalita out of this apathy. Her roommate in Mumbai was the ace steepler and marathoner Sudha Singh, who started her reign at the steeplechase event at the national games from 2007. In 2010, Singh won her first Asian Games medal at the steeplechase, and the prestige and the press attention she received did wonders to push Lalita out of her stubborn inertia.

The second, and equally significant, thing was the coming of the marathon economy to India. In 2004, Mumbai hosted India's first prominent full-fledged marathon with handsome corporate sponsorship and press notice. (Technically, Pune had organized the first marathon event in India, but this was a much smaller affair.) It set off a series of copycat long-distance running events across Maharashtra and, in a couple of years, other metropolitan cities in India. Maharashtra in particular has a culture of sport, inspired, arguably, by the stories of the Maratha king Shivaji, celebrated for his nimble guerrilla warfare across the rocky hills of the Western Ghats. There were 5- and 10-kilometre races, and half-marathons.

And all of them offered decent cash prizes replicating the Mumbai marathon format.

For Lalita, starved of cash after sending money home, it was fruit for the picking, increasingly low-hanging, as she resumed training. With this money, she had the disposable cash to buy better-quality shoes, eat better, travel in the occasional cab. As she started placing regularly at these events (and the cash flow became consistent), her focus shifted. Her energy returned, and with it the fortitude to compete seriously. In five years, she emerged as the finest marathon runner in India, notching up a hat-trick of wins at the prestigious Mumbai marathon from 2012 to 2014 (in the Indian section), in addition to winning other long-distance events such as the Delhi half-marathon. She also returned to national competition in long-distance events on the track, placing at the 5,000- and 10,000-metre events in 2009 and 2010.

In 2012–13, when Lalita was in peak form in the marathon road-running circuit, she asked the national women's long-distance team coach Nikolai Snesarev if she could try the steeplechase. Perhaps it was her old rivalry with Sudha Singh or perhaps it was a strategic choice—the women's steeplechase is an unusual and fairly new race. The men's steeplechase, on the other hand, has been an Olympic event since 1900, the second edition of the modern Games.[9] It was included in the programme of events at the World Athletics Championships for the first time in 2005, and debuted at the Beijing Olympics in 2008. When a race is newish in world competition, it has fewer contenders, and the chances of doing well are relatively high. This was the same logic that Usha's coach O.M. Nambiar used to enter her name for the women's 400-metre hurdles event, which was included in the 1984 Olympics for the first time. The 1984 Olympic final that Usha placed fourth in by a hundredth of a second was only the fourth international hurdles race of her career.

Snesarev, a wiry, bespectacled Belarusian who was a believer in the former Soviet Union's tradition of unreasonable levels of discipline but not their reliance on doping, was known for remaking the Indian women's athletics team's fortunes from a bunch of participants to medal contenders. Certainly, this would be true for Asian competitions. His appointment as coach in 2005 led to the maturing of a fine cohort of middle- and long-distance runners such as Santhi Soundarajan, O.P. Jaisha, who won medals at the 2006 Asian Games, Preeja Sreedharan, Kavita Raut and Sudha Singh, who medalled at the 2010 Asian Games. Snesarev, an outsider in India's sports bureaucracy, was seen as unconventional and open-minded. For one, he had taken an interest in the non-glamorous long-distance events and made his wards shine.

He agreed to let Lalita have a go. And Lalita discovered that she had an unexpected gift—an ambidexterity with hurdles. Most of us have a dominant leg, although it is less evident than our dominant hand. But our dominant leg becomes amply evident when we play a sport such as football or jump hurdles, where we find that we rely on one leg more than the other. Lalita could clear a hurdle with ease no matter which leg was in front. She didn't have to break her stride. Under Snesarev's stern eye, her results were immediate—like instant noodles served at the snap of the fingers. In 2013, she placed second in the national championships after Sudha Singh. By 2014, she was the best in India, overtaking her former roommate Singh to win silver at the Asian Games in Incheon while Singh got bronze. In 2015, she made the finals of the World Championships in Beijing, the second-most prestigious athletics competition after the Olympics, and finished eighth. Next year, she ran the Olympic steeplechase final, the first Indian woman since 1984 to make an Olympic final.

Lalita paved a new trajectory for athletes in India—from the new cash-rich marathon and road-running circuit to the more elite (and conventional) track. Making the Olympic final made her India's first long-distance running star. The marathon economy in India, estimated to be worth Rs 2,900 crore as of 2020, has instituted a vast new ecosystem of sport and enabled a far larger number of people to make careers in it. The big money from corporate sponsorship has made possible different dreams and life choices, full-fledged careers in sport with Plan Bs and Plan Cs. It is plausible now to think of becoming a coach in a corporate academy (Plan B) if you don't make it as an athlete, or crack that elusive government sports coach's job. If this doesn't work out, you could be a physical education teacher in school with a reasonable private practice as a coach after hours (Plan C). Some may even think of working as fitness instructors or physiotherapists (Plan D?). The prize money in marathons makes many want to have a slice of it.

In fact, long-distance running also presents a viable option for retiring track athletes. Sprinters tend to peak in their early to mid-twenties. Long-distance runners typically run well into their thirties. For many retiring athletes, then, a shift to long-distance running extends their playing days. One of the first prominent elite track athletes to shift to marathoning is Lalita's old roommate Sudha Singh, a nice way to reciprocate the compliment Lalita paid her.

When I asked Lalita how she saw her place in history, she looked surprised at first, and then a bit hurt. Take your time to think about it, I said, and she nodded without speaking. She would never articulate her response to me. Perhaps she felt it was too soon to be asked this question. She was only in her early thirties. She wasn't done yet.

It may be clearer for us to see, those of us who are watching from the outside. A woman makes it to the final of an Olympic event after thirty-two years. One woman in a country of 1.3 billion people. One woman in approximately 624 million Indian women. She is one among the select band of Indians who are the subject of quiz questions in high school and general-knowledge papers for government jobs. In her state, Maharashtra, which has developed a serious subculture of road-running, hers is the story that rural girls and boys, and indeed their parents, tell. She has already made her place in India's history. A Marathi biopic on her life is in the works.

But put yourself in Lalita's shoes. You are the one who arrived after thirty-two years. You are called the dark horse in the Indian contingent by some journalists, and you prove them right by pulling off a terrific performance in the heat. When you call home the day before the final, you hear that a battalion of reporters has camped out in your tiny village overnight to watch the final with your family. You don't tell them much about the orb of pain, pulling ceaselessly at your knee. You make deals with yourself to keep running with a throbbing pain that combusts into fire every time you jump, and, yet, you carry on till the finishing line. You place tenth in that final race out of 15 of the world's finest, your performance watched by a village full of reporters sitting next to your parents and aunts and uncles and neighbours, broadcasting it to millions of strangers.

For several years, you live in a dizzying metropolis on Rs 2,000 a month, surviving on junk food and fruit juice, after sending most of your salary home. Then you pull yourself up like an underdog in a mythological story and begin running marathons, competing with the unbeatable Kenyans and making your own mark— the finest woman marathoner in India. You then shift to something new again—the steeplechase—and do whatever your coach says. You wake up at 3 a.m., sleep at 6.30 p.m., eat nothing you love—and win a major medal for India at the Asian Games in 2014. You crash your calf into a hurdle in your terrific heat at the Olympics and decide not to tell people because it sounds like an excuse. You negotiate with a lacerating, white-hot pain every time you jump and, yet, you run till the finishing line. You end the race tenth out of fifteen participants.

You take a break afterwards, waiting for your injury to heal, and get married. But when you return to serious competition, you realize your injury hasn't healed. And that it may never do.

All these years you train for six to eight hours a day in all weather. Sustain injuries in your joints and ligaments and bones, wait anxiously in recovery, work doubly hard to make up for the lost time. You listen to your coach, don't take calls from your family, live a hostel lifestyle with strict rules, lose touch with your friends. As if you are living in suspension from the real world. All because you have to achieve something in sport.

Then one day you realize it is over. The body you spent so many hours training and looking after has betrayed you, although the mind is still keen, the heart still hopes. Tenth at an Olympic final is the best you may ever be.

It cannot be an easy realization. Do you answer that your place in history was to be tenth in the world?

By now we know why the life of elite athletes at national camps is highly sought after in India—decent accommodation, reasonable nutrition, regular professional coaching. But the regimented hostel lifestyle is permanent, unlike even the armed forces, where there are certain provisions to stay with your family in peacetime postings. Institutionalized restrictions take away far more from women than from men—hostel rules are much more strict for women, not only in sports hostels where residents are expected to be disciplined. Windows for going out are narrower and more rigidly enforced for women's 'own safety', as it is invariably justified. Violations are punished more harshly. All of this allows little room for the natural rhythms and familiar desires of life as we know it—falling in love, having a relationship, marriage, children, building a family. And women, unlike men, are aged out of the marriage market in the subcontinent by the time they are thirty years old.

Lalita wanted the normal things too—marriage, a home of her own. Sandeep was her choice from a growing stack of marriage proposals her family received as her sporting achievements grew. Her family had preferred one with more landed property, but Lalita had liked Sandeep's serious face and educated profile, and initiated contact with him on her own. She kept in touch with him from the national camps, but had limited access to her phone. When she returned from Rio, she decided this was it. No one could say no to her now—not her family, not her coach Snesarev. And she married Sandeep. In 2018, when she realized her knee might never return to what it was, she decided it was time to try for a baby. Her body had already started to betray her—what if it got too late for her to have a child later on?

'Lalita lacks the killer instinct,' a coach at a corporate initiative for boosting Indian Olympic chances told me when I asked him what Lalita's legacy in Indian sport would be. 'Most Indians are happy to be good enough. They don't want to be the best.' A handful of other sports officials in public and private positions repeated a version of this and wrote her off when I spoke to them. It's likely that this sentiment has reached Lalita, adding to her own inarticulated disappointment.

When I put the same question to the headmaster of Mohi Kanya Vidyalaya, where Lalita had studied from Class VI to Class XI, I got a different answer, free of any uncertainty, the clearest answer so far. 'At least fifteen girls who graduated from this school have gone on to get government jobs after Lalita,' said Sukhdeo Deokar, 'including her two younger sisters. All of them have done this through the sports quota, because Lalita showed this was possible.'

Some of your girls must have gone to college and found jobs too, I said.

'No, that does not happen here,' said another man present in the room. Rajendra Deokar, no relation to the principal, was the school clerk who sat in the principal's room where I was showed in. Mohi Kanya Vidyalaya is a one-storey rectangular building with the classrooms in one line, a courtyard in front, where the students assemble, and a tennis-court-sized patch of land about 150-odd metres alongside. This was the ground where Lalita trained. About 130 students are enrolled in the school as of 2022, 58 of them girls. Although it carries the name of a girls' school, from 2016, the school has become co-educational, because the number of girls enrolling was small. The school had secured government funding, which they would have had to give up if they could not maintain a minimum number of enrolments. Hence, the decision to go co-educational.

'As soon as a girl nears eighteen here, she is married off. Because there are very few girls in number. We had a student of sixteen years of age who got married last Sunday. Some of us teachers went to her home and requested her parents to wait for her to turn eighteen, but they had already decided. They had a very good match, they said. Girls [women] getting a job after studies just doesn't happen here. Perhaps such jobs are more possible for [city] people like you? But people here now know about the sports quota, that if they are good in sport [sic], they may get a government job. Then the families may wait a little. Because they saw Lalita.'

Is it because of dowry that girls are married off, I asked.

'No, no, we don't have *that* problem here,' Rajendra said. 'In fact, there are such few girls that their parents get nice gifts instead.'

'If girls are valued, that is a good thing, no?' I said.

'Yes, they are valued very highly. That's why the parents get a lot of cash and expensive gifts,' he said.

It struck me then, when he repeated the point about the gifts. 'Do you mean the girls are few in number because they have been aborted?' I used the Hindi phrase, '*gira diya* (dumping the foetus)'.

'*Hahn, wahi* (yes, exactly),' he said, looking relieved. Principal Deokar nodded vehemently. 'It was such a problem in the 1990s when the new technology came in. Doctors were greedy and the government had no regulations. For about five years, there was no restriction, and that was enough to create this situation. Most boys in this village and around will not find a bride.'

Technology means the ultrasound machine?

'Hahn, USG,' Rajendra said.

'The situation was very bad,' the principal Deokar added.

'Now it doesn't happen. The government has made rules and everyone is very strict,' Rajendra said. 'But it helps to have someone like Lalita. To say, look at what a girl can achieve. That means much more than a government rule, no?'

None of this should have been new to me. India's dismal gender indices and barbaric son preferences were among my premises for writing this book. Yet it came as a nasty surprise. The Marathi-speaking people are renowned for a number of nineteenth- and twentieth-century educationists, such as the anti-caste activists and women's educationists Jyotirao and Savitribai Phule (husband and wife); the widow remarriage and women's education advocate Dhondo Keshav Karve; the freedom fighter and teacher Sane Guruji; and the legal scholar, caste abolitionist and architect of India's constitution Dr Babasaheb Ambedkar. Ahilyabai Holkar of the Maratha kingdom was one of the only women rulers in eighteenth-century India when the British were growing their control by stealth and the Mughal empire was crumbling. Her father-in-law had prevented her from immolating herself at her husband's funeral pyre and becoming a sati, entrusting her with leading military campaigns.

It was because of this history that I was especially unsettled by what I heard in the school about the large-scale abortion of female foetuses. I expected this kind of homicidal misogyny in the states of Haryana, Punjab and Uttar Pradesh, where the news and gender statistics have been frightening for decades. Not in the land of the Phules and Maharshi Karve and Ahilyabai Holkar.

Lalita's village Mohi is hilly, free of garbage and full of a quietness that wraps you like velvet. The air was crisp on the late December afternoon when I visited and there was no sign of the drought that stalks the rain-shadow village. It had rained that year, and everywhere it was a lovely dark green. It was the quiet time of afternoon, when everyone was deep in the hum of work before the light fell away in the early evening. The thought of the aborted girls felt especially incongruous in this serene, handsome landscape.

'This road is because of Lalita, you know,' said Chavan, who accompanied me in the car to her family home. 'It wasn't paved earlier.'

I thought he was being metaphorical, and nodded. 'Yes, she really has paved the way for everyone—girls, boys, parents, the entire community, no?' I said.

But Chavan was speaking of the actual tarring of the road. He wasn't being metaphorical. 'When the press arrived to report for her Olympic final, it was a kachcha road. Pagdandi, we call it,' he said. 'The television vans could hardly move. There was a traffic jam here! A few days after they went back, work started, and the road was laid out. Now it takes just five to seven minutes by bicycle to school. When Lalita was growing up, she would run behind the boys who had cycles to go to school. It was a full warm-up before her practice session. In fact, many girls would drop out once they became teenagers because their parents felt the distance was too long.'

The literalness of it was unexpected and delightful, and it made me think of the question Lalita never answered. What if one answer to the question of Lalita Babar's place in history was that she mattered enough that the government rolled out a road to her village, right up to her home, in her honour? They did it to save face, so that the press would not point out how little the village had. But it made it easier for everyone in the village to go to school, to travel outside, to think of working in the world out there.

The practical, hard-working, straight-talking Maharashtrian in her would likely approve.

9

SUNRISE PROJECT:
THE GIRLS WHO RISE BEFORE
THE SUN

Photo © Sagroli Sunrise Project

WHEN DURGA KUMBHARVAD was five months old, her father Linguram Linganna Kumbharvad died. The news that he had been suffering from AIDS got out in the village of Kundalwadi in Andhra Pradesh in the way that such news always does. It confirmed the feeling in the village that the Kumbharvad family was bad news—first the couple had two girls one after the other (Durga was the second) and then the father died of a little-understood, dirty disease that they knew was contracted through sex. Later, Durga's mother, Shobha, would be detected as HIV+ too, but the neighbours in Kundalwadi needed no medical evidence. They knew. This was a bad family and it had no place in the village.

A couple of months after she was widowed, Shobha came away with her girls, Lakshmi and Durga, to the village of Sagroli 30 kilometres away in neighbouring Maharashtra to stay with her brother. Shobha came from a family of agricultural labourers in Sagroli. Her brother, Moglaji Ushkelvar, married with children of his own, worked as a daily-wage farm hand there. His wife, also called Lakshmi, was unhappy to have more mouths to feed. Between his wife's reasonable apprehensions and the sinking feeling in his stomach every time he saw his younger sister Shobha, still in her teens, Moglaji did what many men in the subcontinent do—he stayed quiet and outside his home as much as he could. Naturally, this angered his wife even more.

One evening, when Moglaji and his wife Lakshmi returned from a full day's work on the farms, they found their children, Shobha and her daughters, and their belongings bundled outside their home, locked out of their rented room. Moglaji's landlord had evicted them for the reason they had feared—the news of AIDS/HIV had travelled to Sagroli as well.

Overnight, rental accommodation in the village seemed to gain in value. Each home Moglaji rented—and over the next few years there would be several—was more expensive and cramped than the one before it. And with each move, Shobha, Durga and Lakshmi became more peripheral to the household, like the cattle tied outside.

It was during one of these moves that Nandu Jadhav, head of the sports department at the Sanskriti Samvardhan Mandal (SSM) School in Sagroli, came to hear of the family and realized that he knew who they were. Shobha Kumbharwad (then Ushkelvar) had been his classmate in school until about Class V, when she dropped out and disappeared from his circle of friends and, gradually, his mind. Jadhav didn't know much about AIDS and HIV, but asked his colleagues in the school and learnt what he could. He enrolled Shobha in the Nanded government hospital's free anti-retro viral therapy (ART) programme for HIV-affected persons. To his relief, both the girls Lakshmi and Durga tested negative. He admitted them to his school, where he had been a student himself, as had Shobha.

More than anything, he wanted to enrol the girls in the Sunrise Project, a training programme for long-distance running that was started in 2005. The previous year, the inaugural edition of the Mumbai Marathon had been a snazzy affair—the first major athletics event in India with big press attention and corporate sponsorship. The 2004 Mumbai Marathon gave away generous cash prizes not only to the first-, second- and third-place winners, but also to the next ten best finishers.

A long-time donor of SSM, the late Deepak Kanegaonkar, an entrepreneur in Mumbai, had loved the shiny, anything's-possible vibe of the marathon—cash prizes and media spotlight for seemingly unknown young people. It was just the sort of thing the students in

Sagroli would excel in, he felt, with their sports facilities, ex-army teachers and strict discipline. It was only a matter of funding their diet and sports kits. He funded the Sunrise Project to train a cohort of fifty to sixty students every year, both girls and boys. Over the next decade and more, this policy would reshape the community—from their food habits and marriage plans to their views on raising girls. But for the donors, it was a decision made without thinking, the default choice.

'I don't think of it as a feminist commitment, specifically,' said Carlton Pereira, an investment banker and a friend of Kanegaonkar's, who is now the Sunrise Project's main donor after his friend's passing. 'I don't think Deepak did either. Perhaps it is my urban upbringing, but I've always thought that girls are the same as boys.'

The Sunrise Project provides a protein-rich diet comprising soya milk and cow milk, four eggs a day, sprouts, almonds, walnuts and seasonal fruit to each student on the programme, in addition to the regular meals provided on campus. More than anything else, Jadhav wanted Lakshmi and Durga to eat well. He knew that they rarely ate a full meal. Besides, what if their test results were incorrect? What if the virus had, in fact, snared the girls? Despite the relief he had felt at the negative HIV test result, a gnawing doubt remained. What if there was something else, some other disease? The good food would help.

At nine years old, Durga was the youngest recruit to the Sunrise Project when she joined. At ten and a half, Lakshmi was the second-youngest. The Sunrise Project focuses on training teenagers, because long-distance running can be damaging to growing bodies. But the school made an exception for them because of their circumstances. Lakshmi dropped out after the first year, unable to sustain the demanding routine. Durga stayed on, running her first 6-kilometre race at ten years of age and slowly growing the patience for long-distance running, a form of exercise that can feel tedious to a child.

When I first met Durga, she was nearing sixteen years of age, about to appear for her Class X board exams, which were ultimately cancelled on account of Covid-19. Her record as an athlete was not yet spectacular—she had won local races and placed in school competitions. But there was one thing that was striking. She was easily a head taller than her classmates, indeed as tall as some of the older boys in the project. She is taller than me too. I say this not because my height is remarkable, but I am more than double her age, of average height and have grown up in urban affluence with an abundance of food. Durga is still in her teens and may yet grow taller. Jadhav's faith in nutrition appears to have paid off.

It was a January afternoon when I met her, and the sun in Sagroli village was lovely and strong, the skies clear and a chill wind gave my skin goosebumps. At the Ushkelvar home where Durga was visiting for the long Republic Day weekend, the air was thick with flies. There was no humidity, no heat, it was not the weather for flies, but the buffalo shed with fodder and animal waste was a haven for them. Indeed, it was hard to say where shed ended and home began. The same uneven mud floor and walls, the same straw-covered shaggy roof—there was only the long indent on the floor for the liquid refuse from the shed to flow out, to mark the divide between shed and home. A withered old woman lay on a cot, seemingly undisturbed by the flies that had settled on her. The children, too, cousins of Durga and their friends, seemed used to the flies, occasionally raising a hand to swat a particularly noisy or annoying specimen. The adults were out at work.

This was the current residence of her maternal uncle Moglaji's family. About half of the space in the home housed the animals. They belonged to Moglaji's landlord, whose terms of rent included the work of looking after his animals. In fact, the space they had on rent was probably an animal shed, with an added semi-pucca room for the human residents. Durga is an occasional visitor to her uncle's home on the school's rare long weekend. When school breaks for holidays twice a year at summer and on Diwali, she travels to the village of Kundalwadi, where Shobha and her sister Lakshmi now live. She looked happy to be with her uncle's family. The earlier animosity had mostly subsided, Jadhav told me. It was the financial strain of three additional members that had ruptured the family. Without the financial obligation, the rage and mean-spiritedness had fallen away. But even if the inflammation had ceased now, the scars had not gone, he felt.

It was hard not to feel for Durga's aunt Lakshmi—how much would we be able to give away if we lived in such privation?

The village of Sagroli is bordered by the Manjeera river, a tributary of the mighty Godavari that spans the width of India from Maharashtra on the west to Odisha on the east. It is the second-longest river in the country (after the Ganga). The SSM school complex is nestled amid the soft, cool green of the Maharashtra countryside, a hardy land growing jowar, bajra, legumes and sugarcane, with stout hills in the distance and the strong light of the sun glinting off the surface of the Manjeera. Herds of donkeys and goats move grudgingly across the landscape, like school kids reluctantly trailing a teacher. The sun shines in a suspiciously blue sky. Here it is hard to shake off the sense that you have stepped into a child's drawing of the countryside.

SSM was established in 1959 after the school's founder Keshavrao Babasaheb Deshmukh went to meet Dhondo Keshav Karve, the twentieth-century educationist after whom one of south Mumbai's most prominent roads, Maharshi Karve Road, running parallel to Marine Drive, is named. Deshmukh wanted his daughter to study in Karve's institution. 'You are leaving your daughter in my care. Who will look after the daughters of your village?' Karve is said to have asked Deshmukh, whose family were the local landlords of Sagroli. Moved by Karve's sentiment, Deshmukh set about establishing the school on his return and planted a rubber tree on the day the foundation stone for the first school building was laid.

At the time, it was meant to only be a girls' school, taking inspiration from Karve's work in women's education and spiritual validation from the Saraswati temple 30 kilometres away in Basar, in the neighbouring state of Andhra Pradesh (now Telangana). The idol at the Gnana Saraswati temple in Basar looks nothing like the elegant swan-escorted deity we identify with the goddess of learning, and is said to have been made by Vyasa, the chronicler of the Mahabharata, from the sand on the banks of the Godavari river. The name of the town Basar is said to have been derived from Vyasa. Temples dedicated to Saraswati alone are extremely rare in India. Apart from the one in Basar, there is only the Sharada Peeth shrine in Pakistan-Occupied Kashmir. These must be distinguished from the figurines of Saraswati and small shrines to her that are housed in government educational institutes, chiefly in eastern India, a practice that likely began in independent India to suggest that Western-style school education was aligned to the values of traditional Indian society.

That rubber tree is now majestic—a towering, graceful symmetry of branches and dark green leaves with a statuesque trunk—a god in dark green and ebony regalia watching over the complex. It is an obvious, and effective, embodiment of the institution. The SSM complex has grown over the past six decades to become an impressively equipped residential school with an Olympic-standard fifty-metre pool, a stable of horses and a competitive exam workshop for students beyond Class XII, among other facilities. It would match any of India's exclusive residential schools, including Lawrence School in Sanawar, the Doon School in Dehradun or the Scindia School in

Gwalior, modelled on the public school system in England in terms of the facilities provided.

There are two crucial differences between these schools and SSM, though. First, SSM is a wholly rural school established in a location that was not a British colonial hill retreat. Second, although education is imparted in English, SSM is not primarily an English-language institution. This means that while English may be the medium of education, it is not the medium of thinking and existing there.

In the 1990s, SSM received government funds to become a Sainiki Vidyalaya, or an armed forces preparation school. In 1961, the first Sainik school in the country was opened in the Satara district of the state, thanks to the initiative taken by then Maharashtra chief minister Y.B. Chavan. Later, Chavan would become the defence minister in the Union government. The armed forces have a special place in the Marathi mind, shaped by the hallowed legacy of Shivaji, the seventeenth-century Marathi king who launched several successful guerrilla campaigns against the Mughal emperor Aurangzeb.

In time, as the boys graduated from the Sainiki Vidyalaya in Sagroli, some of them succeeded in securing posts in the armed forces and the paramilitary forces. These jobs, mostly in the lowest ranks, are highly coveted. There is the high prestige and the security of tenure of government employment, but it is also the unforgiving terrain of their homeland. The cinematic, pastoral village of Sagroli lies in Marathwada, a region that has rivalled Vidarbha as a node of bad news over the past decade.

In 2014, each of the 8,100-odd villages constituting Marathwada was declared drought-hit, wrote the journalist Kavitha Iyer in her book *Landscapes of Loss*.[1] Mental-health records in the state note that 48,095 farmers from the Marathwada region were referred for hospital admission in 2015–16. This number rose more than three times, to 162,234, in 2017–18, and climbed to 274,369 in 2018–19. In 2018, there were 947 farmer suicides reported from the eight districts of Marathwada compared to 1,297 reported from the eleven districts of Vidarbha, Iyer wrote.[2]

Marathwada—comprising the eight districts of Aurangabad, Jalna, Beed, Latur, Osmanabad, Hingoli, Parbhani and Nanded—was an arid region in premodern times, but drought has stalked the land persistently only in recent decades, primarily the result of callous policymaking after Independence, most of all. Topographically, the region lies on the Deccan plateau, which receives sporadic rainfall and has black, porous soil that cannot hold much water. From the early decades of the twentieth century, large farmer-industrialists in Maharashtra chose to grow sugarcane, a lucrative but thirsty cash crop, likely influenced by the British empire's nineteenth-century push for sugar cultivation. Post Independence, the Indian state, too, encouraged the growth of sugarcane, and Maharashtra's cooperative farming initiatives responded eagerly to the incentives offered by the Union government, making the state one of the two largest cultivators of the crop alongside Uttar Pradesh. A large part of Marathwada is part of the sugarcane-growing belt.

Furthermore, in the 1990s, the Maharashtra government encouraged fruit cultivation because it offered farmers a relatively higher return on investment—but fruit, too, is a water guzzler. These policy choices have dehydrated an already arid land. Irrigation initiatives have not been adequate for these policy choices to be successfully implemented. In this context of drought, cash crops, indebtedness and impoverishment, government jobs that offer secure payment are, naturally, treasured.

These jobs, however, are overwhelmingly open to boys. Indeed, the Sainik school programme itself is only meant for boys. Much of the paramilitary forces is still not open to women, although women were inducted into two forces—the Central Industrial Security Force (CISF)[3] and the Central Reserve Police Force (CRPF)[4]—in the 1980s. In February 2020, the Supreme Court ordered that women be given permanent commissions in all branches of the armed forces, barring combat roles.[5] The Indian Navy has 6.5 per cent women in its personnel, the Indian Air Force has 1.08 per cent and the Indian Army 0.56 per cent, the government's official Press Information Bureau noted in 2021.[6]

For all the resources and security it brought, Sagroli's Sainiki Vidyalaya had, for a very long time, likely widened the difference in the community between boys, with their government-job prospects, and girls, with their dowry liabilities. SSM has struggled to retain girls until the higher secondary level, although it was initially set up only for girls. Many girls, such as Durga's mother Shobha, stop coming to school around ages ten to twelve, as they step into adolescence and are either swallowed up in household work or married off early. Over the past decade or so, school officials said stricter state action against child marriage has led to girls staying in school until they are eighteen, the Indian state's legally mandated minimum age for marriage.

This is not a mean achievement in itself. The chief minister of West Bengal won a United Nations award, out of 562 such submissions received, for her initiative to give cycles to middle-school girl students with the objective of keeping them in school longer.[7] Since the onset of the pandemic and the accompanying lockdowns, several news reports have indicated the sharp rise in child-marriage numbers in India. According to a report in The Wire, the months of June to October 2020 saw child marriages increase by 33 per cent, compared to this period in 2019.[8]

But beyond the high-school graduation rate improving, not much has changed in SSM. Prabhakar Rao, head of the Plus Two (Classes XI and XII) in SSM, told me, 'One or two girls get married every year even now. When we go to their homes, their parents say, "But she is eighteen now! We have followed the law." Many students remain enrolled in higher education after Class XII—they opt for a diploma or a correspondence course, some even for degree courses. But the main objective is marriage—the diploma may be continued or stopped after marriage. It is a time filler.'

One Saturday afternoon when I was in Sagroli, Rao invited me to speak to the students of Plus Two in the last hour of school before class broke for the weekend. But I was a curiosity—an outsider and a woman—and the double class listened with gratifying attention. I asked them the evergreen interaction question: What do you want to do after finishing school? Most of the boys said software engineering; some mentioned other branches of engineering; a handful said other things. The girls primarily said Maharashtra Public Service Commission, or MPSC—the Maharashtra state civil service exams. Rao was present in the class during this interaction, encouraging the students to be less shy with me, reminding them to look at me while speaking.

'No one says I will get married and have children and serve my husband. They will say MPSC [civil servant]; some will say fashion designer; everyone will say something or the other. How many of them do it?' Rao said, pursing his lips. 'That's why whenever a woman visitor comes, I ask them to speak with the students. They need to see women who do things outside of the house.'

This is not only true about for the women of Sagroli. Or indeed, women in general. Steady salaried jobs have always been scarce in India, even after the decisive turn of 1991. That year, the Government of India liberalized its economy, opening it up to the global market and beginning a process of doing away with domestic regulations. The trigger was a balance-of-payments crisis, to which the International Monetary Fund agreed to bail out the

Indian government with a package that insisted on structural reform in the Indian economy. But Montek Singh Ahluwalia, the Union commerce secretary in 1991, has written[9] that the reforms undertaken were partially in operation in India already, shaped by the East Asian Miracle—the remarkable, sustained growth achieved by Taiwan, South Korea, Hong Kong, Singapore and even China from the 1960s to the 1990s.[10] In recent years, scholarship has shown that the economic policies of liberalization have shaped jobless growth—growth without a corresponding increase in jobs. As well as skewed growth—growth that has perpetuated the inequality between prosperous urban centres with decent infrastructure and rural areas without basic facilities such as electricity, piped water and public transport.

What this disparity means became clear to me when I travelled by road from Pune, Maharashtra's second-largest city after Mumbai, to Marathwada. In the first hour and some more, the area that was visible from the (gloriously smooth) highway appeared built-up and urbane—newish townships, the odd engineering campus, mid-range eateries of the sort that would have a usable women's toilet and advertisement hoardings for real estate, cement and other construction material. Soon after the district of Solapur, the landscape became entirely agricultural and the road bumpy for long stretches. The hoardings are replaced by cloth banners for political parties and occasionally one can spot an eating establishment. The traffic comprises trucks and tractors swaying with the weight of overladen sugarcane and the only rest stops are tea shanties and beer bars. Certainly nothing with the prospect of a women's toilet.

The area around Pune has become a hub for software and financial services, and Solapur is a centre of the textile industry. Beyond this, as I travelled into the interior of Maharashtra, it was still agriculture that defined the economy. Interestingly, there were far more women visible on this stretch of the highway than near the urban centres—these women were all agricultural labourers travelling atop the sugarcane loads or loading cane on to vehicles on the highway.

The landscape suggested little work opportunities other than agriculture. Agriculture may look like equal-opportunity employment for men and women, given the visibility of women, when, in fact, the daily-wage rate for men was Rs 320 and for women Rs 160, as residents in Sagroli told me. The pay gap is, of course, a worldwide reality. In 2018, the International Labour Organization (ILO) estimated that women worldwide are paid 20 per cent less than men on average, the highest pay gap being in the region of 45 per cent.[11] The agricultural pay gap in Marathwada surpasses this by far, it is 100 per cent.

India's female labour force participation rate in January–March 2023, the latest figures available from our Central government, was 22.7 per cent.[12] It would rank among the lowest in the world. A global comparison by the World Bank from 1990 to 2022 showed that only a handful of countries, such as Afghanistan, Algeria, Egypt, Iraq, Iran, Somalia, Yemen, and the West Bank and Gaza territories administered by Palestine, had rates lower than India, listed at 24 per cent.[13] Several of these regions have been affected by war in recent years. World Bank data shows that India's rate fell continuously from 31 per cent in 2000 to 21 per cent in 2018. There has been a brief rally upwards from 2019.[14]

Perhaps this is the most significant change that the Sunrise Project has brought to the village of Sagroli—the limited but real prospect of young women with government jobs. Four years after the start of the Sunrise Project, Sunita Kanna and Savita Kamble placed fourth and fifth in the half-marathon event of the 2009 Mumbai Marathon, but missed out on their cash prizes because the project had not been able to afford the electronic chips to measure time that the marathon regulations required. It was the kind of story the press loves.

The then Maharashtra chief minister Ashok Chavan led a collection drive to hand Kanna and Kamble the exact sums of money the Mumbai marathon's official prizes would have fetched them. This was the start of a brief period of national reckoning for the project. In a couple of years, both Kanna and Kamble secured jobs as van rakshaks, or forest guards, in the Maharashtra forest department.

The next year in 2010, Jayashree Boragi, who briefly joined the training programme, placed first among Indian women in the half-marathon event. The next year, she represented India at the 5,000 metres in the 2011 World Universiade, placing eleventh. She secured a job with the Maharashtra Police the same year. In time, the younger sisters of Kanna and Kamble also joined the Sunrise Project and secured government jobs in the forest service. Indeed, a number of young women from the project have gone on to secure jobs in the lower ranks of the state police, forest department and local municipal corporations, including the Brihanmumbai Municipal Corporation in Mumbai. The project has not scored a national medal yet. But it has not only achieved what it set out to do—help its students score government jobs—but it has also closed the gender gap a tiny bit.

Maharashtra is the richest state in the country in absolute terms, but this wealth has not made it immune to the tradition of patriarchy that prevails in the subcontinent. Nor has the state's formidable list of nineteenth- and twentieth-century educationists and reformers, all of whom emphasized education, especially for women. Maharashtra fares only middlingly on the enrolment of women in higher education. In 2015–16, Maharashtra's figure of 27.6 per cent enrolment of women in higher education or post-secondary education was fourteenth in a list of thirty-six states and union territories, as per a 2018 report by the Ministry of Human Resource Development.[15]

The state has an especially poor sex ratio at birth—913 females to 1,000 males, lower than the all-India average of 929; it ranks twenty-third out of thirty-six states and union territories, as per data from the 2019–21 round of the National Family Health Survey (NFHS).[16] The standard sex ratio at birth is 952 females to 1,000 males. In clearer words, this means a significant number of female foetuses are aborted.

There also remains a stubborn commitment to paying dowry in the Marathwada region. There exists an established rate chart for grooms, Iyer has written in *Landscapes of Loss*—doctors are the most expensive category of son-in-law. The going rate was Rs 51 lakh, plus a kilo of gold. Teachers cost Rs 10 lakh plus some gold. Government-job holders are particularly valued. Families that owned land typically sold some to afford dowry. According to Iyer, girls with degrees 'do not have better marriage prospects in the community unless the parents can afford a large dowry'.[17]

Education does not have a pay-off in this sense. There is no discount on dowry for advanced degrees. That is why the financial burden of continuing education is too much for the parents of many girls to bear. In 2015, a nineteen-year-old woman named Swati Pitale killed herself because she couldn't afford to pay Rs 260 for the bus commute to college, Iyer noted. In a letter to her father, Pitale wrote she didn't want him to incur the exorbitant expense of her wedding.[18]

One in four women from the state—25.2 per cent—reported facing domestic violence in the fifth round of the NFHS. This was lower than the all-India average of 29.1 per cent, as well as lower than the figure in wealthy, relatively developed states such as Karnataka (44.4 per cent), Tamil Nadu (38.1 per cent) and Telangana (36.9 per cent). What is striking is that, unlike in most states, the domestic-violence figures in Maharashtra increased from round four of the NFHS, which reported 21.3 per cent.

It would be premature to say the Sunrise Project has changed the situation for the better. But over the past five years, Jadhav noticed that quite a number of parents of girls were approaching him, asking how they could get their daughters into the project. It was the prospect of government employment, he realized. The community was beginning to view girls not as a dowry liability alone, but as a potential asset—someone who might secure a coveted government job.

It made him think once again about food. 'Feed them like you would feed your boys, I told them,' he said. 'Feed them properly if you want them to compete.' A job is in the future, but for now, at least the girls would eat well, he thought.

Jadhav has the build and temperament of a sports administrator—shaven head, paunch held aloft, a gruff air of authority. It is impossible to make much small talk with him. But I noticed that he softened visibly when he interacted with younger children. Perhaps they reminded him of his eleven-year-old daughter. He invited me to watch her perform malkhamb in a group, a traditional form of gymnastics said to have originated in the twelfth century and revived by the Maratha empire in the eighteenth century. Or maybe they reminded him of the girls who studied with him at SSM before they dropped out and disappeared into marriages. Girls like his friend Shobha.

When I returned to Sagroli a year after my first visit, Jadhav took me to meet Shobha at her home, accompanied by Durga. Shobha now lives in Kundalwadi, a village so full of big stores and paved roads that it feels like a small city at first. As we travelled inwards, the lanes got progressively narrower. The area where Shobha lives in a one-room semi-pucca tenement, the lanes have the width of Mumbai balconies, the sewage is uncovered and families of pigs frolic around blithely without much motorized traffic to disturb them. Shobha is a tall, still youthful woman, who looks only a bit older than Durga. But she spoke with an air of resignation and exhaustion that aged her.

'Durga doesn't like to come home. It is difficult for her to adjust here,' Shobha said, looking at me apologetically. The home didn't have a toilet, and she had been unable to secure the grant given by the government of India to build one. When Durga visited, she had to go down to the river to perform her ablutions. 'My older daughter Lakshmi says that I only speak of Durga, but she doesn't come home. She says I don't think of her. That I don't love her. "I will also work. I will be a nurse. I will go abroad," she tells me.'

I got the sense that Shobha was both close to Durga and distant from her, a little intimidated, too, maybe. But Durga was her usual self, the way she was with her hostel mates and class friends—quiet but affectionate, teasing her mother gently and smiling shyly. When Shobha made tea for us, she got up to help her mother and followed her instructions unobtrusively. Next to each other, mother and daughter looked like sisters. Durga seemed genuinely unconscious of the difference in her surroundings, from the wide open spaces and solid buildings of her school to her family's gloomy one-room tenement.

'I am preparing Durga for the police exam,' Jadhav said as we sipped tea. He had told me this earlier, but this was for Shobha's ears. One of the plans he had was to take Shobha back to Sagroli with him, so she could rest for a few days at his home or with her brother Moglaji if she agreed. 'One can apply for police posts right after Class XII. Her mother needs rest. Nursing also costs money. Durga can pay for her sister's degree too.'

On the walk back to our cab, Shobha turned to me and said, 'You tell Durga to work hard and be a good girl.' Once again there was that apologetic smile.

'She is already such a good girl. She should be allowed to have fun, actually,' I said.

Shobha's comment had taken me by surprise. The dynamic between Shobha and Durga was unlike parent and child—they were more like sisters, where Durga was the protective one and Shobha the one who needed looking after. Later it struck me that I had spoken without thinking. That Shoba was painfully aware of the dynamic with Durga, how dependent her little household was on her younger daughter. The hesitancy in her manner, the apologetic smiles, that remark about asking her daughter to be good were all a reflection of her embarrassment. She was trying to say the things a mother is supposed to say. And I had taken away that moment too.

I first read about the Sunrise Project in 2009, when it received a burst of English-language media attention. When the idea for this book took root in my mind from 2014–15, I knew I had to write about the project. For one, it was a rural story and, for another, it was not an individual story. I wanted to understand how communities received the idea of young women playing sport and how it shaped the sense of self in young girls. It was also a story of the new marathon economy of contemporary liberalized India. It also provided an arc for my narrative of runners—from extraordinary individual athletes to a culture of running as a hobby sport and career, shaped by the market.

It is clear that the marathon economy is a neoliberal project, an extension of the belief that the market is a more rational and efficient distributor of resources than the state. The New York City Marathon became a road race in 1976 (it was earlier run in Central Park), a year after the city's municipality went bankrupt. The Marxist scholar David Harvey, writing about the proliferation of city marathons in the late 1970s and the early 1980s, observed that the races were meant to showcase the host cities—Chicago, London, Tokyo, Singapore—as investment destinations, rather than as inclusive urban communities.

In India, over the past fifteen years, the marathon economy has come to be worth Rs 2,900 crore annually, said Vivek Singh, co-founder of Procam International, which organizes several marathon events, including the Mumbai Marathon. The figure he cited included accounting for the sports shoes, athletic gear and fitness equipment sold to hordes of hobby runners. Participation fees, advertising along the running route, a boost to tourism—all of this adds up too.

Then there are the optics of the marathons—thousands of bodies clocking miles around the city, shaping the impression of individuals striving for fitness, taking responsibility for their health and not burdening the healthcare system.

For decades, sport in India had just a handful of funding sources. The biggest was the state, which offered employment through a 'sports quota'. Athletes entered into regular employment with the government, often representing their department in competitions, and advanced their sports career with the backing of a monthly salary. The best example of this is the Indian Army, which has a long tradition of sport and nurturing Olympians. Another source of funding was large family-owned corporate houses, which also instituted a sports quota for their employee pools. Many of them set up and funded academies and professional clubs. The Tatas run a football academy in Jamshedpur and a hockey academy in Odisha. Smaller concerns, from bicycle manufacturers in Tamil Nadu to cloth mills in Punjab, have also funded teams and infrastructure in sports such as football and hockey. The mining giants of Goa run storied football clubs named after their families—which, however, have seen better days. More recently, Jindal Steel Works pumped money into the Inspire Institute of Sport; it also runs club franchises in cricket and football leagues.

The only anomaly is the Board of Control for Cricket in India (BCCI). It is neither a government body, nor backed by a single corporate house, but it is the richest sports authority in India and so enormously successful that sports such as football, badminton and kabaddi have no hope of keeping up. The best they have been able to do in recent years is try and emulate the stupendous success of the Indian Premier League—a BCCI franchise—with their own professional leagues. This is the neoliberal reordering of sports.

However, private concerns and sports associations have not yet displaced the importance of government jobs and the primacy of government funding, which has led to a surfeit of bureaucracy. That bureaucracy's dismissiveness and disinterest in sport plays on loop around us every year, perhaps even every few months. A national or international athlete is found serving tea or performing menial work for their department. The press report leads to some outrage and then it wanes, until another such story is reported.

The results of state support have been meagre in terms of international medals—we all know this. And neither has it facilitated a culture that encourages young people to take up sport as a career either.

What has translated into sports success in recent years has been individual effort, sponsored by private interests. India's medals at the recent Olympics were largely the result of private academy training (the badminton medals for Saina Nehwal and P.V. Sindhu) or a prosperous and supporting family background (as in the case of the shooter Abhinav Bindra). The case of Neeraj Chopra, India's only Olympic gold medallist in track and field, is an exception in that he has a government job. At the time he competed in the Tokyo 2021 Games, he was a subedar in the Indian Army. In an interview in June 2021 before the Tokyo Olympics, Chopra's coach Uwe John said that the Indian government's top sports organizations, namely the Sports Authority of India and the Athletics Federation of India, provided inadequate training and a diet unfit for elite athletes.[19] Chopra could go to Europe for training only because of JSW's Inspire Institute of

Sport, which supports and manages him. Chopra had the stability of a government job and a sports-friendly environment in the army, as well as the big-money push of corporate sponsorship.

The marathon economy is of a piece with the latter—the private, high-end push to sport. For me, Sagroli was a chance to see what it meant to those who fell outside the old networks of government and big-city opportunities—what they call 'the grassroots'.

$$\psi$$

One glorious January evening on the SSM grounds, the school authorities gathered the Sunrise Project cohort for the year 2020–21 to meet me, the visiting journalist. Most of the students were shy, but the few who spoke all articulated clear plans for a career in sport. Becoming a competitive athlete with a government job was their Plan A. Plan B was to take up a coaching role at a private academy. Even the fall-back option was now a life in sport. If the sportsperson hadn't 'made it', they would no longer have to accept whatever fate had in store.

There's also the visible triumph of Lalita Babar, whom we meet in the previous chapter, the first Indian woman to make an Olympic track and field event final after P.T. Usha in 1984. The one who came after thirty-two years. When I told the students at Sagroli that I would be meeting Lalita in Mumbai, the mood shifted visibly. They had been awkward with me—I was an outsider and potentially an authority figure like their teachers. (One more thing set me apart—I was wearing a face mask, unlike anyone else around.)

'We have met her, you know,' said Vishnu Lavale, who was introduced to me as the most promising athlete in the project, and was certainly the most vocal member of the cohort. 'She comes to competitions as the chief guest. We have eaten with her too.

Village athletes are always the best. We are more tough. City people cannot compete with us. They are soft. Lalita Ma'am is the start.'

Some days later, I met Babar at her apartment in Navi Mumbai, located in a towering building complex nestled amid what remains of the Sahyadri hill range.

Although Babar is not sentimental about it in the least, her story is *the* beloved Bombay stereotype. She was the girl from the remote drought-prone village who made it in the big city. In her case, it was literally the city's branded marathon that put her in the limelight. Now she owns a home there—the unambiguous marker of making it in Bombay.

Only about two decades earlier, trekking enthusiasts from Mumbai took day trips up here in Kharghar, where Babar was staying. Now the city itself had arrived, with multilane roads, cab-booking apps and cafés exuding warm, yellow light. This, too, was the neoliberal project advancing—the city claiming extensive areas for development and investment at the cost of the natural environment. Across the country and South Asia, corporate forces looking to profit off land, water and natural resources are in conflict with communities who have worked and known the land for generations.

Sport comes bundled as part of this development, and not only through marathons to showcase the shining cities in which they take place. Sport is a peace offering, part of legally mandated social-responsibility initiatives in the countryside. As big money travels deeper into communities, leaving unambiguous evidence of ecological impoverishment, sports grounds and athletic achievements are one of the answers set to be furnished for what has been gained.

In fact, the city had arrived in Sagroli too. When I visited in January 2022, panchayat elections in Maharashtra were under way. In Sagroli, the results were unprecedented. Nine of the seventeen seats in the gram panchayat went to candidates aligned with the

Deshmukhs of SSM; the remaining eight went to the opposition. This is the first time since panchayat elections began in the 1960s that any seats have been won by candidates standing in opposition to the Deshmukh family's candidates, teachers in SSM said. This time, the central issue was the mining of the Manjeera river for sand, and its attendant erosion, not only of the soil but also of the community. The Deshmukhs had opposed the sand mining for several years, but things had come to a head in the recent months. Income from the mining industry was leading to increased alcohol consumption and unregulated construction, and was pulling labour away from agricultural work. Mining is also polluting by nature—its machines and construction lead to the erosion of land, raising the possibility of agricultural cultivation in the adjoining areas becoming difficult with time. But most of all, the effect was political—the infusion of cash by the mining industry was eroding the long-unquestioned caste-based authority of the Deshmukhs.

The Deshmukhs and SSM oppose the aggressive cash-rich mining industry eroding the traditional, agricultural and, in recent decades, education-centred community in Sagroli. It is an interesting confrontation. In any other place, the mining industry would sooner or later provide a sports facility for the community there. But in Sagroli, that is already present, and a sponsorship of SSM's sports projects, while not impossible, is unlikely. Across the Global South, industry is offering sports and education projects as a token of investing in communities. The story of SSM suggests that when communities, or the state, have arranged for education and other forms of community development, these inroads may not be so easy for capital-rich industry.

In my travels as a reporter, I have often come across small grounds and stadiums maintained by companies working in cement, mineral refinement, car production and industrial goods. These are lovely

IN THE SWIFTLY failing 5 o'clock light of an April evening in Kolkata, the staircase of the cream-yellow government housing quarters on CIT Road was shrouded in darkness. Summer days and afternoons burn white-hot in Bengal, but evenings descend quickly here, the light retreating almost apologetically, as if to offer some relief from the fierce heat of the summer day. The thrifty white tube lights of the stairway were yet to be switched on. The air was thick with sleep—the exhausted sleep of a city haemorrhaging through a terrifying pandemic and a hot summer.

I tapped my mobile phone's torch on and slowly felt my way up the steps—broad, gentle steps made to the measurements of a different age. The deep-red cement floor was thick with dust, the corners marked by shiny pan masala packets, cigarette stubs and the reddish stains of chewed tobacco juice. This was not a building that afforded daily cleaning maintenance. At each landing I checked the door for the name or number. On the second floor, in the gloomy circle of light cast by my mobile phone, I saw the name I was looking for written in the Bengali alphabet: Ila Mitra. A woman's name on the door is unusual, so is the Bengali lettering, even in a city whose airport celebrates the Bengali alphabet. Mitra was one of the most formidable communist activists in India, one of the earliest members of the mothership Communist Party of India (CPI), which gave birth to the later Marxist, Leninist and Maoist factions of the party in India and her neighbours in the subcontinent—Pakistan, Bangladesh, Nepal and Sri Lanka.

When I began this book in 2014–15, Ila Mitra nee Sen's name popped up in a blog in one of my earliest internet searches for women athletes in the subcontinent. She was a basketball player and a star track athlete in the 1930s, and later a politician. The first blogs led to a handful of other blogs, but there was nothing more substantial than that—not even a Wikipedia page with thin references. There were no newspaper reports on her, not even obituaries. I moved on to women who had left a more substantive trail in physical news archives and the internet—news stories, blogs and Facebook pages. How do you trace the threads that draw out a memory, a story, a figure from history? On the internet, one link dissolves into another until you find the trail that takes you inside the story. But with Mitra, there was no trail—the links led to blanks. She had popped up suddenly on my radar but, eventually, faced with dead end after dead end, she receded from my mind.

Then one day deep in the midst of the Covid-19 pandemic, I woke up with her name on my mind again, as if she had tapped me in my sleep to remind me that I had once gone looking for her. This time when I typed in the names Ila Mitra and Ila Sen, a number of links popped up, some of them quite detailed. What had happened in the intervening years? Had someone digitized a forgotten archive? Had someone written about Ila Mitra after my trail went cold? As I explored the links, I realized that nearly all of them were from Bangladesh. And nearly all of them were in Bengali. I had relied only on the English-language links, I had not pursued the Bengali ones. She had been lost in translation, it would seem.

My Bengali used to be elementary, learnt as a distant third language for a couple of years in school before the syllabus allowed me to forget it. Although I am Bengali, I had become like much of the upper middle class in post-liberalization India—monolingual. For a long time, the only language I was comfortable in was English. I thought in English, I wrote in English, I read in English. This changed somewhat during the first year spent in lockdown during the Covid pandemic in India. I was among the most privileged, who did not have to spend the year battling for life or to make ends meet or scramble to go home. Like much of my upper-middle-class ilk, I amused myself with a lockdown challenge. Instead of baking sourdough bread, whipping up cold coffee or recording music, I taught myself to read in Bengali again. Over six months, I read three stout Bengali novels in succession—the first took me three months to finish, the second two months, the third a month. By the autumn of the year, I had started to prefer reading Bengali novels to English, unimaginable at the beginning of my language adventure.

This time I found a good bit of online material on Ila Mitra. As a schoolgirl, she was a star on the Calcutta track in the 1930s. In 1937 and 1938, the sports club Jatiya Juba Sangha awarded her successive junior championship titles for girls in Bengal. In 1938, the Bengali journal *Sachitra Bharat* featured the thirteen-year-old Ila in a collage of senior sports achievers, which included the British Indian hockey team, a mountaineer setting off for Tibet and 10-mile walking champions. Later, when Ila would become a well-known name in the 1950s and the 1960s in Bengal and erstwhile East Pakistan, several Bengali newspapers and periodicals would describe her as the first Indian woman to be selected to compete at the Olympics. She was slated to represent British India at the 1940 Olympics in Tokyo, which was cancelled for the Second World War. I would find no official report of Ila's selection, only the later news stories that retrospectively mention her selection.

She was also a front-line leader of one of the most vital peasant movements in the subcontinent, the Tebhaga Andolan. A revolutionary who was jailed on charges of murdering four policemen. She was perhaps the first woman in the subcontinent to publicly articulate the experience of rape when she gave testimony before the Rajshahi court in 1951. She was a communist legislator, who won four elections after coming out of jail, where she was savagely gang-raped. This time, I found so much on her that it was surprising how I had missed all of it.

One of the blogs in Bengali turned out to be written by Ila's grandson Riten, a professor of bioinformatics based in the US. When I e-mailed him, he responded immediately, connecting me to his father, Ila's son Ronendranath, who lived in that flat where I found myself that evening. How did it fall into place so easily this time? As if Ila was connecting us personally.

I pressed the bell outside the door. From within came the muffled, groggy sounds of a household waking up. Outside, a human voice swelled slowly, filling the air with a familiar song. The human voice in song, unembellished by accompaniment, is so stirring. My phone told me it was almost 6 p.m., time for azan. I knew this sound so well from my childhood. Kolkata is the proverbial city of mosques, churches and synagogues and Kali temples—including Chinese and Portuguese Kali shrines. But it is a sound that has grown unusual to me now. From the new millennium, upper-middle-class Kolkata has increasingly gated itself into closed communities. Even communist Bengal was not untouched by the post-liberalization economy of India after 1991. The affluent, glossy jobs in the new economy, which drew away members of the upper middle class to other cities, meant substantive remittances sent back home. Moreover, liberalization brought the one truly global industry of the twenty-first-century economy—real estate development—to the city. With it came the new urban design of exclusion—gated complexes and their attendant security guards. Kolkata was always a segregated city, despite the many communities living alongside one another. Now it had been putting up physical walls and gates. Privileged by caste and class, I had in recent years lived in localities where the azan could not be heard. As it happened, I heard the call to prayer more often in popular Hindi films.

In the vicinity of the Linton Road post office bus stop, where I had been instructed to get down, I counted three mosques. About two streets away, and five minutes by car without traffic, is Christopher Road, with its row of large laundry and dry-cleaning stores with Chinese-style lettering in their signage. This is the main road of Tangra, the sole surviving Chinatown in India. Ila's home was in Entally, historically one of Calcutta's truly mixed localities, with a history of large European residences (from the mid-nineteenth century—1830s or so), a living Chinese settlement and the homes of lower-caste Hindu and Muslim communities.[1] This was the area where the Albanian-born missionary Anjeze Gonxhe Bojaxhiu first worked when she arrived in Calcutta in 1929, teaching at the Loreto Convent school, where she eventually set up her organization The Missionaries of Charity and came to be known as Mother Teresa. Entally is, in brief, a snapshot of the Calcutta that you hear of in beloved stereotypes, indeed of India itself—that place where mosque and church and Kali mandir and piggery sit cheek by jowl without inflaming into physical violence. A place of miracle, almost.

Kolkata was not like Calcutta any more, not by far, except for this little pocket that felt like something out of a fairy tale. It felt deserving of Ila Mitra.

In the photograph of hers that is most commonly found on the internet, Ila is wearing plain plastic-frame spectacles, her wispy hair parted at the centre, a few strands astray behind her left ear. Her neck is thin and long, her collarbones conspicuous from her neck to her shoulders, her cheeks barely there. She gazes directly at you without smiling—a frail old woman with tired eyes and a determined set to her jaws.

It's hard to tell whether she is in her sixties or her seventies.

It's a look I recognize from my own grandmothers. Both were thin in a way that my parents' generation of the upper middle class was not, and that slenderness kept them youthful looking. When age hit them, a point that came early in my childhood, they became frail, bird-like, and seemingly ageless. You couldn't put a number to their years. When they walked, you always found yourself watching, because it was the feather-light walk of a small bird and you never really got used to seeing it in a human being.

But the photo that brought me to her doorstep was different. A moon-faced girl in a white shirt and soft, crinkly shorts, smiling shyly at the camera with forty-odd trophies arranged around her. The star athlete who was anointed junior girls' champion in the Bengal Presidency in 1937 and 1938. It gives you a start to realize that the thin, tired old woman looking straight at the camera was once the cheerful, full-cheeked girl who had won all those trophies. But something of the athlete always remained in her, her son Ronendranath Mitra told me.

When I visited the matchbox-sized flat in Entally allotted to her by the CPI, Ila had been dead for twenty years. Ronendranath was seventy-three, a slim, elegantly straight-backed man with a quiet, affectionate manner. Ronen, as he is called, never saw his mother walk without the shadow of a limp, although she walked fast and a lot. His first memory of her was when he was taken to a hospital to visit her, a feeble bundle on a bed who, he was told, was dying.

'I think I was about five when I was told my mother was on her deathbed. I was taken to Dhaka jail to see her,' Ronen said. 'It was confusing for me, because I lived with my paternal grandmother and had no memory of my mother. I always thought of my grandma as my mother, and the woman I saw lying listlessly on the hospital bed was a stranger. I felt bad for her, but I was relieved that my "real mother" was not dying. The first time I lived with my mother and father was when I was seven years old. My mother would mostly lie on the bed and could only walk with the help of my father. Then, as she got better, she started walking with a stick. Then she started hobbling without one. At the time I did not know how ill she had been, but I watched her progress on her feet. It was like watching a baby learn to walk, except the roles were reversed. Her willpower was amazing! It was all very exciting for me anyway, my first time living with my mother and father, as other children did.'

Ronen took out two pristinely maintained scrapbooks, his maternal grandfather's labour of love. Nagendranath Sen had diligently archived his daughter Ila's news clippings, annotating with a neat hand the dates and names of the publications. Over the years 1937 to 1940, Ila Sen was a somewhat familiar presence on the sports pages of Bengali- and English-language newspapers and journals in Calcutta. Several of these were photographs—of Ila arching skywards at the finishing line, or on the podium, or posing with her contemporaries on the field. It is possibly the only visual evidence of Ila in action on the field—there probably exists no video evidence of her career in sport.

Born in 1925, Ila was the eldest of six siblings—three sisters and three brothers. Calcutta was no longer the capital of British India from 1912, but remained its largest and wealthiest city, the second most important city of the British Empire. By virtue of being the deputy accountant general of the presidency, her father Nagendranath was an influential and powerful official.

Ila studied in the historic Bethune School that opened in 1849, only the second girls' school in colonial India after Jyotiba and Savitribai Phule started their own at Bhide Wada near Pune in the Bombay Presidency in 1848. In 1879, Bethune was expanded to become the first women's college in Asia. Although the first principal of the school was the Englishman John Elliot Drinkwater Bethune, after whom the institution was named, the initiative came from the energy and enterprise of the reformer Ishwar Chandra Bandyopadhyay (known as Vidyasagar). From Kadambini Ganguly, the first female Indian medical graduate, and Chandramukhi Basu, the first woman to earn a postgraduate degree in Asia, to firebrand nationalists such as Kalpana Dutta and Pritilata Waddedar, who accomplished daring acts of rebellion against the British colonial government, Bethune has produced women who seem to have walked out of the writings of Bankim Chandra Chattopadhyay, Ishwar Chandra Vidyasagar and Rabindranath Tagore.

Even by the standards of this school, Ila was consistently an overachiever. From 1937, when she was about twelve years old, she was an almost regular presence on the sports pages of newspapers in Calcutta for her triumphs on the track. Nagendranath was invested in his daughter's sports career, working around his office schedule to escort her to College Square for swimming practice and to her many track competitions around the city. He would cut out news stories of his daughter and paste them in a scrapbook, noting the date and publication with an ink pen. Her photographs, too, appeared in the sports sections of newspapers—standing with other winners, and a couple of times in the thick of action in a race, her eyes scrunched in effort, torso arching skywards in that swan-like posture of athletes at the finishing line. Aside from track athletics, Ila also excelled in badminton, basketball, the tenniquoit throw and swimming.

Much of what I had found on the internet—the blog posts and the media stories—likely took their information from Nagendranath's scrapbooks and photo albums, which his grandson Ronendranath has preserved beautifully in Kolkata's murderously humid climate. It was most likely he who arranged for that photograph of Ila's, her trophies organized neatly on a table next to her—to my mind, the most evocative visual record of one of the Bengal Presidency's finest athletes. Without this photograph, it would be easy to miss just how much and how often Ila had won. It's one thing to note and count her photos and mentions in newspapers and journals, quite another to see her surrounded by rows of trophies reaching up to her shoulders.

In 1940, when Helsinki was preparing to host the twelfth Summer Olympics and war had broken out in Europe, Nagendranath received news through his colonial administration network that his fifteen-year-old daughter was being considered for the Olympic contingent that would represent British India. But the outbreak of the Second World War led to the Olympics being cancelled, and there remains no official communication from the British government about Ila's selection.

She was fifteen that year. At that age, disappointment hurts. There is nothing she has left behind to tell us how she felt—nothing in writing, no conversations with her family that they recall, no regrets listed out. 'I feel foolish about it now, but I used to try to stay out of her reach when she was home,' her grandson Ritendranath told me over a Zoom call from Louiseville in the US, where he lives. 'She would wake me up at the crack of dawn to take me swimming, and I hated it. She would sit me down to pore over my Bengali lessons if I was home in the evenings. My favourite grandparent was my [paternal] grandfather. He taught me lessons too—in maths and science—but he was less impatient, less in a hurry. Thakma was always in a hurry, always going somewhere.'

Whatever she felt, she jumped into college with energy. She won the badminton intercollege championship in 1940 and 1941, and was part of the Bethune College team that won the basketball championship in 1941. In addition, she passed her Intermediate examination—the equivalent of Class XII examinations today—in the first class and enrolled for a degree in Bengali at the same college.

It was these years in university that shaped her life. Reports of food shortage, hunger and rising prices had already started coming in from the countryside by 1940, but the British colonial government was preoccupied with the war with the Axis powers. In December 1941, the Japanese bombed Rangoon in Burma (now Yangon in Myanmar), marking an advance in the east that would not be halted until the Battle of Kohima in 1943. In the winter of 1942, a vicious cyclone hit the district of Medinipur in Bengal. The cyclone, the refugees from Burma and the war sparked a devastating shortage of food, leading to an official death toll of three million people in the man-made famine of 1943–44. The official figure is believed to be a massive undercount of the starvation deaths that took place between 1942 and 1944.

'And when I got admission in Bethune College, I joined the Girl Students Committee. There we began to discuss Marxism,' Ila had told the academic Kavita Panjabi in an interview for her book *Unclaimed Harvest*. 'We did this secretly. Gradually, through my relief work, I became a party member.'[2]

The Mahila Atma Raksha Samiti (MARS) of the CPI was formed in 1942, at first to prevent the trafficking of women for sex to soldiers of the Allied Forces, by desperate families pushed to starvation by soaring food prices and scarcity. Soon, the idea of atma raksha (self-protection) was extended to protection from hunger, poverty and violence. MARS travelled across Bengal for relief work, standing vigil at night to safeguard women, setting up langarkhanas (community kitchens) to feed the starving and advocating for individual rights and community action. For the first time in modern India, as Kavita Panjabi writes in *Unclaimed Harvest*, women became participants in public relief work. It was a horrific time, yet also a heady moment in history.

In 1944, the year Ila graduated from college, Nagendranath went to meet a prospective groom named Ramendranath Mitra, the son of a landowning family in Ramchandrapur Hat, Nawabganj district, who had decided never to hold a job because he identified as a worker of the CPI. Presumably the two held opposing political convictions, but Nagendranath came back and told his family that he would not find 'a ratno', a gem, like Ramendranath again. Though Ila identified as a feminist, she did not appear to oppose the idea of being married or, indeed, agreeing to an arranged marriage. Or perhaps she agreed to the match because she approved of the groom's party affiliation. She did not write her thoughts on her marriage, but it would be, by every account, a very happy union.

In 1947, Ila's mother-in-law Biswamaya Mitra made an unusual decision. She decided that the family would stay on in Nawabganj and not come away to India after the subcontinent was partitioned into India and Pakistan. The Mitras' zamindari estate fell to the right of the Radcliffe Line, the boundary between India and Pakistan on the eastern side of the subcontinent. The line was named after Sir Cyril Radcliffe, the British government official who mapped the boundary, a man who was said to have 'never travelled east of Paris'.

Most land-owning Hindu Bengali families chose to come away to West Bengal, likely imagining that they would be more secure in a country that did not identify itself as an Islamic state. Quite a few of them were like the Mitras—Hindu zamindar families with land tilled by Muslim peasant tenants. Biswamaya believed the trust between the family and its tenants could not be broken by an arbitrary line drawn after five weeks of work by a British government servant.[3] So the family stayed back in East Pakistan.

For Ila, the first couple of years of marriage were suffocating. Biswamaya, a powerful widow who had managed her estate since her husband's passing, expected her to stay home and perform the role of a zamindar household's daughter-in-law—cooking and caring for the family and looking the part of a wealthy bride. She was not permitted to step out or talk to those outside the household without permission, maintaining the upper-caste distinction between the andarmahal and baharmahal (private and public areas) of the home. Used to conquering the swimming pools and sports grounds of Calcutta and then working in the langarkhanas of the CPI, Ila chafed at these controls.

Eventually, she secured permission to start a school for children in the village of Krishna Gobindapur, less than 400 metres from her new home. She was not permitted to walk, however, and had to travel the few hundred metres in an assigned bullock cart. She started her school with three students, but within three months, the number of students swelled to fifty. Eventually, Ila also received the permission to walk to school and back by herself. Both boys and girls studied with her and this caused a fissure in the Muslim community in the area. Wealthy landowning Muslims raised objections to girls stepping out of the house to study, clearly using sharia law as a cover. But Muslim peasants resisted. They pointed out that if the sharia did not permit girls to study, it also held that charging interest on the loans the landowners gave them was haram.

The clarity and conviction of the peasants gave Ila the purpose she was looking for. Now that she had the permission to step out of the estate, she, alongside her husband, worked on mobilizing the peasants—even after she gave birth to her first (and only) child Ronendranath in 1948. She found a shelter in the Santhal leader Matla Majhi's home, and husband and wife helped the movement grow around Chandipur village. Their infant son lived under Biswamaya's care. Ila would occasionally visit her son after dark, clandestinely, at their estate.

Unlike her husband Ramendranath, whom the farmers and landless labourers knew as their zamindar's son, Ila struggled to gain their trust. She was a strange new entity to them, not only as a person but also as a figure—a zamindar's daughter-in-law who worked amid the subjects. '[S]ince I was the daughter-in-law of a zamindar family, no one talked to me, and neither did they believe that I could do anything good for them,' she told Bangladeshi writer Maleka Begum, who wrote the biography *Ila Mitra*. 'Anyway, I continued to sleep with them on the same bed, eat the same food with them, wear the same kind of clothes—dirty clothes—as they did. Then, as I gradually started to talk to them about my organisation, I began earning their trust and they started listening to me. But for one whole year, they hadn't trusted me ...'[4]

Here, her experience in famine relief proved useful. She had gained some ideas of solidarity across classes, but she seemed to have retained some of the biases of an upper-caste urban woman of privilege. Her remembrance of the time clearly suggests her discomfort at adjusting to their way of life, their 'dirty clothes'. The name she acquired among them is perhaps a reflection of both the affection the peasants had for her and the distance they sensed— 'Ranima', or queen mother.

The Tebhaga Andolan centred on the demand that peasants would give landlords one-third of the harvest (one of three portions, or 'teen bhaag') and not half, as had been the practice until then. The movement began in the harvest season of 1946, when the memories of the horrific hunger of the Bengal famine of 1943 were still strong. The CPI halted the movement in 1947 for Independence, but in March 1948 the movement was renewed on both sides of the border.

The peasants had other resentments too. It was common practice, for instance, for a peasant's newlywed wife to be called to have sex with the 'borokhoda' (jotedar or zamindar) on the first night after the wedding, Panjabi writes in *Unclaimed Harvest*. At first, the CPI was reluctant to address what it viewed as personal or domestic problems, but discussions about the outsized sense of proprietorship of landowners led to the party adopting resolutions against such sexual exploitation. Gradually, the party would also address acts of domestic violence by their own members, listening to women members who complained of being beaten by their husbands.

Ila and Ramendranath were well positioned to take up the movement in their area. It was to their *own* family that the peasants would refuse to submit half the harvest, a relatively easy beginning to the protest, given that the son and daughter-in-law of the zamindari were asking them to retain two-thirds of the share. If there was opposition from within the Mitra household, it has not been recorded. But other zamindars and jotedars in the area were naturally angered by the work of the Mitras. By the end of 1949, there were unmistakeable signs of a battle on the horizon, Begum has written in *Ila Mitra*. The number of Tebhaga supporters grew, reaching thousands at one point. Armed with bows, arrows and a kind of spear called 'ballam', the volunteers patrolled the villages to guard the villagers from the henchmen of zamindars, jotedars and the police. This created a sense of confidence and perhaps daring among the villagers. It was decided that if there was an attack on the participants of the movement, a red cloth would be hoisted on a bamboo pole and the madol drum would be beaten as a call for villagers to gather.

The occasion for this arose quite soon. On 5 January 1950, the officer-in-charge (OC) of the Nachole police station arrived in the Kendua Ghechua village in the area accompanied by three constables to search for the leaders of the movement. They entered the home of a peasant named Suren Barman, and beat him and two other farmers on the charge of sheltering Tebhaga leaders. The red flag was hoisted and the madol drum played. Four or five thousand men and women gathered with bows, arrows and ballams. All four policemen were killed in the confrontation.

In response, 2,000 policemen gathered at the Amnura police station and surrounded the villages around Nachole. With far more potent ammunition at their disposal, the police set fire to twelve villages and assaulted several men and women. The brute force of the attack left the villagers only one option—escape. Ila, dressed as a Santhal woman, left with 300–400 villagers of Chandipur with the intention of crossing the border into India. Her husband Ramendranath was elsewhere, as husband and wife typically moved separately to avert attention.

At the Rohanpur station, where Ila was waiting to board a train with a group of Santhals on 7 January 1950, she came to the attention of the police because she was the only person wearing a wristwatch.

She was arrested and taken to the Nachole police station, where she was kept nude in a solitary cell and given no food or water. That night, the sub-inspector (SI) and a few other policemen entered her cell and hit her on the head with the butts of their rifles. She bled from the nose and the head, but her clothes were returned to her. Later that night, she was taken to what was likely the SI's personal quarters and administered the 'Pakistani injection'—a handkerchief was stuffed into her mouth as her legs were crushed between two lathis. Afterwards, the policemen carried her to her cell because she was unable to walk.

The SI was waiting in Ila's cell. On her arrival, he ordered four freshly hard-boiled eggs. 'Now she shall speak,' he said. Four or five policemen held her flat on the floor and one of them placed the steaming egg inside her vagina. She lost consciousness. Six decades later, in 2011, when the Adivasi schoolteacher Soni Sori detailed her experience in police custody before the media, she spoke of stones being inserted into her vagina. The medical report from the public

Nil Ratan Sircar Medical College and Hospital in Kolkata confirmed
the presence of stones in her vagina and rectum.[5] Sixty years apart,
how similarly the governments of Pakistan and India treated the
bodies of women in their custody.

When Ila regained consciousness, the SI and his colleagues
kicked her in the stomach with their boots on. Then they stabbed
her right ankle with a nail. Later, four or five men held her down
and a policeman began to rape her. She lost consciousness soon after.

This routine continued for four days. Ila burnt up with fever and
slipped in and out of consciousness with little sense of day or night.
Then she was transferred to the Nawabganj jail. She registered this
change because a policeman kicked her awake when she was being
taken in and she read the name 'Nawabganj Jail' at the gate. But the
jail warden there, O.C. Rahman, had been her batchmate at Calcutta
University. They had met in the heady days of famine relief. He
arranged for a doctor's visit to her cell. She learnt she was running a
temperature of 105 degrees Fahrenheit. Although she remained jailed
until 1954, she would receive medical treatment thereafter.

'I was able to withstand those days, that torture, because of
my fitness as an athlete, I think,' Ila later told her biographer.
The 'Pakistani injection' left her with a slight limp for the rest of
her life. Even before the arrest, it had not been an easy life. The
police, working at the behest of the government, which backed the
zamindars and the jotedars, were always on the lookout for the leaders
of the Tebhaga movement. As the movement gathered momentum,
the chase did too. Ila and her comrades were always on the move and
often on the run. They hid in wells, slipped into rivers, walked miles
in the night, and sometimes simply ran for hours to evade capture.
It was not the kind of life a deputy accountant-general's daughter
would be used to.

In January 1951, Mitra testified about her custodial torture before the Rajshahi court, possibly becoming the first woman from the subcontinent to publicly articulate her experience of gang rape. Begum wrote that Ila was reluctant to speak of the rape and abuse, but the CPI coaxed her into it. Since the case was subjudice, an in-depth news story was not possible. But the party published her testimony as a pamphlet and distributed it in West Bengal and East Pakistan.

It proved to be a brilliant move. Her story moved the citizens of East Pakistan to protest against their police and the government's treatment of her. Bengali poets from both sides of the border, Subhash Mukherjee from West Bengal and Ghulam Khuddus from East Pakistan, wrote poems about her. More importantly for Ila, not a single Muslim or Santhal peasant gave testimony against her. In fact, not a single credible account testifying against her was registered. The prosecution produced some clearly tutored witnesses in court, some of whom were so nervous that when asked to identify Ila Mitra, they repeated their own names. Short of evidence, the court could not convict her of the murder of the four policemen. She was, however, sentenced to seven years for the violence that had led to the killings.

Ila's landmark 'joban-bondi (testimony)' probably moved the judge and authorities to a degree of leniency as well. In 1953, when her health deteriorated so sharply that it was thought she was close to death, the police moved her to a hospital in Dhaka. Then, in 1954, she was given parole to go to Calcutta for treatment. She would only return in 1996, on the twenty-fifth anniversary of Bangladesh, as a state guest, when the cases against her were no longer in effect as they were lodged by the erstwhile government of East Pakistan that had ceased to exist.

In Calcutta, Ila began life anew, although the first several months passed like in Dhaka—horizontal on a hospital bed. When she was permitted to go home, Ramendranath took her for 'hawa bodol', the delightful Bengali expression for a change of scene (and air), to the stout, plateau-like hills of Ghatshila in present-day Jharkhand. There, for the first time, husband and wife lived with their son Ronendranath. He was then seven years old.

Gradually, as Ila recovered, she took her MA exams as a private candidate, scoring first-class marks with the help of notes from her MA classmates, the celebrated actor Soumitra Chattopadhyay and the distinguished poet Sankha Ghosh. By 1962, by sheer force of will (and daily exercise), Ila completed her MA degree, secured a job as a lecturer at Sivanath Sastri College in south Calcutta, contested elections as a legislator from Maniktala constituency and won her seat. She represented this constituency until 1977, participating energetically in the Khadya Andolan of the 1950s and 1960s, which demanded adequate public distribution of food by the government and stringent anti-hoarding measures, because people were still going hungry in independent India.

In her biography, Begum quotes Ila about an incident that reshaped her understanding of political work:

After our arrest, I watched the police [at the Nachole police station] beat a farmer called Hawrek to death, asking him for information about the leaders of the movement ... about me. He didn't name me. Some months ago, the party had stopped assigning work to Hawrek after he failed to fulfil a responsibility handed to him. His cows had got lost, he had said, and it took him so long to find them that he could not do the party work. It made the party take him less seriously. Some days later, when he realised he was no longer given party responsibilities, he was hurt. 'Who do you think of yourselves,' he had said in a meeting one day. 'I can give my life for the party.' And he did, right before my eyes.

Hawrek's courage made her feel so small. She could never forget him, and the fact that parties and movements are most of all made up of the people, not leaders. Perhaps that is why Ila never got bitter, even when she found herself sidelined when the communists stormed to power in West Bengal in 1977, led by the new Communist party, the Communist Party of India (Marxist), or CPI(M).

After 1977, she was no longer a legislator, but remained a committed party worker, sitting at the CPI party office every afternoon after finishing her work in college. Indeed, she maintained a packed schedule for much of her life—teaching in college until retirement, doing party work in the afternoons, offering private tuition in the evenings and translating party-approved books from Russian to Bengali late into the night. She was her family's only earning member, which explains her name on the apartment door in part. Her husband Ramendranath helped her prepare her lessons for college and tuitions, and assisted with translation work. But he held firm to his commitment to never work a job himself, because he identified himself as a communist worker. Even until a fortnight before her death in 2001, she woke up every day before dawn, caught the first bus from Entally to Golpark, and swam at the Anderson Club before taking another bus to college.

In the decades when she no longer held public office, she was an annual or semi-annual presence in Bengali newspapers and magazines, featured or interviewed for her views on feminism and sport. She was almost always asked for her views on India's Olympic performances when the quadrennial event came around. Her views were reliably socialist and critical of the government for its chronic

underfunding of sport, and she never pointed fingers at individuals
for not being as disciplined as she was in her time—that convenient
generational denunciation.

After the Seoul Olympics, Ila wrote in an op-ed in the Bengali-
language newspaper *Ganashakti* in October 1988,

> Only one swimming pool. The central or state government does
> not have the resources to build more. Whatever one does is the
> individual's own striving. These are the conditions in many Third
> World countries. But their sense of identity, of national pride is
> such that they invest in learning new techniques to improve their
> performance.
>
> Today, sport has reached a standard where talent and
> commitment are not enough to excel. You need scientific training
> and the latest equipment and infrastructure, and nutrient dense
> food …
>
> Actually, we lack a national sports policy, the imagination
> to develop a culture of sport. The results of this myopia are in
> front of us.

Easily the most memorable feature on Ila was a full-page Sunday
special in October 1988 on her life and work in *Aajkal*, a small
influential Bengali broadsheet daily known for its sport and political
coverage in particular. The package comprised personal essays by
Ila's colleagues in teaching and politics, and profiles of her legacy
by political reporters, anchored with a lead image of Ila swimming.
Another image featured her in a one-piece swimsuit on a pool ladder.
Images of women in swimwear were unusual on the news pages of
pre-liberalization India. When a woman did appear in a bathing
suit in the public sphere, such as the actor Sharmila Tagore in the
Hindi film *An Evening in Paris* (1967), it was written about for years,

albeit admiringly for Tagore's confidence and oomph. Even in the film, Tagore's character wore the bikini overseas in the heady precincts of Paris, not in India.

In this special package, Ila wrote about herself:

> I am 63 but guess why I am not an old woman yet? There's only one reason. I know the rules to keep myself fit and I follow them diligently. Every day I wake up kaak bhorey [that hour just before dawn when the crows call] and step out of my government housing flat in Entally to catch the first bus that brings me to Golpark. To the Anderson Club to swim. I swim for 40 minutes straight. I have a swimming costume but not a swimmer's cap. It doesn't bother me to swim without one. As I swim, I feel my age being peeled away. I tell myself I am fighting age with each stroke. Fight! At the same time, swimming is also my hobby. Every stroke fills me with joy and resolve …
>
> … It was because of my mental strength and my training in sports that I could withstand the police torture I faced.

The most public tribute to her sports career came at the South Asian Games in 2010 in Dhaka. Bangladesh was the host country, and the opening ceremony included a fifteen-minute dance drama on Ila's work with peasants in the Tebhaga Andolan, and her subsequent arrest and custodial gang rape.[6] The voice-over introducing her described her as an athlete who was selected for the 1940 Olympics in Tokyo, which was cancelled for the Second World War.

It was an apt venue for remembering her. The South Asian Games is a political event rather than a sporting one. It marks an economic bloc of postcolonial nations that were part of the British Empire until seventy-five years ago. The sports on offer is not the point, the political statement is. In 2010, the host was Bangladesh, a place that

Ila felt especially close to. She had come of age as a political activist with the Tebhaga Andolan there, and when she was charged with the murder of four policemen, the farmers and agricultural workers in Nachole had refused to name her in their testimony, enabling her to avoid a murder charge. And indeed, it is Bangladesh that seems to remember Ila Mitra with great fondness today. India, even West Bengal, barely so. This is the reason almost all the material available on Ila on the internet is in Bengali: It comes from Bangladesh.

There is no greater theatre of national pride than sport. Sportspersons who compete at the national and international level are celebrated as heroic, and they themselves (usually) demonstrate pride in their national identity. This is natural, given the ceremonies of high nationalism in sport. The national anthems of the competing teams or winning sportspersons are broadcast at the start of play or during the prize ceremony, sports uniforms display national motifs, international sports competitions typically kick off with a flag parade of participating nations. From the 1940s to this moment, India's sports record has been largely dismal. This is understandable, given how poor we are as a nation. Moreover, the culture of competitive sport is wholly imported from the colonial project. Excellence in sport, as against simply playing sport, is not a cultural habit.

Yet, from the 1980s in particular, the media in India and the Union government have projected sports stars as hallowed beings. The 1980s were a special decade in sport for India—not only because Prakash Padukone won the prestigious All England Open Badminton Championships in 1980, India won its first World Cup in cricket in 1983 and P.T. Usha blazed her way to what is arguably the most celebrated fourth-place finish at the Olympics in 1984, but also because live sports telecasting began with the 1982 Asian Games in Delhi. To my mind, the act of watching changed the status of sport in India. As viewers enjoying the beauty and thrill of sport, we also started following and admiring sportspersons. Corporates doing business in India began to choose sports heroes as brand ambassadors. The first of these is World Cup-winning cricket captain Kapil Dev, who appeared in a popular advertisement for a Palmolive shaving cream. Post-liberalization, when Pepsi arrived in India, it signed up Sachin Tendulkar, Mohammad Azharuddin and Vinod Kambli, the most prominent members of the Indian men's cricket team, as brand ambassadors. Over the past decade and more, a handful of other sports stars such as boxer Mary Kom, badminton players Saina Nehwal and P.V. Sindhu—all Olympic medallists—have also bagged prominent advertising campaigns.

Popular Hindi films of the past decade are another indication. Sports stories have yielded mammoth blockbusters such as *Lagaan, Chak De! India, Bhaag Milkha Bhaag, Dangal, Sultan* and *M.S. Dhoni,* and smaller hits such as *Mary Kom.* These films are often critically acclaimed too. In 2002, *Lagaan* became the first Indian film to make the shortlist for the best foreign film Oscar after *Mother India* in 1958. Several other sports projects in Hindi, with major A-list stars, are in the making. Typically, these films have at least one sequence where the Indian flag is shown fluttering, sometimes overlaid with the Indian national anthem.

But over the past decade, with the ascent of Prime Minister Narendra Modi and his brand of muscular nationalism, a further layer of influence has accrued. Sportspersons have become prominent political voices on behalf of the BJP-led government of India. On 3 February 2021, badminton Olympic medallist Saina Nehwal tweeted a mass-circulation message put out by the BJP government, hours after pop star Rihanna posted an even-tempered question about the farmer protests, the longest-sustained protest in independent India. 'Why aren't we talking about this?' Rihanna had asked, and shared a link to a CNN story about the movement against the farm Bills rammed through Parliament in 2020 giving corporates greater control over the agriculture sector. In response, Nehwal wrote, 'Farmers constitute an extremely important part of our country. And the efforts being undertaken to resolve their issues are evident. Let's support an amicable resolution, rather than paying attention to anyone creating differences. Folded hands#IndiaTogether #IndiaAgainstPropaganda.'[7]

On 15 April 2020, during the first long lockdown amid Covid-19, the Commonwealth Games medal-winning wrestler Babita Phogat tweeted saying India's biggest problem was not Covid-19 but Jamaatis, implying Muslims.[8] When she was criticized on social media for her Islamophobia, Phogat posted a video saying she stood by her tweet. On 23 December 2019, when the protests against the explicitly anti-Muslim Citizenship Amendment Act 2019 were taking place, the largest movement led by women in post-Independence India, badminton star Saina Nehwal tweeted once again what appeared to be a mass-circulation message put out by India's ruling party BJP's social media cell. 'I m hearing a thought provoking speech from @narendramodi sir #RamlilaMaidan.'[9] The message was clear: Nehwal supported the government, not the protesters resisting the government's move to weaken India's proud secular tradition. Usha, too, as I have written earlier, was critical of the citizens' movement against the Citizenship Amendment Act in person, although she did not articulate this in public.

What makes these sportspersons so beholden to the state? Is it the reverence and substantial wealth they now deservedly receive? Is it the coveted government jobs? Or, increasingly, the land grants and other institutional support for sports academies and tickets to political office? Perhaps it is for these considerable incentives that sportspersons in India are rarely outspoken or heroic like Muhammad Ali, the great boxer who criticized his government in America for the war on Vietnam, among many other issues.

Ila never got to go to the Olympics, the most exalted arena of sports nationalism. Perhaps this is why it was easier for her to make her allegiance to the people and not to the mighty state administration that represented them. For the peasants on the ground, who wanted their daughters to go to school and retain a fraction more of the crop they harvested for themselves. And for the party worker slighted by the high command that felt he was not good enough for Communist Party membership.

In the ceaseless summer of 2021, when my pulse was always too rapid, I found myself thinking often of Ila Mitra. We had a pulse oximeter at home, and Covid had arrived in the household, infecting my comatose eighty-nine-year-old grandfather. I was not ill myself; my test result was negative, but the anxiety never left me—the helplessness all around had stuck itself to me. It was during this time that Ila returned to me in a dream. Once the internet led me back to her story, I found myself obsessed with her. Not much of Ila's life remained in physical archives. The sole archive that claimed to hold some of her work was the CPI library at the Bhupesh Bhawan office of the party in Kolkata, named after Rajya Sabha lawmaker Bhupesh Gupta. This was the office in which Ila spent most of the afternoons of her adult life in Calcutta, taking a bus after finishing her classes in college to do her work for the party.

But a curious thing awaited me at the gracious, high-ceilinged Bhupesh Bhawan, adorned with striking red textile posters of Karl Marx, Friedrich Engels and Vladimir Lenin. When I searched for the party journals and magazines where Ila had published some of her translated works and political essays, the precise volumes where her work had appeared could not be found. Even the edition of the party's daily newspaper *Kalantar*, where her obituary must have been published on 14 October 2002, was missing. Only those particular volumes were misplaced, the remaining volume numbers were all available. It was as if someone had come looking for Ila before me, found her and taken her carefully away.

I should have been disappointed, and I was. But I was also pleased, strangely relieved that Ila was still remembered and cherished. That someone had cared enough to take Ila away from the dusty, poorly catalogued library, and keep her close.

In all the women I met, all the remarkable athletes, there was so much to admire, so much to emulate, but respect proved harder. In Ila, I found that elusive thing. How convenient, you could argue, to like the dead woman best. The person you never had to interview but only interpret. The one who never got annoyed by your questions. And you would be right, in a sense.

The truth is, I had grown very attached to her. Bombarded by news of the brutal apathy of the Indian state in the pandemic, I found a shelter in her, a figure of integrity and empathy who had the conviction to grab anyone by the hand, no matter how large or powerful, and ask: What's wrong with you? Don't you know right from wrong?

I found in her the thread of hope that things could, after all, go from worse to slightly better, as they did after the long, ruinous 1940s. That a sense of community, like the one she had sown with education and ground-level resistance in the Tebhaga Andolan, could help us reclaim some of what was lost in the wreckage.

In the last decade of her life, Ila was increasingly troubled by the rise of Hindutva politics, her grandson Riten (short for Ritendranath) has written in a poignant personal essay. The toppling of the Babri

Masjid and the communalism that came with the rise of the BJP was poison to the sense of community she had worked to build throughout her adult life. With the rise of Hindutva, in particular, communists in India have been criticized for their articulated antipathy to religion and adherence to the textbook separation of religion and political practice. Their textbook secularism is seen by some observers as a musty, old-fashioned value that no longer holds in the rough and tumble of the 'real world'.

Her own life was testament to the kind of syncretic community that is now seen as a Nehruvian fantasy. The peasants she led in the Tebhaga Andolan, for whom she was 'Ranima', were Muslim and Santhal. In the four years she spent in police custody, many of them were subjected to torture to reveal the names of their leaders, specifically the names of Ila and Ramendranath. So many were beaten to death, but no one gave away the real name of their Ranima, even when Ila was often forced to be present to witness the torture. Perhaps this is why she felt the kinship that did with Bangladesh, because the people there had claimed her as their own.

In the frenzied days after 6 December 1992, when the mosque in Ayodhya was trampled and danced upon and brought down, Calcutta was mostly quiet under the iron fist of the Left Front, which quickly brought in the army to maintain peace. But there were stray incidents of violence, especially in mixed localities such as Entally, where the Mitras lived. One evening, a bus was set ablaze outside their building, Riten has written in the essay, and the voices of an angry mob rent the air. When he ran down to lock the gate to the apartment complex, he found his grandmother standing in front of the mosque opposite, scolding the mob that had gathered armed with stones and bottles, wagging her finger at them like a schoolteacher disciplining a noisy class. To Riten's surprise and relief, it worked. The mob disintegrated.

Walking through Ila's neighbourhood in a similarly desolate city deep in the pandemic—with the sounds from the mosques and church bells somewhere out of sight—my mind played these stories back to me. I had never seen Ila in action on the track. There are no videos of her sporting days. Only a handful of still photographs in faded newspapers. Yet, when I closed my eyes, I saw her running down the deserted streets, wisps of hair blowing behind her ears, to scold a screaming mob that had gathered in the distance. A frail, bird-like woman with hollowed-out cheeks, she was surprisingly quick on her feet, even though she dragged one foot more than the other.

11

A CODA

Photo © Getty Images

YOU HAVE PROBABLY sensed the absence, haven't you? There is Mary D'Souza, an east Indian Catholic from Mumbai. Kamaljit Sandhu, a Punjabi Sikh from Chandigarh. Pilavullakandi Thekkeraparambil Usha, a Malayalam-speaking Hindu from Calicut in Kerala. Santhi Soundarajan, the daughter of a Sri Lankan Tamil refugee, a Dalit who grew up in the Pudukkottai district of Tamil Nadu. Pinki Pramanik, a Bengali-speaking Hindu from Purulia, among the most backward districts of West Bengal. Dutee Chand, an Odia-speaking Hindu from Chaka Gopalpur, a village of weavers in the Jajpur district of Odisha. Lalita Babar, the daughter of a community of landless Hindu agricultural labourers in the Satara district of Maharashtra. Durga Kumbharvad, from a village near the Maharashtra–Telangana border; her father's side is a Telugu-speaking fishing community and her those from her mother's family are Marathi landless labourers. (Almost every student of the Sunrise Project in the Sagroli village of eastern Maharashtra is from a similar background—lower-caste Hindus who work in manual labour and own little or no land.) The late Ila Mitra, an upper-caste Bengali communist who worked in West Bengal and Bangladesh.

Where is the Muslim woman?

If this book is a window into the a history of women's citizenship in the Indian republic, as I see it, why is the Muslim woman absent from the roster?

One explanation is straightforward—there are no Muslims among the elite women athletes in India from the 1940s to this moment in the decades that I looked at. Indeed, there is still no promising Muslim woman in the ranks of elite national athletes, a surprising thing considering a handful of Muslim women from India have

313

emerged to compete at the highest international level in other sports. Among them is Sania Mirza, who made the national headlines in the mid-2000s with a series of impressive performances on the ATP Tour. On the strength of this she played in the early rounds of a number of Grand Slam singles competitions. In January 2006, she became the first Indian woman to be seeded for the singles competition at the Australian Open, or, indeed, any Grand Slam tournament.[1] She is a doubles superstar, winning six Grand Slam titles and spending ninety-one weeks (a little less than two years) ranked as the number-one women's doubles player in the world.

Then there is the right-arm off-break bowler Nooshin Al Khadeer, who debuted for India in January 2002 in a one-day international against England in Hyderabad.[2] She was a consistent presence in the Indian cricket team until 2007, and played her last match for the country, a one-day against Australia, at the Wankhede cricket stadium in Mumbai in 2012. She picked up her hundredth ODI wicket in this match, the third Indian woman to reach the milestone and one of only twenty-three women in the world, as of June 2023.[3] Two more Indians are inches away from the milestone, albeit eleven years after Al-Khadeer. In 2005, she was part of the Indian team that reached the finals of the one-day World Cup in South Africa, where the Indian women lost to Australia to finish as runners-up. Interestingly, in the Hindi biopic on Mithali Raj, the legendary captain of the Indian women's team, Nooshin is portrayed as Raj's best friend, who introduces her to the game but never plays for India because her family is conservative. In reality, it was Nooshin's father who asked her to try for the Karnataka women's-team selection in 1997.[4]

In 2022, Nikhat Zareen became the world boxing champion in the flyweight category (51 kg), the fifth Indian woman boxer to hold the world championship after Mary Kom, Sarita Devi, Jenny R.L. and Lekha K.C. In 2019 Nikhat came to national attention for intrepidly reaching out to the Union sports minister Kiren Rijiju via Twitter, requesting a match against six-time world boxing flyweight champion Mary Kom, who had been selected for the Tokyo Olympics that were held in 2021.[5] Mary Kom won that match 9–1, and was headlined 'ill-tempered' by *The Times of India*,[6] but one thing was clear—Nikhat had what it takes to challenge a living legend, face a resounding defeat and move on from it.

Sania, Nooshin and Nikhat. Three successful Muslim sportswomen in seventy-five years of independent India.

The Sachar Committee Report of 2006 suggests the most likely reason for this small number—the ghettoization of Muslims in India due to historical and political reasons, their own sense of insecurity and the attitude of 'neglect' that government and municipal authorities had towards these ghettos. 'Water, sanitation, electricity, schools, public health facilities, banking facilities, anganwadis, ration shops, roads and transport facilities are all in short supply in these areas. In the context of increasing ghettoization, the absence of these services impacts Muslim women the most, because they are reluctant to venture beyond the confines of "safe" neighbourhoods to access these facilities from elsewhere,' the report noted.[7] Muslims had conspicuously poor indicators of higher education, formal-sector employment, particularly government and large private sector jobs, access to bank credit, standard of living, consumption and poverty. The Sachar Committee was tasked by Prime Minister Manmohan Singh's government with studying the relatively backward status of Muslims compared to other communities across national, state and district levels.[8]

The perceived orthodoxy of Islam towards women in particular, a notion strengthened by news from Afghanistan, Iran and Saudi Arabia, is assumed to be the principal reason for the relative absence of Muslim women in the public sphere in India. We see this implicit assumption in popular Hindi films, jokes on social media, in news reporting and even in government policy. But when a community worries for its safety, it would be anxious about its women stepping out of 'their neighbourhoods'. Isn't that one of the most natural fallouts?

Are a handful of Muslim sportswomen who have hit the big league in the past twenty years enough to suggest the community's growing participation in sport? Wouldn't that be like looking at the superstardom of Shah Rukh Khan, Salman Khan and Aamir Khan, and concluding that Muslim men are very successful in the Hindi film industry? In other words, a hypothesis based on the very limited evidence of outliers. There is no data that looks at women in Indian sport in terms of their religion—indeed, there is little data on women in Indian sport in general. The three outliers are all I have, and I am going to take it. Sania, Nooshin and Nikhat are here now, and I'd like to believe there will be more Sanias, Nooshins and Nikhats in the next few years. That if this book is ever reissued in a new edition thirty years later, it would be incomplete without a chapter (or two) on Muslim athletes.

Two further things. Consider the media reporting on these three outliers. Every story on Nikhat published in the reliable mainstream press—from BBC and *The Hindu*'s *Sportstar* magazine to the website News18—noted her Muslim background and the discouragement from her community for taking up sport. 'People would object to a Muslim girl wearing shorts to play sport and we learnt to ignore them. But when she won the youth championship, people changed their minds and said she'd proven herself,' Nikhat's father was quoted as saying by the BBC.[9]

Compare this with Lovlina Borgohain, Nikhat's Hindu contemporary who won bronze at the Tokyo Olympics in the welterweight category (64–69 kg) one year earlier in 2021.[10]

'Born on October 2, 1997, in a remote hamlet called Baromukhia in the Golaghat district of Assam, Lovlina Borgohain's family struggled to make ends meet during her childhood,' her profile on the Olympics website says. 'But that did not stop Lovlina's father from supporting his children's sporting ambitions. Lovlina and her two elder sisters took up Muay Thai, a form of kick-boxing. Both her siblings even competed at the national level.'[11]

Incidentally, both Lovlina and Nikhat come from families where their fathers introduced them to sport. Nikhat's father initiated her into athletics at first and supported her move to boxing when she expressed interest in the sport. No media story on Lovlina mentioned her religious identity or the discouragement she may have faced from her community for taking up a combat sport such as boxing. The only challenges mentioned are the so-called secular ones—the lack of paved roads and development infrastructure in her village in Assam, and her mother's ailing health.

News reporting on Sania Mirza has always included commentary by clerics. 'The dress she wears on the tennis courts not only doesn't cover large parts of her body but leaves nothing to the imagination,' said Haseeb-ul-hasan Siddiqui of the Sunni Ulema Board. 'She will undoubtedly be a corrupting influence on these young women, which we want to prevent,' he was quoted in the UK newspaper *The Guardian*.[12] The paper reported the fatwa Siddiqui had issued against her for 'indecent dressing' on the court and in advertisements, describing him as a leading cleric of the Sunni Ulema Board. The same year, there were news reports, including in the BBC, that security had to be beefed up at a Kolkata tournament because a group called the Jamiat-Ulama-i-Hind had reportedly threatened to stop Sania from playing if she did not change her dress. 'These are rumours, we have not threatened to stop Sania or anybody else from playing,' Siddiquallah Choudhary of the group was quoted as saying in the BBC. 'Though it is true that the kind of dress Sania wears offends us—we don't expect a Muslim girl to wear such skimpy clothes in public.'[13]

Some months later in 2006, the All India Muslim Personal Law Board, a non-governmental body, clarified that Siddiqui's 'fatwa' had no meaning. 'Every sports has its specific dress code and it does not come under the purview of the Muslim personal laws,' AIMPLB general secretary Maulana Nizamuddin told a news agency.[14]

But this did not stop the media from reporting on the subject. In 2010, the same Sunni Ulema Board expressed its views on Sania's conduct with her then fiancé and now husband Pakistani cricketer Shoaib Malik, and news reports dutifully carried them. 'The kind of actions the two are indulging in, like living together and addressing media together, are haram in Islam,' said Moulana Haseebul Hasan Siddiqui, a religious scholar. 'Islam permits a man and woman to see each other only once before marriage and it does not allow them to live together and indulge in these sort of activities before marriage. Muslims should stay away from such gatherings where men and women mingle freely in violation of Islamic principles.'[15]

'If a sport requires women to drop their burqas, then women should not take part in the sport,' a maulvi, Sajid Rashid, said in a TV show in 2017, and the media once again carried it diligently. 'Do you think Sania Mirza's attire is legal? Is it legal? It is sexual and hence, un-Islamic.'[16]

What explains the media's commitment to keep reproducing this commentary, publicly discredited by the Indian Muslim community themselves?

The anxiety about young women outside the home, engaging in physical exercise (vis-à-vis physical labour) and wearing sports clothes is universal in India. Nearly every athlete and coach I spoke to for this book, including the many I could not profile or quote, spoke of how women are shamed for playing outdoors and wearing sports clothes. Indeed, this is a custom shared by most religious faiths in India. Mary D'Souza's east Indian Catholic family and neighbours in Bandra anointed her a tomboy because she was most frequently seen playing hockey in the parks and municipal grounds of Bandra. The most Westernized, indeed so-called progressive families signal their sense of awkwardness about women who play sport with the term, 'tomboy'. It is seen as a term of affection, but it is, to my mind, an expression of unease. It signifies that old distinction—that boys and men are meant to be outdoors, and girls and women indoors.

It is far less commonly noted, on the other hand, that from the 1940s to the 1970s, women from Hindu families were rare in Indian sport. That it was Indian Christians, Anglo Indians and Parsis who dominated Indian women's sport from the 1940s to the 1960s. Kamaljit Sandhu, the queen of Indian sport in the 1970s, is a Sikh. (No one seems to remember either that Nawal El Moutawakel of Morocco, who won gold at that 400-metre hurdles race in Los Angeles in 1984, was a Muslim, celebrated as the first Arab woman, the first African woman and the first Muslim woman to win an Olympic gold.)

'To demonize and dehumanize a whole culture on the grounds that it is "enraged" at modernity is to turn Muslims into the objects of a therapeutic, punitive attention,' wrote the Palestinian-American scholar Edward W. Said in his book *Covering Islam*.[17] In the introduction to a new edition of the book, Said described how the Western media, led by the Americans, portrayed Muslims and Islam with 'highly exaggerated stereotyping and belligerent hostility'. In the 1990s, in particular, after the fall of the Soviet Union, prestigious media outlets, including *The New York Times,* projected Islam (used as a monolithic thing bereft of variations) as the great threat facing the West, replacing communism in this regard.

The English-language media in India has faithfully followed this template. Examine the reporting on Sania and Nikhat yourself. Don't go by my references. Do it systematically—compare like with like, look for the anecdotes of family and community disapproval in all the stories of sportswomen.

The second thing: Look at the Bombay film industry, which began in the early decades of the twentieth century, only a few years before the start of organized sports activities in India. *Raja Harishchandra*, recognized as the first Indian feature film by the Government of India, was released in 1913; and the first edition of the All India Olympic Games, essentially the first national competition of sport in India, was held in 1924.[18]

In the first four decades of the Bombay film industry, the women who emerged as big names in the industry were non-Hindu. Arguably the first international female star on the Indian screen was Renee Smith, an Anglo-Indian from Calcutta billed as Seeta Devi on screen. She appeared in the first three films of the filmmaker and actor Himansu Rai—*The Light of Asia* (1925), *Shiraz* (1928) and *A Throw of Dice* (1929)—which travelled to Europe.[19] It is said that the actor known as Seeta Devi was actually two sisters—Renee and Percy Smith. Patience Cooper, another Calcutta Anglo-Indian, whose career spanned the 1920s and the 1930s, was a star in both silent and sound cinema. Unusually for the time, Cooper did not adopt a non-Western screen name.

The undisputed female superstar of the 1920s was the Jewish actor Ruby Myers, who was christened Sulochana for the screen. The action star of the 1930s and the 1940s, Nadia, whose fans were known as the 'chavanni audience (25-paise audience)' but also included those such as the celebrated playwright and actor Girish Karnad, was British and Greek by parentage. Her real name was Mary Ann Evans. The Jewish actor Esther Victoria Abraham, who went by the name Pramila, was another star of the 1940s, typically cast as the Westernized flirtatious woman who served as the counterfoil to the traditional Indian heroine. Florence Ezekiel, who became popular as the vamp figure Nadira in major Hindi films in the 1950s, was another Jewish actor.

One of the first recognized known women composers in the Bombay film industry was Saraswati Devi, a Parsi woman whose name was, in fact, Khorshed Minocher-Homji. Much like the landscape of sport from the 1940s to the 1970s, non-Hindu communities such as Jews, Anglo-Indians and Parsis abounded. But unlike sport, Muslim women were a major presence in Bombay cinema in these decades, both in front of the camera and around it. A brief list: Fatima Begum is possibly the first woman to set up her own production company, Fatma Film Company, in 1925.[20] She was also possibly the first credited woman scriptwriter in Bombay cinema, as well as an actor. Her daughters Zubeida and Sultana were also actors. Zubeida also has a first to her credit—she played the lead in *Alam Ara* (1933), the first Bombay film with sound.

A contemporary of Saraswati Devi's, Jaddanbai is also known as the first woman composer in Bombay cinema. Who came first is immaterial to this argument—they were both pioneers. A noted singer, Jaddanbai also holds direction and production credits in Hindi film. Unlike Saraswati Devi, she went by her own name on screen. Jaddanbai's daughter Nargis is one of the triumvirate of female superstars who owned the 1950s in Hindi cinema; the other two, of course, are Madhubala (Mumtaz Jehan Dehlavi) and Meena Kumari (Mahjabeen Bano). The only Hindu star contemporary of the triumvirate was Vyjayanthimala Bali. The 1940s had a couple of other Hindu women stars—producer and actor Devika Rani and actor Sadhona Bose—but they were the exceptions. Both came from highly influential families. Devika Rani was a relative of Rabindranath Tagore, and Bose was the maternal grand-daughter of the Brahmo reformer Keshub Chandra Sen. There may be a couple of other Hindu names, but there most certainly are many more Muslim, Jewish, Anglo-Indian and Parsi names. This is not an encyclopaedic list, but an outline of the picture from the start of the cinema industry in the 1910s to the 1950s.

There were also Muslim women pioneers outside of the cinema. The Hindustani classical singer Gauhar Jaan is considered to be the first Indian woman to have recorded her voice in 1902. Her birth name was Eileen Angelina Yeoward, but her mother converted to Islam and became Malka Jaan and renamed her daughter Gauhar Jaan.[21] Her contemporary Janki Bai Allahabadi, also likely Muslim, was another gramophone star. Both women performed for King George V at the Delhi Durbar of 1911. Several decades later, in 1947, the first Indian woman to record her voice on the radio was Saeeda Bano.[22]

What does film and the performing arts have to do with sport? I'd argue two things. Both the performing arts and sport involve bodily labour—to sing, dance or act, you use the body, just as you do while playing sport. And second, both involve the public sphere. You display your labour—hence the verb 'perform' is used for both— to a public that watches. Indeed, if so many Muslim women were pioneers in the use of the new technologies of the performing arts that emerged in the early twentieth century, could it be because a number of Muslim women were public-facing figures by virtue of their role as performing artists—courtesans with aristocratic patronage—in the eighteenth and nineteenth centuries? The 'nawabi' culture of north India and the zamindari culture of Bengal are associated with the patronage of song, dance and poetry performances by courtesans. Popular Hindi cinema suggests that these courtesans were wealthy women with their own establishments, and often Muslim. In pre-independent India, these would appear to be the few women who were financially independent and socially influential.

The absence of the Muslim sportswoman in today's India is likely to be read as the consequence of Islam's conservatism, and this may be right to a degree. The politics of this moment perceives the Muslim woman to be a citizen who needs to be liberated—from the burkha, the hijab, legally sanctioned polygamy, genital cutting and a thousand other restrictions that the Islamic faith is perceived to have placed on her. And so the Indian government has passed the Muslim Women (Protection of Rights on Marriage) Act, 2019, criminalizing men who abandon their wives without taking legal divorce.[23] There is a petition pending in the Supreme Court that asks to ban the practice of female genital cutting, prevalent in the Bohra community of Muslims. There was a political movement in the state of Karnataka to prohibit Muslim women from wearing the hijab, which has led to a case being heard, at the time of writing, in the Supreme Court of India.[24]

But I want to point to a time less than a century ago in pre-independent India, when Muslim women were among the only public-facing women in the subcontinent. Pioneers of the use of technology. Influential performers and artists, who made the so-called disreputable profession of cinema, singing, dancing, performing arts thrilling and sought-after avenues of aspiration for generations of Hindu women today. Women whose performances bring joy and pleasure.

No matter what the story of women in Islam has been in other parts of the world in the modern period, the history of Muslim women in the Indian subcontinent is wondrously, defiantly distinct. Their legacy of distinction in the performing arts is something to celebrate and remember. And indeed, invoke and encourage in every field, including sports.

That is the day I am waiting for.

ACKNOWLEDGEMENTS

LONG BEFORE THIS idea crystallized into a book, when I had thought I may have to publish these as separate profiles for a magazine, several athletes and some coaches gave me their time. My first and unrepayable debt is to them. Mary D'Souza and her daughter Marissa, and her son's family who live in Mumbai. Kamaljit Sandhu and her husband, who welcomed me into their home in Chandigarh and fed me through my interviews. P.T. Usha and Sreenivasan sir in Payyoli, for their time and recommendations for the best seafood thali and jackfruit chips in Kozhikode. Saraswati Chand in Chaka Gopalpur, Odisha, and the government of Odisha's sport publicity department. Sports Authority of India coach and Dronacharya award winner Nagapuri Ramesh sir, for making time to speak on Zoom interviews. Lalita Babar and her husband Sachin Bhosale in Mumbai, not least for the 'kharvas' she cooked for me. Her family in Mohi village and her former teacher Bharat Chavan, for their time and a superb rustic Marathi meal. Dayanand Kamble sir of the Maharashtra government's publicity department, who helped me with the logistics of travelling in Maharashtra in the high noon of the pandemic, and Sachin Raut, his colleague in the same department, who accompanied me to Mohi village. What's more, he is a schoolmate of Lalita's, a particularly thoughtful deputation from Kamble sir. Rohit Deshmukh and his family in Sagroli village, and the staff of the Sanskriti Samvardhan Mandal School complex, who made me feel like I was on a rustic resort holiday. A list of names in particular: Nandu Jadhav sir, Dyaneshwar Kondlade, Prabhakar Rao, Durga Kumbharvad and her mother Shobha Kumbharvad in Kundalwadi village across the border in Telangana. Ritendranath and Romendranath Mitra, for sharing the memories and scrapbooks of Ila Mitra so graciously and patiently. Pinki Pramanik for giving me her time amid her workday.

A special note for Gopi Shankar Madurai and Santhi Soundarajan, who explained the terrain of sex-testing and intersex identities with great patience. And fortitude, because these are not happy memories or experiences. It helped me put in perspective the complex section in the middle of the book. The errors, if any, are mine.

Virtuoso photographer Ashish Shah, who patiently explained his artistic process to me, taking out time amid shoots in remote locations with limited connectivity.

The International Women's Media Foundation (IWMF) and the Howard G Buffett Fund for Women Journalists gave me a grant for Rs 230,000 ($3,190) to report the last four chapters of the book during the pandemic when travel coats soared. (And they haven't come down since then.) Further, their questions during the interview gave me clarity and the insistence to publish two stories in the press before the book helped me develop the structure for two chapters. Thank you also to Priyanka Dubey, true writing and reporting comrade, for telling me about this grant and helping me prepare the application for it.

Dinesh Thakur, healthcare activist and intrepid whistleblower who blew the lid off the goings-on in Ranbaxy, gave me a no-strings-attached grant of Rs 1.2 lakh simply on the basis of my book proposal and the chapters I had written until 2020. The confidence that this kind of act bestows is hard to measure.

The New India Foundation, funded by Nandan Nilekani, is a sanctuary unlike any other. The fellowship sum is handsome, possibly the only one of this magnitude for writing a book outside of the First World. But the intellectual and emotional support is also substantive, should you ask for it. The trustees manage the delicate balance of never sending 'gentle reminders' or questions, yet when you seek their help, they are there. Thank you, Manish Sabharwal, Srinath Raghavan and Niraja Gopal Jayal. Yauvanika Chopra is the comrade that every slightly cynical writer like me needs—she reads your work, she makes herself available to listen to your anxieties (and never dismisses them), she makes sure you are paid before time and wards off the evil eye!

What do I say about Ramachandra Guha that has not been said before? I know he has done for me what he has done for every NIF fellow and, indeed, every non-fiction writer who has sought his help. The acknowledgements pages of the best non-fiction books published in India would tell you that. Still, my experience would be my own—he terrified me by asking to read my manuscript. He then terrified me further by calling directly some weeks after I had sent my darned thing in (after revising it half a dozen more times.) It was to congratulate me and ask if I had an agent. He could so easily have simply written to me, but picking up the phone and speaking is so much more warm and forthcoming and confidence-building. (It is also true that I am ageing, and showing some inevitable marks of sentimentality.) He found me an agent, yet read every chapter of the book and sent each back with comments, and spoke of the book to many individuals whom I didn't know personally. Ram, thank you for the several strangers who told me they had heard of my book from Ram Guha! (Thank you also for finding my grandfather's personal library a permanent home.)

My knight in shining armour is Rivka Israel, the first reader of my book (who informed Ram Guha that my book was done and that he should read it.). But she is also one of the last readers of my book— when I contracted a corneal infection at the proofreading stage of my book, Rivka offered to read the typeset manuscript, although she confessed to not being a good typo-catcher. Moreover, she lost her uncle suddenly the week I sent her the typeset manuscript, but sent me her corrections three days before my deadline. Putting a book out into the world is a realization of how much we owe the universe, but what I owe Rivka is particularly unquantifiable.

My agents Hemali Sodhi and Ranjana Sengupta of A Suitable Agency for backing this with such conviction, and responding to all my lengthy voice notes within twenty-four hours. Every writer waiting months/years for a response from editors, agents, the universe, will find an antidote in A Suitable Agency. They understand that, more than anything, we are worn down by waiting and the rejections that never come.

The staff of the National Library in Kolkata, and specifically, Supriya Sannigrahi, the assistant library and information officer, who made it possible for me to resume my research in the long closure due to Covid-19. Sakti Roy, the well-known archivist of the Anandabazar Patrika group, made available several PDFs of pages from newspapers of the ABP group as well as pages from other newspapers (his suggestions for my reading) without ever meeting me in person. I was told that the ABP library is closed to outsiders due to Covid-19, but he didn't let me feel it. The staff of the library in the Bhupesh Bhawan office of the Communist Party of India in Kolkata, who let me go through their journals and papers for Ila Mitra's work, and Aruna Roy for directing me to it.

Vaishna Roy of *The Hindu*, now *Frontline*, Zuraidah Ibrahim of the *South China Morning Post*, Anupama Chopra and Mohini

Chaudhuri of Film Companion, Supriya Nair of FiftyTwo.in for publishing a version of the Sagroli story, and Anindita Ghose of *Mint Lounge* published my essays and reportage frequently, so I had some money to pay my bills while I wrote this for years and years. Zuraidah, Anupama and Vaishna, thank you also for writing me recommendations.

My parents, for learning to be patient and responding well to the idea that this is their age to follow my instructions, reversing the direction of traffic so far. My late grandmothers. Dipti Mukerjee shared her stories with me, giving me the idea of an unusual personal thread to tie the book with. Shefali Chattopadhyaya, for forgiving me for not being there by her side in her final illness. If she had withheld it, this book would not have been completed the way it was.

Swati Chopra, my editor at HarperCollins India, for championing the book long before it was completed. Udayan Mitra, for reading the manuscript well before it was polished and corrected, and being so generous with his conviction and praise. Ujjaini Dasgupta, who made me think and labour hard with her questions in more than two rounds of copy-editing. The book has gained much (and lost only its self-indulgence), thanks to her sharp copy-editing.

My sage friend Naveen Kishore, for asking me that difficult question—when are you going to finish?—so often that I had to do something about it. Also the first reader of my book outside the circle of my fellowship grantees and editors and publishers. Thank you for your comradeship and calm, Naveen. I can see why you are considered among the best publishers of this moment.

And a big hug to my Labrador brother Raja, who was literally by my side as I wrote this. He is about as old as the idea of the book. He was also physically in my room during every critical interview—with fellowship/grant funders and publishers. His peaceful snoring gave me calm.

NOTES

1. The Bengali Woman's Running Diary

1. A short version of this essay was published in The Ladies Finger in 2014. The conclusions drawn here, based on facts and figures up to 2013–14, are no less true today.
2. Helen Macdonald, *H Is for Hawk* (London: Jonathan Cape, 2014).
3. Sarah Knapton, 'Lack of Exercise Is Twice as Deadly as Obesity, Cambridge University Finds', *The Telegraph*, 14 January 2015, http://www.telegraph.co.uk/news/science/science-news/11345448/Lack-of-exercise-is-twice-as-deadly-as-obesity-Cambridge-University-finds.html
4. 'Actor Kangana Ranaut's Sister Hurt in Acid Attack', *The Indian Express*, 6 October 2006, http://archive.indianexpress.com/news/actor-kangana-ranaut-s-sister-hurt-in-acid-attack/14123/
5. Paying guest, or PG, accommodation, as it is widely known, is possibly the most common living arrangement for young women working in Indian cities, where landlords largely do not let out homes to unmarried young women. They believe this will encourage young women to enjoy independent lives and, more worryingly, enable sexual encounters outside of marriage. Instead, young women pay for lodging within people's households, where there are strict curfews for coming back home and rules against bringing in male friends.

6. Vishwanathan was a journalist with the Indian national news network TV Today. She worked in their New Delhi office. She was murdered in 2008 when she was driving home after a late shift at work. For a comprehensive account of the attack, see PTI, 'Soumya Vishwanathan Murder Case Cracked: Cops', Rediff.com, 24 March 2009, https://www.rediff.com/news/2009/mar/24soumya-vishwanathan-murder-case-cracked-four-held.htm

7. Sohini Chattopadhyay, 'Diary of a Newly Thin Person', *OPEN*, 23 June 2011, https://openthemagazine.com/essays/true-life/diary-of-a-newly-thin-person/

8. Priyanka Pulla, 'Our Basic Bug Instinct', *OPEN*, 27 December 2013, https://openthemagazine.com/features/living/our-basic-bug-instinct/

9. Haruki Murakami, *What I Talk about When I Talk about Running* (New York: Vintage International, 2009).

10. Paula Cocozza, 'Menstruation: The Last Great Sporting Taboo', *The Guardian*, 21 January 2015, https://www.theguardian.com/sport/shortcuts/2015/jan/21/menstruation-last-great-sporting-taboo

11. Aarefa Johari, 'As UK Tennis Player Breaks Silence on Menstruation, Indian Sportswomen Speak Out on Taboo Subject', Scroll.in, 7 February 2015, https://scroll.in/article/703877/as-uk-tennis-player-breaks-silence-on-menstruation-indian-sportswomen-speak-out-on-taboo-subject

12. 'Are Telomeres the Key to Aging and Cancer', Genetic Science Learning Center, University of Utah Health Sciences, https://learn.genetics.utah.edu/content/basics/telomeres

13. Sooraj Barjatya, a director-producer who has helmed several Hindi-language blockbusters, including the all-time hit *Hum Aapke Hain Koun..!*, is known for the depiction of traditional Indian family values. The films are often mocked for their regressive views of women.

14. The Bullerei, Hamburg, is an elegant full-service fine-dining restaurant run by the celebrated German chef Tim Mälzer.

15. Restaurant kitchens have infamously few women, most of them in the 'pink ghetto' of the dessert station. This story details the rise of

certain women up the professional kitchen ranks in New York. See Julia Moskin, 'A Change in the Kitchen', *The New York Times*, 21 January 2014, https://www.nytimes.com/2014/01/22/dining/a-change-in-the-kitchen.html

16. A.R. Rahman is a double Oscar-winning composer. Even before the Academy Awards, he was widely regarded as a prodigy in the Tamil- and Hindi-cinema music landscape.

17. Photograph from www.kathrineswitzer.com. Image used without permission.

18. Kathrine Switzer, *Marathon Woman: Running the Race to Revolutionize Women's Sports* (New York: Carroll & Graf Publishers, 2009).

19. Charlie Lovett, 'The Fight to Establish the Women's Race', *Olympic Marathon: A Centennial History of the Games' Most Storied Race* (Wesport: Greenwood Publishing Group Inc, 1997).

20. Athanasios Tarasouleas, 'Stamata Revithi, "Alias Melpomeni"', Olympic World Library, https://library.olympics.com/Default/doc/SYRACUSE/353009/stamata-revithi-alias-melpomeni-by-athanasios-tarasouleas?_lg=en-GB

21. Ben Snider-Mcgrath, 'The Women's Olympic Marathon Debuted OTD in 1984', *Canadian Running*, 5 August 2020, https://runningmagazine.ca/the-scene/the-womens-olympic-marathon-debuted-otd-in-1984/

22. These views were not unfounded. The story of Gretel Bergmann, a German record holder in high jump in the 1930s, was recently retrieved from the footnotes of history when the German government named a stadium and a sports complex after her in 1999. A Jew, Bergmann was recalled to Germany for the 1936 Games after she had gone to the UK. But she was dropped from the German Olympic team two weeks before the Games for poor performance, and her name was withdrawn from the German national record she had equalled. In 1937, she emigrated to the United States.

23. Ben Johnson's most enduring rivalry was with his American counterpart Carl Lewis. His 100-metre gold finish at the Seoul Olympics, defeating Lewis, is considered by many to be the most exciting race ever run.

Three days later, however, he was disqualified as officials found traces of drugs in his urine. The 1988 race was documented in the book *The Dirtiest Race in History* by Richard Moore.

24. Rachel Bachman, 'The Half-Marathon Achieves Its Personal Best', *The Wall Street Journal*, 20 October 2014, https://www.wsj.com/articles/the-half-marathon-achieves-its-personal-best-1413825711

25. 'Running USA Marathon Report: Minor Drop in U.S. Marathon Finishers Reported in 2016', Running USA, 2 August 2017, https://www.runningusa.org/running-usa-news/running-usa-marathon-report-minor-drop-in-u-s-marathon-finishers-reported-in-2016/

26. Ibid.

27. Carl Bialik, 'More People Are Running; Fewer Are Playing Bar Sports', Fivethirtyeight, 2014, https://fivethirtyeight.com/features/more-people-are-running-fewer-are-playing-bar-sports/

28. Richard Askwith, *Running Free: A Runner's Journey Back to Nature* (London: Yellow Jersey Press, 2014).

29. The Madrid train terror attacks took place on 11 March 2004, killing 181 persons, by most commonly stated estimates.

30. The London train attacks took place on 7 July 2005, killing fifty-two, according to most estimates; a series of blasts took place in suburban Mumbai trains on 11 July 2006, killing 209 people.

31. Niraja Gopal Jayal, *Citizenship and Its Discontents: An Indian History* (Hyderabad: Orient Blackswan, 2017).

32. 'What Is the Olympic Creed?', International Olympic Committee, https://olympics.com/ioc/faq/olympic-symbol-and-identity/what-is-the-olympic-creed

33. Sabyasachi Dasgupta, 'Delhi Protests Are by "Dented and Painted" Women: President Pranab's Son', NDTV, 27 December 2012, https://www.ndtv.com/india-news/delhi-protests-are-by-dented-and-painted-women-president-pranabs-son-508663

2. Mary D'Souza: The Woman Who Danced Her Way to Helsinki

1. '62 Years Later, Mary Dsouza: Pioneer of Women Athletics in India, Will Finally Be Honored', Goenchi Mathi, https://goenchimathi.wordpress. com/2013/08/08/62-years-later-mary-dsouza-pioneer-of-women-athletics-in-india-will-finally-be-honored/?fbclid=IwAR0MloND_yQGlr8a8tJh11l6ww4lbj2-fs5hwE0UxgKZqVRvRIp9zYtVZ5c

2. Edited by Joanna Lobo, 'Hail Mary: Hockey Player Mary D'Souza Being Honoured with Dhyan Chand Award', *DNA*, 21 November 2013, https://www.dnaindia.com/lifestyle/report-hail-mary-hockey-player-mary-d-souza-being-honoured-with-dhyan-chand-award-1882611

3. Leon, 'Sports News and Views of the Day by Leon', *The Times of India*, Bombay edition, 25 April 1951, p. 8; PTI, 'Funds for Indian Olympic Contingent to Helsinki', *The Times of India*, Bombay edition, 15 May 1952, p. 9.

4. Leon, 'Bori Bunder Gossip: While Other Countries Prepare for Achievements We Are Pressing Claims for Trip to Helsinki', *The Times of India*, Bombay edition, 27 April 1952, p. 11; Leon, 'Bori Bunder Gossip: Despite Those Pious Resolutions Our Olympic Team Is Ever on the Increase', *The Times of India*, Bombay edition, 18 May 1952, p. 11.

5. G. Ezekiel, 'Women's Sports in India Poised for Great Heights', *The New Indian Express*, 1 July 2010, http://www.newindianexpress.com/opinion/article162863.ece

6. 'Four Bombay Athletes in Danger of Losing Places on the Team', *The Times of India*, Bombay edition, 24 September 1956, p. 19.

7. V. Anand, 'Alex Silveira, 400m Athlete Who Beat Milkha Singh, Passes Away', *The Times of India*, 24 December 2022, https://timesofindia. indiatimes.com/city/mumbai/alex-silveira-400m-athlete-who-beat-milkha-singh-passes-away/articleshow/96469410.cms

8. Reuters, 'Mary Leela Rao Wins Favour', *The Times of India*, Bombay edition, 13 November 1956, p.10.

9. PTI and Reuters, 'Mary Leela Rao Pulls Thigh Muscle in the 100 Metres Heat', *The Times of India*, Bombay edition, 24 November 1956, p. 13.

3. Kamaljit Sandhu: The Woman Who Took Gold Unexpectedly

1. 'Talks on: A.A.F.I. Bid', *The Times of India*, Bombay edition, 29 November 1970, p. 14.
2. PTI, 'Olympian Athlete Ajmer Singh Passed Away', *The Times of India*, 27 January 2010, https://timesofindia.indiatimes.com/sports/more-sports/athletics/olympian-athlete-ajmer-singh-passed-away/articleshow/5506102.cms
3. PMP India, 'PM's Speech on Independence Day from Red Fort', YouTube, 16 August 2014, https://youtu.be/jU3w0jBXSqo (Translated by the author)
4. '1982 Asian Games, New Delhi', Olympian Database, https://www.olympiandatabase.com/index.php?id=305420&L=1

4. P.T. Usha: The Woman Who Came Fourth

1. Personal interview with the author in December 2019.
2. Personal interview with the author.
3. 'Special Bulletin on Maternal Mortality in India 2018–2020', Office of the Registrar General, India, November 2022, New Delhi.
4. 'Key Indicators of Household Social Consumption on Education in India', National Statistical Office, Ministry of Statistics & Programme Implementation, 2019, New Delhi, p. A-6.
5. https://twitter.com/PTUshaOfficial/status/1428348599545393157?s=20
6. M.L. Kaul, 'Pathetic Show by Usha', *The Times of India*, Bombay edition, 26 September 1988, p. 1.
7. Shekhar Gupta, 'Seoul Olympics: Defeat and Recriminations All the Way for Indian Camp', *India Today*, 15 October 1988, https://www.indiatoday.in/magazine/cover-story/story/19881015-

seoul-olympics-defeat-and-recriminations-all-the-way-for-indian-camp-797808-1988-10-14

8. 'Railways Felicitates P.T. Usha for Getting Nominated to Rajya Sabha', *The Hindu*, 9 October 2022, https://www.thehindu.com/news/cities/ Mangalore/railways-felicitates-pt-usha-for-getting-nominated-to-rajya-sabha/article65988710.ece

9. Joanna Slater, 'Police Stormed a University in India. Muslim Students Say the Violence Was an Act of Revenge', *The Washington Post*, 16 February 2020, https://www.washingtonpost.com/world/ asia_pacific/police-stormed-a-university-in-india-muslim-students-say-the-violence-was-an-act-of-revenge/2020/02/16/6727aa24-37e8-11ea-a1ff-c48c1d59a4a1_story.html; Sameer Yasir and Billy Perrigo, '"The Police Did Nothing." Students in India Are Protesting after a Masked Mob Violently Attacked a Top Delhi University', *Time*, 7 January 2020, https://time.com/5760593/jnu-attack-student-protests/; *The Economic Times*, 'Jamia Violence: New CCTV Footage Shows Delhi Police Attacking Students in Library', YouTube, 16 February 2020, https://www.youtube.com/watch?v=P-VUPenZpPE

5. Santhi Soundarajan: The Woman Who Was Erased

1. 'Indian Athlete Fails Gender Test', BBC News, 18 December 2006, http://news.bbc.co.uk/2/hi/south_asia/6188775.stm; Biswajyoti Brahma, 'Is Silver Winner Santhi a Man?', *The Times of India*, Mumbai edition, 18 December 2006, p. 1.

2. Luke Harding, 'Forgotten Victims of East German Doping Take Their Battle to Court', *The Guardian*, 1 November 2005, https://www. theguardian.com/sport/2005/nov/01/athletics.gdnsport3

3. Olympics, 'The High Jumper Who Faced the Nazis | Foul Play', YouTube, 26 November 2017, https://www.youtube.com/ watch?v=2NIoJ5KqKns

4. Maria Jose Martinez-Patino, 'Personal Account: A Woman Tried and Tested', *The Lancet*, December 2005, https://www.thelancet.com/ journals/lancet/article/PIIS0140-6736(05)67841-5/fulltext

5. María José Martínez-Patiño, Covadonga Mateos-Padorno, Aurora
    Martínezvidal, Ana María Sánchez Mosquera, et al., 'An Approach to
    the Biological, Historical and Psychological Repercussions of Gender
    Verification in Top Level Competitions', *Journal of Human Sport
    and Exercise*, Vol. 5 (3), 2010, pp. 307–21, https://www.redalyc.org/
    pdf/3010/301023489001.pdf

6. Eventually, in 2019, Caster Semenya lost an appeal seeking to be
    permitted to run without taking testosterone-reducing drugs. But she
    retains the right to compete.

7. V. Narayan Swamy, 'Asiad Medallist Labours at Brick Kiln', *The Times of
    India*, 24 July 2012, https://timesofindia.indiatimes.com/sports/off-the-
    field/Asiad-medallist-labours-at-brick-kiln/articleshow/15112611.cms

8. 'Prize Money for Medal Winners', Ministry of Youth Affairs and Sports,
    22 July 2019, https://pib.gov.in/Pressreleaseshare.aspx?PRID=1579723

9. 'TN Honours Santhi Despite Controversy', *Hindustan Times*,
    18 December 2006, https://www.hindustantimes.com/india/tn-honours-
    Santhi-despite-controversy/story-eQ0RomGjwC0G7CPVkxsdiO.html

10. 'IOA Takes Back Santhi's Asiad Medal', News18, 18 December 2006,
    https://www.news18.com/news/india/ioa-takes-back-santhis-asiad-
    medal-253836.html

11. 'Best & Co, 7th Federation Cup Athletic Championship, 23rd to
    25th June 2001 Bangalore Meet Results', Indian Athletics, https://
    indianathletics.in/wp-content/uploads/2020/03/7th-FEDRATION-
    CUP-ATHLETIC-CHAMPIONSHIP-23RD-TO-25TH-JUNE.
    pdf; 'Best & Co, 41st Open National Athletics Championship, 18-21
    October 2001, Jawaharlal Nehru Stadium, Chennai', Indian Athletics,
    https://indianathletics.in/wp-content/uploads/2020/03/41ST-OPEN-
    NATIONAL-ATHLETICS-CHAMPIONSHIP-18-21-OCTOBER.pdf

12. V. Narayan Swamy, 'Asiad Medallist Labours at Brick Kiln', *The Times of
    India*, 24 July 2012, https://timesofindia.indiatimes.com/sports/off-the-
    field/Asiad-medallist-labours-at-brick-kiln/articleshow/15112611.cms

13. *Arunkumar vs The Inspector General Of… on 22 April, 2019*, Madras High Court, 22 April 2019, Indian Kanoon, https://indiankanoon.org/doc/188806075/

14. Free & Equal: United Nations for Intersex Awareness, https://www.unfe.org/intersex-awareness/#:~:text=Intersex%20people%20are%20born%20with,definitions%20of%20male%20and%20female.&text=Intersex%20children%20don't%20need,protect%20intersex%20children%20from%20harm

15. Manasa Rao, '"With Every Word, I Have Died and Survived": Santhi's Moving Letter to Alleged Harasser', The News Minute, 30 October 2018, https://www.thenewsminute.com/article/every-word-i-have-died-and-survived-santhi-s-moving-letter-alleged-harasser-90811

16. 'Violence against Trans and Non-Binary People', VAWnet, https://vawnet.org/sc/serving-trans-and-non-binary-survivors-domestic-and-sexual-violence/violence-against-trans-and

17. 'Report of the Expert Committee on the Issues Relating to Transgender Persons', Ministry of Social Justice and Empowerment, 2014.

6. Pinki Pramanik: The Woman Who Was Accused of Rape

1. 'Woman Athlete Faces Rape Charge, Gender Test', *Hindustan Times*, 15 June 2012, https://www.hindustantimes.com/india/woman-athlete-faces-rape-charge-gender-test/story-oXZ93vXtITSJCLRcJWBTlJ.html; 'Arrested for Rape, Asiad Gold Medalist Pinki Presented in Court', *Mid-day*, 15 June 2012, https://www.mid-day.com/news/india-news/article/Arrested-for-rape--Asiad-gold-medalist-Pinki-presented-in-court-168162

2. 'I Underwent Medical Tests with Hands and Feet Tied: Pinki', *The Hindu*, 16 November 2021, https://www.thehindu.com/news/national/i-underwent-medical-tests-with-hands-and-feet-tied-pinki/article3626771.ece

3. 'Report: Pinki Has Male Features', *The Indian Express*, 11 July 2012, https://indianexpress.com/article/news-archive/web/report-pinki-has-male-features/

4. Free & Equal: United Nations for Intersex Awareness, https://www.unfe.org/intersex-awareness/#:~:text=Intersex%20people%20are%20born%20with,definitions%20of%20male%20and%20female.&text=Intersex%20children%20don't%20need,protect%20intersex%20children%20from%20harm

7. Dutee Chand: The Girl Who Challenged the Olympic Rules

1. The British settler colonies of Australia (1969), Canada (1975) and New Zealand (1986) decriminalized homosexuality far sooner—the years in parentheses indicate the year for each.
2. Karan Johar, 'Why a Bollywood Memoir Has Kicked Up a Storm about Being Gay in India', BBC News, 23 January 2017, https://www.bbc.com/news/world-asia-india-38687051
3. 'Dutee Chand Becomes First Openly Gay Indian Athlete', BBC News, 19 May 2019, https://www.bbc.com/news/world-asia-india-48327918
4. PTI, 'Universiade 2019: Dutee Chand Wins Gold at Naples', *Sportstar*, 10 July 2019, https://sportstar.thehindu.com/athletics/dutee-chand-athletics-india-gold-medal-napoli-italy-iaaf-meet/article28336811.ece
5. 'Prize Money for Medal Winners', Press Information Bureau, Ministry of Youth Affairs and Sports, 22 July 2019, https://pib.gov.in/Pressreleaseshare.aspx?PRID=1579723
6. CAS 2014/A/3759 *Dutee Chand v. Athletics Federation of India (AFI) & The International Association of Athletics Federations (IAAF)*, Interim Arbitral Award delivered by the Court of Arbitration for Sport.
7. PTI, 'Athletics Team for CWG Pruned Down to 32, Dutee Chand Dropped', *The Times of India*, 15 July 2014, https://timesofindia.indiatimes.com/commonwealth-games-2014/india-at-glasgow/athletics-team-for-cwg-pruned-down-to-32-dutee-chand-dropped/articleshow/38431867.cms
8. 'Data Transfer of Digital Health Records', Press Information Bureau, Ministry of Health and Family Welfare, https://pib.gov.in/Pressreleaseshare.aspx?PRID=1578929

9. PTI, 'Dutee Failed Test Conducted to Check Androgen Level: SAI', *The Times of India*, 16 July 2014, https://timesofindia.indiatimes.com/ sports/more-sports/athletics/dutee-failed-test-conducted-to-check-androgen-level-sai/articleshow/38495489.cms?from=mdr

10. John Daniel Kelly, 'Testosterone: Why Defining a "Normal" Level Is Hard to Do', The Conversation, 16 April 2019, https://theconversation. com/testosterone-why-defining-a-normal-level-is-hard-to-do-113587

11. CAS 2014/A/3759 *Dutee Chand v. Athletics Federation of India (AFI) & The International Association of Athletics Federations (IAAF)*, Interim Arbitral Award delivered by the Court of Arbitration for Sport, pp. 146–60.

12. 'National Multidimensional Poverty Index, Baseline Report', NITI Aayog, 2021, https://www.niti.gov.in/sites/default/files/2021-11/ National_MPI_India-11242021.pdf

13. T.N. Ninan, 'Deaths in Orissa: Government, Opposition, Press Have All Twisted the Facts', *India Today*, 31 October 1987, https:// www.indiatoday.in/magazine/special-report/story/19871031-deaths-in-orissa-government-opposition-press-have-all-twisted-the-facts-799467-1987-10-30

14. Satyanarayan Pattnaik, 'Mango Kernel Soup Kills Four Tribals in Koraput', *The Times of India*, 22 August 2009, https://timesofindia. indiatimes.com/city/bhubaneswar/mango-kernel-soup-kills-four-tribals-in-koraput/articleshow/4923500.cms

15. 'Three Odisha Tribals Die after Consuming Mango Kernel Cake', *Hindustan Times*, 22 August 2018, https://www.hindustantimes.com/ india-news/three-odisha-tribals-die-after-consuming-mango-kernel-cake/story-ZUKws5mAojTSTfDGXDOmeJ.html

16. Chetan Chauhan, 'Kalahandi: From Hunger Deaths to a Rice Revolution', *Hindustan Times*, 19 May 2013, https://www. hindustantimes.com/delhi/kalahandi-from-hunger-deaths-to-a-rice-revolution/story-EhfBXx90gGYBL4JDB8ju2O.html

17. 'IOA Takes Back Santhi's Asiad Medal', News18, 18 December 2016, https://www.news18.com/news/india/ioa-takes-back-santhis-asiad-medal-253836.html

18. 'Rhea Chakraborty Requests Amit Shah for CBI Investigation into Sushant Singh Rajput's Death', *Hindustan Times*, 16 July 2020, https://www.hindustantimes.com/bollywood/rhea-chakraborty-aks-for-cbi-investigation-into-sushant-singh-rajput-s-death-i-request-you-with-folded-hands/story-3nucScoHVAhKGBxLhVTAIM.html

19. Aparna Banerjea, 'Sushant Singh Rajput's Father Files FIR against Rhea Chakraborty in Patna', Livemint, 28 July 2020, https://www.livemint.com/news/india/sushant-singh-rajput-s-father-files-fir-against-rhea-chakraborty-in-patna-11595943026253.html

20. https://twitter.com/AmanKayamHai_/status/128885299789 2534273?ref_src=twsrc%5Etfw%7Ctwcamp%5Etweetembed%7Ctwt erm%5E1288852997892534273%7Ctwgr%5E%7Ctwcon%5Es1_& ref_url=https%3A%2F%2Fwww.thequint.com%2Fneon%2Fsocial-buzz%2Fmedia-blames-black-magic-rhea-chakraborty-sushant-death-twitter-reaction

21. '"Don't Try to Destroy My Family": Watch Rhea Chakraborty's Full Interview', NDTV, 27 August 2020, https://www.ndtv.com/video/news/news/don-t-try-to-destroy-my-family-watch-rhea-chakraborty-s-full-interview-558776?rdr=1

22. Shobhaa De, 'Rhea's Polished, Glitch-Free Prime Time Performance', NDTV, 28 August 2020, https://www.ndtv.com/opinion/rheas-polished-glitch-free-prime-time-performance-2286614

23. Arvind Gunasekar, 'Rhea Chakraborty, 32 Others Named in Anti-Drugs Agency Chargesheet', NDTV, 5 March 2021, https://www.ndtv.com/india-news/rhea-chakraborty-32-others-named-in-narcotics-control-bureau-chargesheet-linked-to-sushant-singh-rajput-case-2384198

24. Panchali Ray, 'Of Media Trials and Witch Hunts: A Testimony of Survival', The Wire, 8 September 2020, https://thewire.in/media/rhea-chakraborty-media-trial-witch-hunt

8. Lalita Babar: The Woman Who Took the Long Road

1. Tata Mumbai Marathon, https://worldsmarathons.com/marathon/ tata-mumbai-marathon
2. Shahid Judge, 'Lalita Babar Makes History, Breaks National Mark', *The Indian Express*, 25 August 2015, https://indianexpress.com/article/ sports/sport-others/lalita-shivaji-babar-smashes-her-national-record-to-enter-3000m-steeplechase-final/
3. Shweta Sharma, 'Virat Kohli on the Need to Prioritise Mental Health: "Even in a Room Full of People Who Love Me, I've Felt Alone"', *The Indian Express*, 18 August 2022, https://indianexpress.com/article/ lifestyle/life-style/virat-kohli-interview-fitness-asia-cup-mental-health-cricket-indian-team-8091752/
4. 'Virat Kohli's Manager Says Depression Remark Being Used Too Loosely', *The Times of India*, 18 August 2022, https://timesofindia. indiatimes.com/sports/cricket/news/virat-kohlis-manager-says-depression-remark-being-used-too-loosely/articleshow/93646139.cms
5. Abhinay Deshpande, 'Maharashtra Economy to Grow 6.8% in 2022-23: State Economic Survey', *The Hindu*, 8 March 2023, https://www. thehindu.com/news/national/other-states/maharashtra-tables-2022-23-economic-survey-pegs-growth-at-68/article66594838.ece; 'Suicides in India', National Crime Records Bureau, p. 205, https://ncrb.gov.in/ sites/default/files/ADSI-2021/adsi2021_Chapter-2-Suicides.pdf
6. Prasad Joshi, '71 Talukas in Marathwada Parched', *The Times of India*, 14 April 2019, https://timesofindia.indiatimes.com/city/ aurangabad/71-out-of-76-talukas-register-drop-in-groundwater-level/ articleshow/68867850.cms
7. 'Operational Guidelines, Vidarbha Intensive Irrigation Development Programme', Department of Agriculture and Cooperation, Ministry of Agriculture, 2012, https://agricoop.nic.in/sites/default/files/VIIDP.pdf
8. 'Economic Survey of Maharashtra, 2018–19', Directorate of Economics and Statistics, Planning Department, Government of Maharashtra, https://mahades.maharashtra.gov.in/files/publication/ ESM_18_19_eng.pdf

9. '3,000 Metres Steeplechase', World Athletics, https://worldathletics. org/disciplines/middlelong/3000-metres-steeplechase

9. Sunrise Project: The Girls Who Rise before the Sun

1. Kavitha Iyer, *Landscapes of Loss: The Story of an Indian Drought* (New Delhi: HarperCollins Publishers India, 2021).
2. Ibid.
3. 'The Women Power', CISF, https://www.cisf.gov.in/cisfeng/wp-content/uploads/2020/12/women_power.pdf
4. 'Mahila Battalions', CRPF, https://crpf.gov.in/mahila-battalions.htm
5. Krishnadas Rajagopal, 'Women Army Officers Eligible for Permanent Commission, Rules SC', *The Hindu*, 17 February 2020, https:// www.thehindu.com/news/national/women-officers-can-be-given-permanent-commission-sc/article61627070.ece
6. 'Gender Ratio in the Armed Forces', Ministry of Defence, 8 February 2021, https://pib.gov.in/PressReleaseIframePage.aspx?PRID=1696144
7. TNN, 'Didi's Pet Kanyashree Wins UN Award', *The Times of India*, 24 June 2017, https://timesofindia.indiatimes.com/city/kolkata/didis-pet-kanyashree-wins-un-award/articleshow/59293234.cms
8. Mathew Thomas, 'Rise in Child Marriages in the Lockdown: How the Centre Ignored Data of Its Own Nodal Agency', The Wire, 8 April 2021, https://thewire.in/rights/rise-in-child-marriages-in-the-lockdown-how-the-centre-ignored-data-of-its-own-nodal-agency
9. Montek Singh Ahluwalia, 'India's Economic Reforms: Achievements and Next Steps', *Asian Economic Policy Review*, Vol. 14, Issue 1, 14 November 2018, https://onlinelibrary.wiley.com/doi/10.1111/ aepr.12239
10. Simon Rabinovitch and Simon Cox, 'After Half a Century of Success, the Asian Tigers Must Reinvent Themselves', *The Economist*, 5 December 2019, https://www.economist.com/special-report/2019/12/05/after-half-a-century-of-success-the-asian-tigers-must-reinvent-themselves
11. 'What Lies behind Gender Pay Gaps', Global Wage Report 2018/19, International Labour Organization, 2018, https://www.ilo.org/

wcmsp5/groups/public/---dgreports/---dcomm/---publ/documents/
publication/wcms_650553.pdf

12. 'Quarterly Bulletin, Periodic Labour Force Survey', Ministry of Statistics and Programme Implementation, National Statistical Office, p. A7, https://mospi.gov.in/sites/default/files/publication_reports/QuarterlyBulletinPLFS%20JanuaryMarch2023.pdf

13. 'Labor Force Participation Rate, Female (% of female population ages 15+) (modeled ILO estimate)', The World Bank, https://data.worldbank.org/indicator/SL.TLF.CACT.FE.ZS?end=2012&start=1990

14. 'Labor Force Participation Rate, Female (% of female population ages 15+) (modeled ILO estimate) – India', World Bank, https://data.worldbank.org/indicator/SL.TLF.CACT.FE.ZS?end=2021&locations=IN&start=1990

15. 'Educational Statistics at a Glance', Ministry of Human Resource Development, Department of School Education and Literacy, Statistics Division, New Delhi, 2018, p. 53, Table 40.

16. 'Update on Child Sex Ratio', Ministry of Health and Family Welfare, 17 December 2021, https://pib.gov.in/PressReleaseIframePage.aspx?PRID=1782601

17. Kavitha Iyer, *Landscapes of Loss: The Story of an Indian Drought* (New Delhi: HarperCollins Publishers India, 2021).

18. Ibid.

19. Nihal Koshie, 'Too Difficult to Change Anything with People at SAI or AFI: India's Javelin Coach Uwe Hohn', *The Indian Express*, 16 June 2021, https://indianexpress.com/article/sports/sport-others/too-difficult-to-change-anything-with-people-at-sai-or-afi-indias-javelin-coach-uwe-hohn-7360794/

10. Ila Mitra: The Woman Who Missed the Olympics

1. Swati Chattopadhyay, *Representing Calcutta: Modernity, Nationalism and the Colonial Uncanny* (Abingdon and New York: Routledge, 2005).

2. Kavita Panjabi, *Unclaimed Harvest: An Oral History of the Tebhaga Women's Movement* (New Delhi: Zubaan Publishers Pvt Ltd in collaboration with The Indian Institute of Advanced Studies, 2017).

3. Please see the BBC documentary titled *Partition: The Day India Burned*, directed by Ricardo Pollack. Available on Youtube: https://www.youtube.com/watch?v=0ZS40U5yFpc

4. Maleka Begum, *Ila Mitra* (Dhaka: Agamee Prakashani, 1997) (published in Bengali).

5. 'Soni Sori Acquitted in 4th Case; Lawyers to Move HC for Bail', *The Times of India*, 15 February 2013, https://timesofindia.indiatimes.com/city/raipur/soni-sori-acquitted-in-4th-case-lawyers-to-move-hc-for-bail/articleshow/18508556.cms

6. 'South Asian Games Dhaka 2010 Opening Ceremony', YouTube, https://www.youtube.com/watch?v=wPKFmOP6YVo

7. https://twitter.com/NSaina/status/1357010059172040705?s=20

8. https://twitter.com/BabitaPhogat/status/1250390859717021697?s=20

9. 'Saina Nehwal, Others Post Identical Tweets Praising Narendra Modi during His Ramlila Maidan Rally; Badminton Player Mocked on Social Media', Firstpost, 22 December 2019, https://www.firstpost.com/india/saina-nehwal-others-post-identical-tweets-praising-narendra-modi-during-his-ramlila-maidan-rally-badminton-player-mocked-on-social-media-7814811.html

11. A Coda

1. 'Sania Mirza: A Series of "Firsts" by the Indian Tennis Icon", Olympics, https://olympics.com/en/news/sania-mirza-a-series-of-firsts-by-the-indian-tennis-icon

2. 'Nooshin Al Khadeer', ESPN Cricinfo, https://www.espncricinfo.com/player/nooshin-al-khadeer-54286/matches

3. 'Records for Women ODI Matches', ESPN Cricinfo, https://www.espncricinfo.com/records/most-wickets-in-career-283976

4. Juili Ballal, 'In Difficulty, Lies Opportunity: The Journey of Nooshin Al Khadeer | The Pioneers', Female Cricket, 18 August 2020, https://femalecricket.com/the-pioneers/14066-in-difficulty-lies-opportunity-the-journey-of-nooshin-al-khadeer-the-pioneers.html

5. https://twitter.com/nikhat_zareen/status/1184730219103408128?ref_
    src=twsrc%5Etfw%7Ctwcamp%5Etweetembed%7Ctwterm%5E1184
    730219103408128%7Ctwgr%5E385155cfc9318a9b1d5f3485b455c
    0bed39e7b65%7Ctwcon%5Es1_&ref_url=https%3A%2F%2Fwww.
    hindustantimes.com%2Fother-sports%2Fnikhat-zareen-
    writes-to-kiren-rijiju-gets-abhinav-bindra-s-support%2Fstory-
    rEAk2VvHThfpkt3AE0yujN.html

6. TNN, 'Mary Kom Wins Ill-Tempered Bout against Nikhat Zareen',
    The Times of India, 29 December 2019, https://timesofindia.indiatimes.
    com/sports/boxing/mary-kom-wins-ill-tempered-bout-against-nikhat-
    zareen/articleshow/73013590.cms

7. 'Social, Economic and Educational Status of the Muslim Community
    of India: A Report', Prime Minister's High Level Committee, Cabinet
    Secretariat, Government of India, November 2006, p. 14, https://www.
    minorityaffairs.gov.in/WriteReadData/RTF1984/7830578798.pdf

8. Ibid.

9. 'Nikhat Zareen: Indian Wins Gold at Women's World Boxing
    Championship', BBC News, 20 May 2022, https://www.bbc.com/
    news/world-asia-india-61518168

10. 'Tokyo 2020: Boxing Women's Welter (64-69 Kg) Results', https://
    olympics.com/en/olympic-games/tokyo-2020/results/boxing/women-
    s-welter-64-69kg

11. 'Lovlina Borgohain', https://olympics.com/en/athletes/lovlina-
    borgohain

12. Randeep Ramesh, 'Fatwa Orders Indian Tennis Star to Cover Up',
    The Guardian, 10 September 2005, https://www.theguardian.
    com/world/2005/sep/10/india.randeepramesh#:~:text=A%20
    group%20of%20Muslim%20clerics,Islamic%22%20and%20
    %22corrupting%22.

13. Subir Bhaumik, 'Protection for Indian Tennis Star', BBC News,
    17 September 2005, http://news.bbc.co.uk/2/hi/south_asia/4256052.stm

14. PTI, 'Fatwa against Sania Meaningless', *Hindustan Times*, 2 February
    2006, https://www.hindustantimes.com/india/fatwa-against-sania-
    meaningless/story-e6NDqrYndr62nGsiKyhFLI.html

15. '"Fatwa" against Sania, Shoaib for Living Together before Marriage', *Hindustan Times*, 11 April 2010, https://www.hindustantimes.com/india/fatwa-against-sania-shoaib-for-living-together-before-marriage/story-A3LDQNbDpU4sr9vE8pPH5I.html

16. Joshua Arpit Nath, 'Now, Muslim Cleric Claims Sania Mirza's Tennis Dress Is "Sexual" And Hence Un-Islamic', Indiatimes, 17 January 2017, https://www.indiatimes.com/sports/now-muslim-cleric-claims-sania-mirza-s-tennis-dress-is-sexual-and-hence-un-islamic-269670.html

17. Edward W. Said, *Covering Islam: How the Media and the Experts Determine How We See the Rest of the World* (New York: Vintage, 1997).

18. 'History', Indian Olympic Association, https://olympic.ind.in/history

19. Kishwar Desai, *The Longest Kiss: The Life and Times of Devika Rani* (Chennai: Westland Publications Pvt Ltd, 2020).

20. '40 Short Biographies of Indian Cinema Pioneers Who Worked between the Years 1897–1947', Indian Memory Project, https://www.indianmemoryproject.com/cinema-citizens/

21. Vikram Sampath, *My Name Is Gauhar Jaan* (New Delhi: Rupa Publications, 2010).

22. Saeeda Bano, 'How Saeeda Bano Became the First Woman in India to Work as a Radio Newsreader', Mint Lounge, 12 October 2020, https://lifestyle.livemint.com/news/talking-point/how-saeeda-bano-became-the-first-woman-in-india-to-work-as-a-radio-newsreader-111602431601835.html

23. 'Muslim Women (Protection of Rights on Marriage) Act, 2019: Short Title, Extent and Commencement', India Code, https://www.indiacode.nic.in/show-data?actid=AC_CEN_3_20_00069_201920_1565334896444&sectionId=49419&sectionno=1&orderno=1

24. 'Karnataka Hijab Row: Explained', *The Times of India*, 15 March 2022, https://timesofindia.indiatimes.com/india/karnataka-hijab-row-explained/articleshow/90214058.cms; Krishnadas Rajagopal, 'Supreme Court Delivers Split Verdict on Karnataka Hijab Ban', *The Hindu*, 13 October 2022, https://www.thehindu.com/news/national/sc-delivers-split-verdict-on-hijab-row-case-likely-to-go-to-a-larger-bench/article66004319.ece

ABOUT THE AUTHOR

Sohini Chattopadhyay is a journalist and a National Award-winning film critic. Her work has been translated into German, Bengali, Tamil and Malayalam. She is a recipient of the New India Foundation fellowship, and has been bestowed the Ramnath Goenka Excellence in Journalism Award and the Human Rights Press Awards citation, among others. Her writing is archived on her website.

30 Years *of*

HarperCollins *Publishers* India

At HarperCollins, we believe in telling the best stories and finding the widest possible readership for our books in every format possible. We started publishing 30 years ago; a great deal has changed since then, but what has remained constant is the passion with which our authors write their books, the love with which readers receive them, and the sheer joy and excitement that we as publishers feel in being a part of the publishing process.

Over the years, we've had the pleasure of publishing some of the finest writing from the subcontinent and around the world, and some of the biggest bestsellers in India's publishing history. Our books and authors have won a phenomenal range of awards, and we ourselves have been named Publisher of the Year the greatest number of times. But nothing has meant more to us than the fact that millions of people have read the books we published, and somewhere, a book of ours might have made a difference.

As we step into our fourth decade, we go back to that one word – a word which has been a driving force for us all these years.

Read.